Understanding the Refugee Experience in the Canadian Context

TABLE OF CONTENTS

Understanding the Refugee Experience in the Canadian Context

Edited by, Bharati Sethi, Sepali Guruge and Rick Csiernik

This book first published 2021

Cambridge Scholars Publishing

Lady Stephenson Library, Newcastle upon Tyne, NE6 2PA, UK

British Library Cataloguing in Publication Data
A catalogue record for this book is available from the British Library

ISBN (10): 1-5275-6300-6
ISBN (13): 978-1-5275-6300-1

Understanding the Refugee Experience in the Canadian Context

Edited by

Bharati Sethi, Sepali Guruge,
and Rick Csiernik

Cambridge
Scholars
Publishing

SECTION V: Where Do We Go Next?

LIST OF TABLES AND FIGURES

Tables

Figures

PREFACE

The United Nations High Commissioner for Refugees (UNHCR) estimated that at the end of 2018, approximately 70.8 million people worldwide were forcibly displaced as a result of "persecution, conflict, violence, or human rights violation" (2018, p. 2), primarily from the Middle East and Africa (Table 1a). This displaced population includes refugees (25.9 million); refugees under UNHCR's mandate (20.4 million); Palestine refugees under United Nations Relief and Works Agency for Palestine Refugees in the Near East (UNRWA)'s mandate (5.5 million); internally displaced people (41.3 million); and asylum-seekers (3.5 million). More than half of the global refugee population is under the age of 18 (UNHCR, 2018). In 2018, Canada hosted the largest number of refugees among the five developed nations by taking in 28,100 of the 92,400 individuals who were resettled in 25 countries (Table 1b).

Table 1: Refugee Statistics

Table 1a: Country of Origin

Top 5 Countries of Refugee Origins	Number of Refugees Displaced
Syria	6.7 million
Afghanistan	2.7 million
South Sudan	2.3 million
Myanmar	1.1 million
Somalia	0.9 million

Table 1b: Resettlement Country

Top 5 Refugee-Settling Countries	Number of Refugees Resettled
Canada	28,100
United States of America	22,900
Australia	12,700
United Kingdom	5,800
France	5,600

Source: UNHCR (2019), pp. 3, 32

Based on Canada's 2019–2021 multi-year immigration strategy, potential admissions in the Total Refugees and Protected Persons category are expected to rise from 46,450 in 2019 to 51,700 in 2021 (Government of Canada, 2018). The increasing number of refugee admissions has raised concerns among some political quarters, contributing to social conservative-leaning government victories in Alberta, Ontario, Quebec, and New Brunswick. Jean-Nicolas Beuze, UNHCR Canada representative in Ottawa, told the *National Observer* that "The terminology we hear in Canada lately, like 'queue jumper,' 'bogus claim,' and 'illegal,' just taints refugees as a threat and neglects completely the reason why they come and their individual stories" (Beuze cited in Syed, 2018). The reality is that refugees will continue to play a vital role in Canada's economic and population growth by addressing gaps in the labour market and challenges related to Canada's aging population [Immigration, Refugees, and Citizenship Canada Government of Canada (IRCC, 2018)].

Currently, more than 60% of new immigrants worldwide come from Asia (Table 1), including the Middle East (Statistics Canada, 2017), and 67% of all refugees worldwide originate from Afghanistan, Myanmar, Somalia, South Sudan, and Syria (UNHCR, 2018). Many studies have demonstrated that racialized newcomers to Canada experience racism (Gilbert, 2013; Parker, 2018) and discrimination (Stewart et al., 2015). Racialized refugees bear the additional burdens of emotional and physical trauma, forced separation from loved ones, and political or religious persecution (Murray, Davidson & Schweitzer, 2010). During post-conflict/post-war situations, refugee girls and women experience sexual and gender-based violence including systemic rape, sexual assault, torture, and slavery, trafficking (Forced Migration Research Network, 2017), and "corrective rape of lesbian, gay, bisexual, transgender and intersex (LGBTI) identifying women" is prevalent (Forced Migration Research Network, 2017, p. 1). It is noteworthy that despite these experiences of trauma and sexual and gender-based violence, refugee women are not passive victims. In the absence of men in refugee camps and sites, many courageous women provide financial, economic, social, and physical support to their own families and other refugees. Researchers have found that refugee women arrange for childcare, earn money by running small businesses with no funding or external support, organize basic education classes, and even build physical thorn barriers as protection from enemies (Bartolomei, 2015; Olivius, 2014; Forced Migration Research Network, 2017).

In the context of global policymaking and peace-making affecting the lives of refugees including women and girls, certain members of the refugee population have less social power. Members of the LGBTI community, youth and children, individuals living with disability, people from small ethnic or religious groups, and older adults "have unequal access to decision-making, infrastructure and resources, and have their capacities ignored" (Forced Migration Research Network, 2017, p. 1).

This edited volume includes contributions from 32 authors, with the goal of engaging readers and helping them appreciate the shared and distinct migration and resettlement experiences within refugee communities. It is divided into five sections, and each chapter concludes with key takeaway points that can serve as a useful guide and a source of reflection for researchers, educators, students, service providers, and policymakers.

Section I, "Introduction," includes two chapters. In Chapter One, *What Brought Us Here?*, Bharati Sethi, Sepali Guruge, and Rick Csiernik reflect on their personal and academic experiences, which led to their engagement with this topic and the content of this edited volume. In Chapter Two, *Refugee Demographics,* Karun Karki and Dhruba Neupane provide insights into the global numbers of displaced persons, where they originate, and where they settle. They conclude the chapter by focusing on the real-world situation in Canada, setting the stage for the remainder of the book.

Section II, "Refugee Resettlement,' includes six chapters. In Chapter Three, *Syrian Refugee Reflections on Canada's Sponsorship Programs,* Nimo Bokore evaluates the advantages and disadvantages of Canada's three refugee sponsorship programs: Government-Assisted Refugees (GAR), Blended Visa Office Referred (BVOR) refugees, and Privately Sponsored Refugees (PSR), with specific attention to the objectives of each sponsorship program and their ability to meet the resettlement needs of newcomers.

In Chapter Four, *We Are a Gift to Canada: Refugee Women's Voices of Resettlement and Resilience,* Bharati Sethi and Snežana Obradović-Ratković combine data from two distinct studies to explore the resettlement experiences of refugee women in Canada and resilience strategies they use. The experiences of university-educated refugee women from Africa, the Arab world, Korea, Japan, Latin America, and the former Yugoslavia included individual and structural oppression, racism, and discrimination. Sethi and Obradović-Ratković explored resilience strategies in the face of adversity and the importance of recognizing refugee women's agency and honouring their gifts to Canada,and conclude by stressing the need for collaboration between the government, local community, ethnic community, employers, service providers, and educational authorities.

In Chapter Five, *Parenting in Contexts of War, Displacement, and Resettlement: Refugee Voices from the Syrian Conflict,* Abdelfettah Elkchirid and Bree Akesson explore parenting experiences during the pre-flight, flight, and resettlement stages. Parenting during pre-flight tends to follow cultural and societal norms, with conflicts and issues handled from an intergenerational perspective with extended family and community support. However, during flight and displacement, parents tend to focus on the safety of the family unit, which sometimes leads to them engaging in harmful coping mechanisms to maintain family survival. During the resettlement stage, family roles again tend to shift, challenging 'traditional' family norms related to authority, identity, and culture, and creating additional pressure as the family transitions to life in Canada.

In Chapter Six, *Listening to the Children: Effects of Islamophobia on Muslim Youth*, Siham Elkassem and her colleagues explore the experiences of young Muslims once the family arrives in Canada. Specifically, they focus on the increasing anti-Muslim bigotry within the current political and societal climate, and how Islamophobia has fuelled significant negative attention to young Muslim refugees. This chapter adds to the limited body of knowledge about how Islamophobia affects Muslim youth, drawing directly from the experiences of young Muslim refugees living in a Canadian urban setting.

In Chapter Seven, *The Realities of Queer and Trans Migrants with Precarious Status Living in Canada,* Edward Lee examines the realities and challenges faced by LGBTQI refugees as well as other migrants with precarious status in Canada, including visitors, international students, temporary foreign workers, refugee claimants and protected persons, and individuals who are detained and undocumented. This chapter explores how queer and trans migrants have been ideologically framed as 'non-genuine' by the Canadian immigration regime, along with pathways to critical and anti-oppressive practices that could benefit queer and trans migrants with precarious status.

Section II concludes with Chapter Eight, *Group Refugee Resettlement in Canada: Learning from the Karen,* in which Ei Phyu Smith, Sheila Htoo, Michaela Hynie, and Susan McGrath explore the experiences of Karen refugees from across Canada and settlement workers working with this community. The authors also discuss the implications of the findings for future resettlement of other groups.

Section III, "The Promise of Education," includes two chapters about the education of refugee children in Canada. In Chapter Nine, *Educating Refugee Children in Canada: Toward A Pedagogy of Healing,* Snežana Obradović-Ratković, Dragana Kovačević, Neelofar Ahmed, and Claire Ellis explore how education can serve as a healing process for refugee and war-affected children. Based on their analysis of previous research, they chart a pedagogy of healing for school-aged children, arguing that teachers, resettlement officers, and policymakers must develop cross-cultural competences, a social justice focus, and transformative leadership skills to enhance the role of education as a tool in helping heal refugee children in Canadian classrooms.

In Chapter Ten, *Aiming Higher: The Case for Refugee Access to Tertiary Education in Canada*, Claire Ellis, Courtney Oreja, and Emma Jankowski build on the previous chapter to examine the current landscape of global policy initiatives to address disrupted post-secondary education. They focus specifically on the resettlement process of the World University Service of Canada's (WUSC) Student Refugee Program (SRP), an education-centric refugee resettlement sponsorship model in Canada. They conclude that post-secondary education can serve as a pathway for social and economic inclusion, and that more research is needed to develop pragmatic and holistic ways to address the disparity in post-secondary educational access for students with experiences of forced migration.

Section IV, "Refugee Health," focuses on the Social Determinants of Health. In Chapter Eleven, *Fayyaa-Nagaa: Health and Wellbeing among Oromo Women and Girls in Ontario,* Baredu Abraham, Tolee Biya, Martha Kuwee Kumsa, and Nardos Tassew explore the cultural resources that Oromo refugees in Ontario draw on to redress the disparities they experience in their health and wellbeing. The findings of their community-based participatory action research project provide a holistic understanding of the experiences faced by this population.

In Chapter Twelve, *Refugee Mothers' Perinatal Mental Health Experiences and Access to Health Care,* Joyce O'Mahony and Nancy Clark discuss the multiple contextual factors and structural processes that can lead to negative mental health outcomes among pregnant women refugees. This population has experienced the traumas of war and displacement, followed by social isolation and challenging settlement contexts, and the authors argue that health providers must find best practices to support newcomer mothers who are refugees. This chapter adds to the body of research on mental health among immigrant and refugee women, with a specific focus on how they access and receive health care and support to deal with mental illness during the perinatal period and how contextual factors intersect with race, gender, and class to influence mental illness treatment and prevention.

In Chapter Thirteen, *Considering Primary Health Care as a Social Determinant of Refugee Health Through the Lens of Social Justice and Care Ethics: Implications for Social Policy,* Clark and O'Mahony identify the social determinants of refugee health required for promoting social justice in primary health care for refugees. Based on a care ethics framework, the authors explore primary health care models in Canada and what components of social policy could promote broader social justice in terms of refugee health.

Section V, "Where Do We Go Next?," provides conclusions and directions for next steps. In Chapter Fourteen, *Change Making,* Bharati Sethi demonstrates that refugees are an integral part of the Canadian mosaic: they bring economic, ethnic, religious, and social diversity that enriches the Canadian mosaic.

We hope that the chapters in this volume will inspire researchers, educators, students, service providers, and policymakers to foster safe and nurturing environments for the increasing numbers of refugees within Canada who seek safety from political, religious, and environmental challenges – back home and in Canada.

References

Bartolomei L, 2015, 'Surviving the city: Refugees from Burma in New Delhi', in *Urban Refugees: Challenges in Protection, Services and Policy*, pp. 139 – 163.

Gilbert, L. (2013). The discursive production of a Mexican refugee crisis in Canadian media and policy. *Journal of Ethnic and Migration Studies*, *39*(5), 827-843. doi: 10.1080/1369183X.2013.756693

Government of Canada (2018). Supplementary Information 2019-2021 Immigration Levels Plan. Retrieved from https://www.canada.ca/en/immigration-refugees-citizenship/news/notices/supplementary-immigration-levels-2019.html

Immigration, Refugees and Citizenship Canada. (2018). Annual Report to Parliament on Immigration. Retrieved from https://www.canada.ca/content/dam/ircc/migration/ircc/english/pdf/pub/annual-report-2018.pdf

Murray, K. E., Davidson, G. R. & Schweitzer, R. D. (2010). Review of refugee mental health interventions following resettlement: Best practices and recommendations. *American Journal of Orthopsychiatry, 80*(4), 576-585.

Olivius, E. (2014). (Un)Governable Subjects: The Limits of Refugee Participation in the Promotion of Gender Equality in Humanitarian Aid. *Journal of Refugee Studies, 27*(1), 42–61. https://doi.org/10.1093/jrs/fet001

Parker, S. (2018). "It's ok if it's hidden": The discursive construction of everyday racism for refugees and asylum seekers in wales. *Journal of Community & Applied Social Psychology, 28*(3), 111-122.

Puzic, S. (2017). *Record number of refugees admitted to Canada in 2016, highest since 1980.* Retrieved from https://www.ctvnews.ca/canada/record-number-of-refugees-admitted-to-canada-in-2016-highest-since-1980-1.3382444

Schwarz, D. (2015). *Canada's refugees by the numbers: The data.* Retrieved from https://www.cbc.ca/news/canada/canada-s-refugees-by-the-numbers-the-data-1.3240640#arrivals

Statistics Canada. (2017). *Immigration and ethnocultural diversity highlight tables, 2016 census.* Retrieved from https://www12.statcan.gc.ca/census-recensement/2016/dp-pd/hlt-fst/imm/index-eng.cfm

Stewart, M., Dennis, C. L., Kariwo, M., Kushner, K. E., Letourneau, N., Makumbe, K., . . . Shizha, E. (2015). Challenges faced by refugee new parents from Africa in Canada. *Journal of Immigrant and Minority Health, 17*(4), 1146-1156. doi:10.1007/s10903-014-0062-3

Syed, F. (2018, December 20). Canada's top refugee authorities call out conservation fear-mongering. National Observer. Retrieved from https://www.nationalobserver.com/2018/12/20/news/canadas-top-refugee-authorities-call-out-conservative-fear-mongering

The Forced Migration Research Network, University of New South Wales (2017). THE WORLD'S BIGGEST MINORITY? Refugee Women and Girls in the Global Compact on Refugees. Retrieved from http://www.unhcr.org/59e5bcb77.pdf

United Nations High Commissioner for Refugees. (2018). Global Trends: Forced Displacement in 2018. Retrieved from https://www.unhcr.org/figures-at-a-glance.htmlhttps://www.unhcr.org/statistics/unhcrstats/5d08d7ee7/unhcr-global-trends-2018.html

United Nations High Commissioner for Refugees. (2018). *UNHCR resettlement handbook: Canada.* Geneva: United Nations.

Bharati Sethi, London, Ontario
Sepali Gurugee, Toronto, Ontario
Rick Csiernik, Hamilton, Ontario
September 2020

SECTION I

INTRODUCTION

CHAPTER ONE

WHAT BROUGHT US HERE?

BHARATI SETHI, SEPALI GURUGE
AND RICK CSIERNIK

Reflections: Am I home?
Bharati Sethi

I have lived in Canada for most of my adult life. My reasons for taking asylum in Canada were embedded within the socio-cultural web of gender-based violence. Resettlement is a complex process, as is the question of belonging and home, and until the day I received my permanent residency, I constantly feared deportation. Those nine and a half years living as an alien motivated my community-engaged work with refugees.

In my 14 years as a community-based participatory researcher, I have met people from many different countries. Their unique stories have intersected at the site of trauma (invasion, loss, marginalization, and Othering) and hope (resilience, strength, and perseverance). Many of these people have demonstrated a unique ability to learn to live again in a foreign land, and they often resist the label of 'refugee.' I understand their struggles and loss as they work to replant their roots and make a home for themselves and their family – even after living in Canada from two decades, I still sometimes need to touch the piece of paper that allowed me to stay here. However, I am also aware of my privileged position as an academic, so I sometimes find myself in undefined territory, trying to reconcile my subjective-objective and refugee-citizen positionality – I feel uprooted again.

To feel rooted is to feel safe. To feel rooted is to feel at home. Unlike economic and family-class immigrants who enter Canada primarily out of choice, refugees often have no idea where they will land. It is also important to be careful when using the word 'choice.' For example, my previous work demonstrated that women from India who are sponsored to Canada by their husband may not have the choice to refuse; they are bound by cultural obligations and fear being cast out of the community if they rebel (Sethi, 2014).

Refugees differ from those other immigration categories in that their lives depend on finding a safe territory. Unlike immigrants, who choose to settle permanently in another country, refugees are forced to flee their homeland due to the risk of torture, abuse, persecution, war, and environmental or other disasters. Before the Immigration Act of 1978, which distinguished between immigrants and refugees, Canada did not have a refugee policy. The incorporation of a humanitarian category within this act was a substantive step forward, and continues to reflect Canada's humanitarian ideals by permitting entry to a displaced foreign national or refugees in need of protection. However, it was not until 2012 that a foreign national could apply for permanent residency as a "Convention refugee" or "a person in similar circumstances." Canada's refugee system now offers protection to people who risk torture, loss of life, or unusual and cruel punishment if they leave Canada through the In-Canada Asylum Program, while the Refugee and Humanitarian Resettlement Program assists people seeking protection from outside Canada (Government of Canada, 2017).

Under Prime Minister Justin Trudeau, the federal Liberal Government of Canada rebranded Citizenship and Immigration Canada (CIC) as Immigration, Refugee and Citizenship Canada (IRCC). The inclusion of the word 'refugee' reflects the government's ongoing commitment to upholding its obligation under the Charter of the United Nations and the Universal Declaration of Human Rights to protect the fundamental rights and freedom of refugees. However, the government needs to do more to protect those who are considered 'irregular' or 'not genuine' refugees. Canada's multiculturalism policy also needs more work to reflect Canada's changing demographics and intersectionality of social locations such as race, ethnicity, and gender identity. Although Canada is largely a welcoming nation, some people believe that refugees live free on welfare, do not want to work, are security threats or criminals, and fear that a refugee invasion will make White people a minority in Canada (Samuel, 2018).

With regard to my earlier comments about the complexity of resettlement and home, I am never really 'at home,' and I don't know if I ever will be. I am outside the borders of India (my original home) and of Canada (my current home). When in Canada, I ache for the smell, taste, and love of India; when I am in India, I wonder when I am going 'home.'

What I do know is that the narrative of 'resettlement' involves a complex set of Otherness, identity politics, and social relations of power. As I moved up the socio-economic ladder in Canada, my racialized ethnic body became viewed quite differently than when I worked as a maid, but even after two decades in Canada, I still get asked where I am from. Even after obtaining my permanent residency, I did not feel integrated within the Canadian mosaic – until I began to be heard in social, economic, cultural, and political spaces. Integration into a multicultural Canada is not just about Canadian citizenship: fostering newcomer belonging is about allowing the Other to speak – and then listening. The question is not: Am I home? Rather, it is: How am I perceived?

This edited volume is an investment in individuals and families who deserve safe spaces to have their stories heard. We hope that the information will be valuable to researchers, educators, students, service providers, and policymakers who share our commitment to imagining a nation where refugees and asylum seekers feel rooted and safe in our communities.

Reflections: On divides and imperatives
Sepali Guruge

Both personal and professional interests, as well as a line of thinking and understanding that I have been developing since my undergraduate studies shapes my interest and engagement in research on immigrant and refugee health. According to Thorne and Varcoe (1998), locating the researcher's identity in relation to those of the study participants has been commonly acknowledged as an imperative in feminist research. My venture into immigrant and refugee health research, especially in relation to women's health, that began when I was still an undergraduate student in Nursing arose out of the struggles I endured as a newcomer to Canada.

Even though this book focuses on refugees, my thinking here goes back and forth between immigrant health and refugee health. This divide is based on the presumed, assumed, and real social, political, and economic realities of the lives of immigrants and refugees. Of note is that within the same family, sometimes, some members can be refugees while others can be immigrants Another divide that is prominent in the research literature relates to the insider-outsider positionality of the researcher. This divide and related concerns are based on the premise that insider researcher is a member of the immigrant community that is being 'studied' and the outsider researcher belongs to the majority population (read: white in the Canadian context). As

Jorgen Carling et al (2014) note, one of the underlying assumptions here is that former may lead to more emancipatory outcomes and the latter can (re)create on colonial/neocolonial practices. While it is important to critically examine how the researcher social identity and positionality shape the research we do and their outcomes, these overt divides and dichotomies are problematic.

One of my many struggles during my own engagement in research with individuals and families who are immigrants and/or refugees has been to learn how to portray their shared experiences, while acknowledging the many personal, professional, and socio-economic and cultural differences that shape their experiences and in their 'choices' about building their life in the Canadian context. Many immigrants and refugees experience micro, meso, and macro-levels of violence in Canada. If we are not careful, we may view these experiences from a culturalist lens, further damaging the very lives we, as researchers, educators, practitioners, advocates, and policymakers, hope to improve. Yet, we cannot overlook the cultural, patriarchal, and ethno-religious systems that often create situations of vulnerability for women and children, and older persons. In grappling with such concerns, I have attempted to avoid a dichotomous approach – culturalizing and essentializing versus disregarding the role of culture – and to search for a framework that would help explore the intersectionality of race, gender, class, and culture in the context of post-migration. While taking a reflexive and relational stance to my work has helped to address some of my concerns, and frameworks of interpretation have helped me understand the topic in all of its complexity.

During the last 30 years of conducting research, I have worked with many immigrant and diaspora communities. I was an outsider to the individuals and families from these communities on the basis of ethno-cultural, and religious backgrounds as well as reasons of immigration to Canada. Yet, during these times, I faced many difficulties that I share with some of the immigrants and some of the refugees. For example, I found that a lack of fluency in English (defined differently within each job category, educational institution, and discipline), limited my potential for job security and advancement. In order to obtain university entrance, I had to study Grade 13 in Ontario (which meant that I had written Grade 13 exams or their equivalent three times – and in a different language each time). Lack of fluency in English has been one of the rationales given for the aggregation of refugees, in particular, at the lower echelons of the workforce in Canada. While professionals and especially those with university educations continue to be one of the preferred target groups of immigrants, as Mojab (1999) has noted, their "intellectual capacity had been undermined in

Canada and, consequently, they were seen as a potential source of manual labour" (p.125).

Problematic access to information and services is one that I faced within the first 5 to 10 years of my life in Canada. Having access to information is power, and many newcomers are rendered powerless because of lack of information which in turn limits their access to services, even when they are available. This lack of information and services is the result of exclusionary attitudes of those in power. Refugees face racism at every level of society. As my co-editor Bharati has noted, refugees are seen as a burden to this country. Immigrants are also often seen as a burden to this country, especially the racialized individuals, families, and communities. Racialized individuals and families in general are worse off as immigrants or refugees. The experience of racism is a not-so-rare occurrence in my life in Canada. My first attempt at formally addressing racism was quickly dismissed by someone whose responsibility was to help address students' complaints with a question: "Are you sure you want to go ahead with this – it is after all your word against your teacher's word?" Ng (1994) has elaborated on racism (and sexism) as being systemic in the university. My second (and formal) complaint, which was against a large hospital/institution in the Greater Toronto Area (GTA), was rejected because the hospital claimed that it was a case of nepotism and not racism. My experience of racism now (after being in Canada for 30 years) often comes in more subtle forms, while my encounters on the street is as overt as it was 30 years ago. I believe that my experiences, however, have been minor compared to the horrific stories I was privy to during the in-depth individual interviews and focus groups that I conducted with refugees from many social, cultural, ethnic, and religious backgrounds.

Am I a refugee? Am I an immigrant? Why and how does it matter? After 30 years of being in Canada, would my initial immigration status still matter to you? How do you think my initial immigration status still shape my life? How does my initial immigration status shape my approach to research? Many of the chapters in this book are based on qualitative research; Rigor and trustworthiness of qualitative research involves the critical engagement of the readers with what is written in research reports. This can only be done in the context of their reflection on their own positionality in relation to the phenomena explored and the communities involved in these reports. So, as you read this book, I invite you to think about these questions in relation to who you are and what these study findings mean to you and your communities, and what you can do with this information as you forge alliances in improving the lives of many refugees and immigrants who make Canada one of the best countries in the world.

Reflections: …but you don't look like a refugee
Rick Csiernik

I am a White, able-bodied, university-educated, professional, cis-gender male. My demographics place me in every category of privilege that exists in Canada, despite being the grandchild and child of refugees. This irony is one reason why I contributed to this book, with the goal of encouraging readers to become an ally in what?

From my perspective, which may differ from those of other contributors to this volume, Canada doesn't currently have a refugee crisis, nor has Canada ever had a refugee crisis. What we do have is a historical relationship with refugees who come to Canada to create a new home. This is a relationship that will not abate given the current health, economic, political, and environmental issues that are shaping our planet. However, a minority of people fearfully claim, and have historically claimed, that refugees are a threat to the nation's stability, integrity, and values. Despite these beliefs, refugees (including my family) have made Canada one of the most prosperous nations on the planet. The major difference now is that the refugees are not 'Canadian enough,' meaning that unlike my own family, many contemporary refugees don't 'look' like the majority – a dog whistle word; a symbolically loaded word; a lived reality. Refugees have never been Canadian enough for the minority of 'true' Canadians who object to and fear newcomers invading their home … the irony of this situation is that the only 'true' Canadians are the Indigenous Peoples of Turtle Island.

A quarter of a million economic and political refugees have come to Canada to find new homes. My mother's family were economic refugees who came to Canada during the Great Depression of the 20th century. In order to survive, my great-uncle jumped off a moving freight train during his resettlement process: he had been taken to Saskatchewan to be a farm worker, but he realized this was not possible in February and rode the rails back to Ontario to try to find a home and start again. He would have been called a hobo. Later, he became a sharecropper who, along with his sister and brother-in-law (my grandparents), saved enough money to buy a small business and then a larger business, all family-run, and worked that business 18+ hours a day seven days a week. This is, of course, a story familiar to wave after wave of refugees.

My father was a political refugee, although many would not consider him the smartest of men, for as a young adult he threw rocks at Russian tanks during the Hungarian revolution. As in many popular uprisings against more weaponized and technologically superior regimes, the outcome did not end well for him or his brothers in arms. He was fortunate to escape to a refugee camp in Austria, which was his home for six months. Next, he was shipped to Burlington, Ontario. He spoke no English, but was able to stay with a man from his home village. Later, he changed his 'foreign' name in the hopes of finding work in the Alberta oil patch. Unfortunately, he purposefully chose the Irish-sounding name Paul Kerry, without knowing how Irish refugees had been treated in Canada.

My family's story is hardly unique. It is one that has been repeated by those far older than I am and is being repeated now by those far younger. The commonality is how I, they, and most possibly you and your families have been treated and why now is the time to stand up and address that through the means described by the contributors to this book. In closing, a brief summary to support my earlier claim and to lead you into the book, that despite the purported refugee crisis after refugee crisis, Canada has continued to exist, grow and prosper because of not despite the Other.

1770 - 1779: The first wave of Quakers arrive to what is now known as southern Ontario as refugees from the American Revolution. More arrive in the 1820s escaping religious persecution in England and Ireland.

1776: 3,000 Black Loyalists, among them freemen and slaves, flee the oppression of the American Revolution.

1789: Lord Dorchester, Governor-in-Chief of British North America, gives official recognition to the "First Loyalists": individuals loyal to the Crown who fled the oppression of the American Revolution to settle in Nova Scotia and Quebec.

1793: Upper Canada becomes the first province in the British Empire to abolish slavery, resulting in Canada becoming the final stop in the Underground Railway which over the course of the 19th century will aid thousands of black slaves escape from the United States.

1750: The forced eviction of inhabitants of the highlands and western islands of Scotland, sees an influx of Scottish refugees to Canada throughout the latter half of the 18th century.

1812: Over 500 African-Americans are settled at Hammonds Plain, Nova Scotia escaping the War of 1812.

1830 - 1860: After Poland is annexed by Russia, thousands of Poles flee to Canada, to escape economic, political, and military reprisals.

1847: Hundreds of thousands of Irish flee the country, driven out by starvation during the potato famine. With passage to Canada cheaper than to the United States of Australia, Canada receives a majority of the most destitute many of whom are children whose parents perished prior to or during the escape.

1858: The first significant mass migration of Poles escaping Prussian occupation in northern Poland.

1880-1914: Thousands of Italians refugees arrive in Canada as an outcome of Italy's state reforms that drove peasant farmers from their lands.

1891: The migration of 170,000 Ukrainians begins, mainly to flee oppression from areas under Austro-Hungarian rule, marking the first wave of Ukrainians seeking refuge in Canada.

1899: More than 7,500 Doukhobors arrive in Canada to escape persecution in Russia, aided by author Leo Tolstoy and Canadian pacifist groups such as the Quakers whose ancestors had themselves been refugees.

1920 - 1927: Thousands of Mennonites, fleeing religious and ethnic persecution in the newly created Soviet Union are allowed into Canada.

1948: The first of 10 boats carrying 1,593 Baltic refugees, mostly Estonian, arrives on the east coast of Canada. These refugees sailed from Sweden, where they were living under threat of forced repatriation to the Soviet Union. They were detained on arrival and finally processed through an ad hoc arrangement with all but 12 being granted refugee status.

1947 - 1952: 250,000 displaced persons from Central and Eastern Europe come to Canada, victims of Nazism, communism, and Soviet occupation

1950s: Canada admits Palestinian Arabs, driven from their homeland by the Israeli-Arab war of 1948.

1956 - The crushing of the Hungarian uprising led to over 200,000 Hungarians fleeing to Austria. In response to public pressure, the Canadian government implemented a special program, offering the Hungarian refugees free transport, instead of loans. Thousands of Hungarians arrived in the early months of 1957 on over 200 chartered flights. More than 37,000 Hungarians were admitted in less than a year (including Csiernik's father).

1960s: Chinese refugees enter Canada fleeing the violence of the Cultural Revolution.

1968: Warsaw Pact troops enter Czechoslovakia leading to 10,975 Czechs entered Canada between August 20, 1968 and March 1, 1969.

1969 - 1972: An unknown number of American conscientious objectors flee to Canada to avoid the mandatory military draft that would have forced them into active duty to fight the war in Vietnam after Canada changes its laws regarding individuals conscripted into military service

1970 - 1990: Deprived of political and religious freedom, 20,000 Soviet Jews settled in Canada.

1971: Canada welcomes 228 Tibetan refugees fleeing Chinese persecution after the occupation of their country.

1971 - 1976: Fearing economic instability and persecution following the liberation of East Pakistan (now Bangladesh) hundreds of Bengalis seek refuge in Canada

1972 - 1973: Ugandan president for life Idi Amin announced that Ugandan Asians, primarily Ismaili Muslims would be expelled. Canada responds swiftly, setting up an office in Kampala. By the end of 1973, more than 7,000 Ugandan Asians had arrived, of whom 4,420 come in specially chartered flights.

1973 - Arising from the American supported overthrow of the leftist Chilean government by military dictator Augusto Pinochet's 7000 Chileans are accepted as refugees.

1979: Iranian refugees flee Iran following the overthrow of the American-backed Shah and the imposition of an Islamic Fundamentalist regime.

1979 - 1980: Nearly 70,000 Vietnamese Boat People are offered refuge in Canada after the American withdrawal and democratic government collapse in Vietnam.

1980s: Khmer Cambodians, victims of the Communist regime and the aftershocks of Communist victory in the Vietnam War, flee to Canada.

1992 - 1997: Nearly 13,000 thousand Bosnian refugees enter Canada to escape ethnic cleansing after the breakup of Yugoslavia.

2000 - 2011: Canada resettles 3,900 Karen refugees from Thailand, Myanmar, and Burma.

2015: Over 6,500 Bhutanese refugees arrive in Canada

2016: Canada resettles 25,000 Syrian refugees and commits to accepting 3,500 refugees from Sudan, primarily Eritreans and Ethiopians.

2017: Canada resettles more than 1,300 survivors of Daesh along with Haitians who sought refuge in the United States from the devastation of the 2010 earthquake but were threatened with deportation by the Trump government.

2018: Canada resettles more refugees than any other nation. According to the annual global trends report released by the United Nations High Commissioner for Refugees, Canada took in 28,100 of the 92,400 refugees who were resettled across 25 countries.

Sources: Canadian Council for Refugees (2009); Government of Canada (2018); Nagy (2018); The Canadian Encyclopedia (2019).

References

Carman, T. & Elash, A. (2018). Gender persecution the top reason women seek asylum in Canada. Retrieved from https://www.cbc.ca/news/canada/asylum-seekers-data-gender-persecution-1.4506245

Canadian Council for Refugees. (2009). *Brief history of Canada's response to refugees*. Retrieved from https://ccrweb.ca/sites/ccrweb.ca/files/static-files/canadarefugeeshistory.htm

Government of Canada (2017). How Canada's refugee system works. Retrieved from https://www.canada.ca/en/immigration-refugees-citizenship/services/refugees/canada-role.html

Government of Canada. (2018). *Canada: A history of refuge*. Retrieved from https://www.canada.ca/en/immigration-refugees-citizenship/services/refugees/canada-role/timeline.html

Nagy, A. (2018). *Canada's refugees*. Retrieved from https://www.canadashistory.ca/explore/settlement-immigration/canadas-refugees

Samuel, S. (2018). *There's a perception that Canada is being invaded*. Retrieved from https://www.theatlantic.com/international/archive/2018/05/theres-a-perception-that-canada-is-being-invaded/561032/

Sethi, B. (2014). *Intersectional exposures: Exploring the health effect of employment with KAAJAL Immigrant/Refugee women in Grand Erie through photovoice* (Order No. 3662103). Available from ProQuest Dissertations & Theses Global. (1646467937). Retrieved from https://www-lib-uwo-ca.proxy1.lib.uwo.ca/cgi-bin/ezpauthn.cgi?url=http://search.proquest.com.proxy1.lib.uwo.ca/docview/1646467937?accountid=15115

Simmons, A. B. (2010). *Immigration and Canada: Global and transnational perspectives*. Toronto: Canadian Scholars' Press.

The Canadian Encyclopedia. (2019). *Refugees*. Retrieved from https://www.thecanadianencyclopedia.ca/en/article/refugees?gclid=CjwKCAjwq832BRA5EiwACvCWsXsooawy9decIou6pP4-yzKxHsndGhwJ4vlJFN4DaI6-RFKvrqkBNxoC8ZkQAvD_BwE

CHAPTER TWO

REFUGEE DEMOGRAPHICS: A GLOBAL PICTURE

KARUN K. KARKI AND DHRUBA J. NEUPANE

Introduction

The 21st century is witnessing an unprecedented rise of forced refugees, asylum seekers, and involuntary migrants globally. In countries such as Afghanistan, Congo, Myanmar, Somalia, Sudan, and Syria death, desolation, and trauma make a daily spectacle. And almost routinely, social media and news outlets are filled in with graphic images, tragic, numbing stories of fatal swims, capsized boats, as well as formidable resilience of people fleeing for their lives.

A study conducted by United Nations High Commissioner for Refugee (UNHCR, 2017) shows that world's "population of concern", a term that it uses to signify the displaced people that include refugees, asylum-seekers, internally displaced populations (IDPs), stateless persons, returnees, and people who need protection based on other special grounds, has reached a record high (71.4 million) by the end of 2017 (Figure 2.1). Of the total 71.4 million, 68.5 million were forcibly displaced, making up refugees (25.4 million), asylum seekers (3.1 million) and internally displaced persons (40.0 million). That is, in 2017, one out of every 118 people on the planet were displaced. If all these displaced people were to live in a single country, it would be the 21st largest country in the world (Hilado & Lundy, 2017).

Figure 2.1: The World's Population of Concern

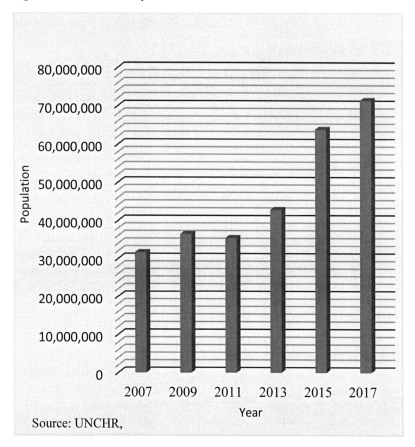

Source: UNCHR,

Table 2.1 provides further insights into the world's refugee crisis by specifying further categories of refugees and by showing the substantial growth of forcibly displaced people over the past decade. For example, in 2007, there were 31.7 million people who had been forcibly displaced whereas in 2017 there were now 71.4 million, an increase of over 125%. While the Syrian conflict can be considered a significant contributor to this increase, there have been many other major displacements throughout the world as illustrated in Figure 2.2.

Table 2.1: The Global Displacement and Displaced Population (2007-2017)

Population	2007	2009	2011	2013	2015	2017
Refugees	11,390,930	10,396,538	10,404,804	11,699,279	16,111,285	19,941,347
Asylum-Seekers	741,110	989,169	897,021	1,164,450	3,224,966	3,090,898
IDPs	13,740,317	15,628,057	15,473,378	23,925,555	37,494,172	39,118,516
Stateless	2,937,315	6,559,573	3,477,101	3,469,278	3,687,764	2,796,204
Others[1]	68,615	411,698	1,411,848	836,100	870,740	1,596,189
Returnees	2,800,758	2,481,018	3,777,711	1,770,736	2,518,729	4,896,352
Total	31,679,045	36,466,053	35,441,863	42,865,398	63,907,656	71,439,506

Source: UNHCR, 2018b

[1]Others refers to individuals who do not necessarily fall directly into any of the groups above, but who need assistance services based on humanitarian grounds.

Figure 2.2: Top Ten Source Countries of Refugees - 2017

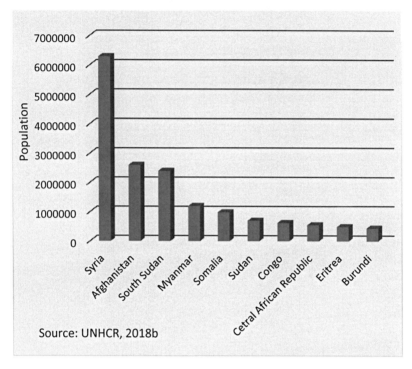

Source: UNHCR, 2018b

It is important to note that the greatest number of refugees are hosted not by the countries that are recognized as having greatest resources or the major United Nations signatories but rather by those who share physical proximity. As Figure 2.3 illustrates, among the 10 largest refugee host countries, Bangladesh, Ethiopia, Sudan, and Uganda, arguably among the world's least developed countries, hosted over 12.5 million refugees in the end of 2017, an approximately 63% of all the refugees under the UNHCR's (2018a) mandate. A comparison among the developed countries who received Syrian refugees shows that Canada, Germany and Norway top of the list of most receiving courtiers (250%, 144%, 118%, respectively of the fair share value of 481,022 total number of Syrian refugees). The countries at the bottom of this list are the United States, Spain, and France, all accepting a mere 10%, and Japan, Russia, and South Korea with zero percent acceptance (Ros, 2017).

Figure 2.3: Top Ten Host Countries of Refugees – 2017

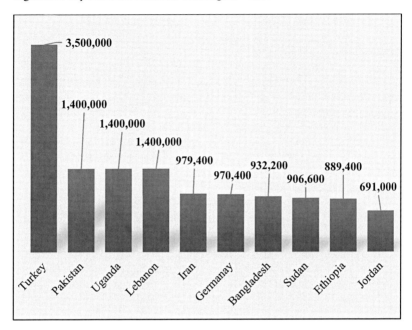

Source: UNHCR, 2018b

How the World is Responding to Global Refugee Crisis

As Marlowe (2018, p. xi) writes, the refugee crisis has triggered a "moral panic" button among the leaders in many leading developed countries. The rise of nationalism, popularism, and protectionist politics in Hungary, Italy. Spain, and the United Kingdom and United States, has made tightened border security a national priority, resulting in new laws to restrict refugees. In contrast, a relative generosity is shown by countries such as Canada."

One way in which to make sense of how the Global North is responding to the refugee crisis is by examining how the problem is perceived, framed, and (re)presented in rhetoric and language, in political and policy debates, as well as in action and practice. The election results in Italy, the United Kingdom and the United States, for example, was a matter of the stark choice between those who held anti-immigration and nation-first sentiments versus those who remained pro-immigrant. These election campaigns saw the political right playing scare tactics which had citizens of those nations perceive refugees as a threat to national security, national values, and identity, following the stereotypes associated refugees and immigrants as a population that breed pollution, that rely on, even misuse, social benefits and governments funds.

While it is useless to have any expectations of political leadership whose rise was based on anti-immigration campaign, even those who appeared to be pro-immigrants have failed their promises. The *Observer* Editorial (July 9, 2017), a sister paper of the British daily newspaper *The Guardian*, points out Europe's response to refugee crisis as "the continent's 'out of sight, out of mind' attitude" (July 9, 2017). The Editorial adds, citing Angela Markel, the German Prime Minister's and other European nations' nonchalance and failure to deliver their promises:

> "Wir schaffen das" – "we can do this" – when she flung open Germany's doors to refugees from Afghanistan, Iraq and Syria for six months in 2015. But she failed to take German public opinion with her, and her words quickly turned hollow. Other European nations, including Britain, chose to free-ride on Germany's generosity rather than follow its example. Led by Germany, Europe's approach to refugees in the last two years has evolved from Merkel's misplaced optimism in "we can do this" to a shameful "out of sight, out of mind" …Meanwhile, Europe, led by Merkel, has recalibrated its efforts towards preventing refugees from reaching Europe. This simply shifts the locus of the problem elsewhere, at a huge humanitarian cost. (July 9, 2017)

Refugee Admission in Canada

Canada has three different resettlement programs: government assisted, private sponsorship, and blended visa[1]. Government-assisted refugees (GARs) are refugees referred by the United Nations Refugee Agency or another referral organization to resettle in Canada. To be eligible under the GAR program, an individual must register for refugee status with the UNHCR or state authorities to be considered by a referral organization. Under the privately sponsored refugee (PSR), an individual or a group of individuals in Canada can sponsor refugee/s to help them adjust to life in Canada. The blended-visa office-referred (BVOR) refugees are identified for resettlement by the UNHCR and are matched with a private sponsor.

In 2016, 46,321 refugees were admitted to Canada in 2016 under its resettlement programs. Of these 23,523 were GAR, 18,362 PSR and 4,434

---

[1] These programs are examined in greater depth in Chapter 3.

BVOR (UNHCR, 2018a). However, this figure does not include an additional 12,116 individuals who were asylum claimants and 3,913 humanitarian and compassionate considerations (Government of Canada, 2018). This total represents an increase of 21% in from 2015.

Canada has accepted refugees and resettled over 700,000 refugees since 1959 (UNHCR, 2018b) with an aim of accepting between 200,000 and 280,000 immigrants annually moving forward. While looking at the 2016 census, of the 225,000 of immigrants accepted that year, only (11.4%) comprised refugee class, compared to a whopping 65% admitted under economic class; the rest consisting of family class. Canada formally organized its refugee policies and management structures in the Immigration Act of 1976. This practice continued in 2002 when Canada implemented the Immigration and Refugee Protection Act, introduced by Minister of Citizenship and Immigration, placing emphasis on the principles for refugee resettlement, including a shift toward protection rather than ability to successfully establish, rapid family reunification, fast track processing for urgent and vulnerable protection cases, and balancing inclusiveness with effective management through a closer relationship with partners (UNHCR 2018a). The resettlement of refugees in Canada from 2008 until 2014 showed a steady linear trend. There was a notable increase in 2015 and again in 2016 with the number stabilizing just under 45,000 in 2017 (Figure 2.4).

However, the selection or determination processes are quite complicated. The fact that inclusion always already is predicated on exclusion shows that many more people in need of immediate protection may have been left behind.

Figure 2.4: Number of Permanent Resident Refugees in Canada (2008-2017)

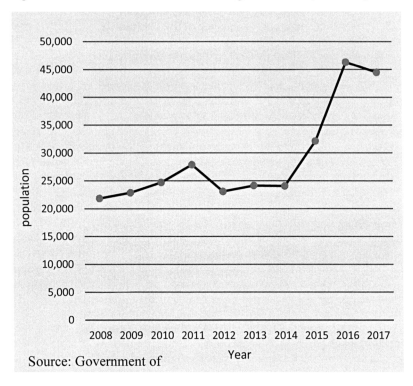

Source: Government of

Canadian State and Public Response to
the Current Refugee Crisis

Whereas recent changes in policies pertaining to refugees have been impacted by growing populist and nationalist sentiments in the United States and major European nations, Canada under the first term of Prime Minister Justin Trudeau presented itself as a more generous nation. This was reflected in Trudeau's pledge to resettle more than 40,000 Syrian refugees by the end of 2017, in responding to the unfolding humanitarian crisis. The following tweets exemplifies the approach and attitude a leadership level has shown toward refugees. The context of Prime Minister Trudeau's response in the tweet below was following President Trump's threat to his 'Executive Order' to ban Syrian and Muslim refugees entering the United States.

Figure 2.5: Twitters Showing Leadership Stances to Refugees Crisis

Justin Trudeau himself welcomed Syrian refugees at the airport, garnering international attention.

According to a survey conducted by the Environics Institute, although there is a section of population who hold newcomers to Canada as a burden, a gradual attitudinal change towards refugees has occurred over the last decade with a majority of Canadians across political isles not being either anti-refugee or anti-immigrant (Perreaux, 22 March 2018). This study found that Canadians were less polarised over immigrant issues than were Europeans or Americans (Perreaux, 22 March 2018).

Following the Trump Administration's immigration policy, the number of asylum-seekers to Canada increased exponentially (Table 2.2). This had led some to believe that Canada is facing what some news outlets describe as "a new crisis" (Ballingall & Boutilier, 21 July 2018). As Samuel writing for *The Atlantic* (May 26, 2017) cites Wendy Ayotte, "there's a perception that Canada is being invaded…the perception is that these people are illegal and that they're violating Canada's borders and that they're just queue jumpers trying to get freebies on welfare".

Crowley warns of the danger Canada may be facing, with an illustration of what is happening in the United States because of its failure to surveil borders in time. Crowley believes that advocates of liberal immigration are foolish to downplay this danger as public opinions regarding policies refugees remain divided within Canada.

Refugee Demographics: A Global Picture

Table 2.2: Asylum Claimants by Claim Office-Type and Province (2013 – 2018)

Province	Claim office	2013	2014	2015	2016	2017	2018
Ontario	Airport	790	1,490	1,885	2,420	2,380	3,735
	Border	1,930	2,565	2,840	4,955	6,165	4,390
	Inland	4,070	5,175	6,365	8,830	11,635	11,610
	Total	*6,790*	*9,230*	*11,090*	*16,205*	*20,180*	*19,735*
Québec	Airport	350	285	325	440	1,125	2,915
	Border	730	805	960	1,660	3,645	15,040
	Inland	1,325	1,540	1,670	2,550	19,955	8,525
	Total	*1,405*	*2,630*	*2,955*	*4,650*	*24,725*	*26,480*
British Columbia	Airport	85	55	60	75	180	115
	Border	110	125	150	215	340	295
	Inland	320	515	565	1,050	1,810	1,545
	Total	*515*	*695*	*775*	*1,340*	*2,330*	*1,955*
Alberta	Airport	50	35	45	55	100	90
	Border	140	185	245	330	545	475
	Inland	305	400	665	810	1,085	990
	Total	*495*	*620*	*955*	*1,195*	*1,730*	*1,555*
Manitoba	Airport	--	--	--	5	--	10
	Border	25	15	80	145	860	430
	Inland	40	60	55	80	220	150
	Total	*65*	*75*	*135*	*230*	*1,080*	*590*

Other Provinces	Airport	--	5	0	40	75	55
	Border	25	15	15	65	75	25
	Inland	50	55	75	105	140	145
	Total	*75*	*75*	*90*	*210*	*290*	*225*
Total	*Airport*	*1,280*	*1,885*	*2,325*	*3,040*	*3,875*	*6,930*
Total	*Border*	*2,960*	*3,715*	*4,295*	*7,375*	*11,630*	*20,660*
Total	*Inland*	*6,110*	*7,750*	*9,395*	*13,435*	*34,845*	*22,965*
Grand Total		**10,365**	**13,440**	**16,060**	**23,870**	**50,350**	**44,315**

Source: Government of Canada, 2018

Note: Government of Canada has used "--" to all values between 0 and 5 and also has rounded other values to the closest multiple of 5 to prevent individuals from being identified when data is compiled. So, the data may not sum to the totals indicated.

Discussion

The greatest number of refugees are hosted by low-or middle-income countries, primarily neighbouring nations, rather than countries with the most economic resources. This reality conveys a powerful message to international communities, particularly to the developed countries in the Global North, that they are not taking a fair share of their global humanitarian responsibility with respect to refugees. This is not to dismiss the past and ongoing achievements that have been made in this direction but rather illustrate the ongoing issues arising from this arena.

International communities need to further activate collective commitments and efforts to resolving the needs of refugees and displaced people by exploring all potential range of options and opportunities. A wide range of partners inclusive of governments, refugees, and United Nations agencies, the private sector, international financial institutions, civil society, academic, faith leaders, social organizations, and relevant partners can work together to address the world scale problem and refugee needs. Moreover, the negative image associated with refugees need to change through such a collective effort. Building on this point and in concluding, it is emphasized that the aforementioned international communities, governments, private sectors, and civil society need to adopt an approach called the 'sharing opportunity and resources' in settling refugees. This approach views refugees not as a burden but rather as a series of opportunities for nations to explore their potentials. Refugees bring with them diversity talents, skills, abilities, and cultures that strengthens the richness of the host country. A more respectful and more generous approach to dealing with the most vulnerable population is long overdue.

Take Away Points

1. The reality that 84% of refugees are offered shelter in the developing world points to the need for the developed countries to open themselves up to humanitarian crises. However, in recent years, particularly with the rise of populism, the global cooperation over refugee issues have been the matter of the sovereign decision of a sovereign state. A partnership among government, international communities, migration organizations, private sector and civil society is critical to a joint action in alleviating the humanitarian crisis. In that spirit, the chapter also informs substantial collaboration among global communities and nation-states, the governments of these countries need to put more effort

and work in collaboration to ensure that the refugee crisis is a collective problem demanding collective action.

2. The chapter apprises an urgent need to address reintegration challenges the refugee populations face in the host countries. Humanitarian response, including to refugee and displaced populations are generally designed to be lifesaving, providing basic necessities of food, shelter, water and sanitation which are intrinsically short-term in scope. A long-term solution to addressing the multitude of refugees in their socio-economic, psycho-social and civic integration is the utmost priority.

3. Finally, this chapter stresses on the need for international communities and host nations to develop a better framework that addresses legal and socio-economic dimensions of refugees and stateless people. In particular, it is important to identify and address barriers for refugees in their effort to fully participate in the socio-economic life in the host nation and enjoy equal rights and respect as the nationals of host nations. This would provide them with opportunities to foster social capital within the host communities.

References

Ballingall, A., & Boutilier, A. (2018, July 21). Is Canada in the midst of a refugee crisis? Experts say it's important to keep things in perspective. Retrieved from https://www.thestar.com/news/canada/2018/07/21/is-canada-in-the-midst-of-a-refugee-crisis-experts-say-its-important-to-keep-things-in-perspective.html

Crowley, B. (2018). *Does Canada have a refugee crisis? Yes.* Retrieved from https://www.thestar.com/opinion/contributors/thebigdebate/2018/07/17/does-canada-have-a-refugee-crisis-yes.html

Dummett, M. (2011). *On immigration and refugees.* London: Routledge Print.

Government of Canada (2018). Asylum claimants processed by Canada border services agency and immigration, refugees and citizenship Canada offices, January 2011 - December 2018. Retrieved from https://open.canada.ca/data/en/dataset/b6cbcf4d-f763-4924-a2fb-8cc4a06e3de4

Hilado, M., & Lundy, M. (2017). *Models for practice with immigrants and refugees: Collaboration, cultural awareness, and integrative theory.* Thousand Oaks: Sage Publications, Inc.

Marlowe, J. (2018). *Belonging and transnational refugee settlement: Unsettling the everyday and the extraordinary.* New York: Routledge.

Perreaux, L. (March 2018). Canadian attitudes toward immigrants, refugees remain positive: Study. Retrieved from *https://www.theglobeandmail.com/canada/article-canadian-attitudes-toward-immigrants-refugees-remain-positive-study/*

Ross, M. (2017, April 9). The borgen project: 15 statistics on refugees. Retrieved from https://borgenproject.org/15-statistics-on-refugees/

Samuel, S. (2018). There's a perception that Canada is being invaded: Justin Trudeau's government has started rejecting more refugee claims from migrants who cross the U.S.-Canada border on foot. Retrieved from https://www.theatlantic.com/international/archive/2018/05/theres-a-perception-that-canada-is-being-invaded/561032/

The Guardian (2017). The observer view on Europe's shameful response to the growing refugee crisis. Retrieved from https://www.theguardian.com/world/2017/jul/09/observer-editorial-europes-shameful-response-to-growing-refugee-crisis

United Nations High Commissioner for Refugee (February 2018). *Canada: By the government of Canada.* Retrieved from https://www.unhcr.org/3c5e55594.pdf

United Nations High Commissioner for Refugee (2018a). *Global trends: Forced displacement in 2017.* Retrieved from https://www.unhcr.org/5b27be547.pdf

United Nations High Commissioner for Refugee (2018b). *Canada refugee resettlement facts.* Retrieved from https://www.unhcr.ca/wp-content/uploads/2018/09/Canada-Resettlement-Fact-Sheet-2018-En-8August.pdf

Yakovenko, N. L. (2017). Brexit and its impact on contemporary Europe. *Scientific Developments, Future Technologies, Innovations.* Retrieved from: http://sried.in.ua/uploads/magazine/konf-05-2017.pdf#page=532

SECTION II

REFUGEE RESETTLEMENT

CHAPTER THREE

SYRIAN REFUGEES:
REFLECTIONS ON CANADA'S
SPONSORSHIP PROGRAMS

NIMO BOKORE

Canada presently has three types of refugee resettlement programs:

- Government-Assisted Refugees (GAR): resettlement of Convention refugees referred by the United Nations High Commissioner for Refugees (UNHCR) through 100 percent financial assistance by the federal government;
- Privately Sponsored Refugees (PSR) program: resettlement of refugees and those in refugee-like situations through the assistance of organizations and private individuals; and
- Blended Visa Office-Referred (BVOR): resettlement of Convention refugees referred by the UNHCR through 50 percent financial assistance from the federal government and 50 percent by private sponsors.

All three of these programs are part of Canada's humanitarian tradition to find solutions for prolonged displacement, emerging refugee situations, and final resettlement (Immigration, Refugees and Citizenship Canada [IRCC], 2016).

This chapter will explore these three programs using findings from a research initiative entitled the "Emerging Voices Project: How Syrian newcomers and other key stakeholders perceive Canada's three sponsorship programs for refugee (re)settlement." This collaborative project, led by the chapter author (Ottawa), Sepali Guruge (Toronto), and Bharati Sethi (London), was funded through a SSHRC Connection Grant to explore key issues involving refugees and settlement workers in the three cities.

Canadian Resettlement Projects

Government-Assisted Refugees

Several substantive changes have occurred in Canadian refugee policy since the 1967 Immigration Act, which replaced the race-based criteria for accepting immigrants and refugees into Canada with a point-based system. Though it did not come into effect until 1978, the Immigration Act focused, for the first time, on who should be allowed to enter Canada – rather than who should be kept out. This began the move toward a more humanitarian tradition of refugee resettlement, further solidified with the Immigration and Refugee Protection Act (IRPA), which was passed in 2001 and came into force in 2002. The IRPA placed greater emphasis on the vulnerability and protection needs of refugees. Through these changes, those who are considered vulnerable or with greater needs are referred by the UNHCR or other designated referral agencies, to be accepted as GARs (IRCC, 2016). The government of Canada provides resettlement support for members of this group for at least the first year after arrival. Organized services, including housing, employment, educational information, are provided for these refugees starting with the initial reception at the port of entry. Temporary accommodation, orientation, and other integration needs are usually followed by permanent accommodation, adaptation services to aid with life skills, and links to both federal and provincial programs, including employment services.

In the city of Ottawa, arriving GARs are received at Sophia House, the city's designated reception centre, which typically refers them to the Catholic Community Service (CSS) and the Catholic Center for Immigrants (CCI) to address their immediate and long-term needs. GARs are provided with services including funds for health care, English as a second language classes, and daycare, all of which are covered by the Resettlement Assistance Program [RAP] (CCI, 2019).

Table 3.1: Resettlement Phases of GARs in Ottawa

Initial	Mid-Term	Long-Term
Sophia House or a hotel	Catholic Community Service (established 1953)	Catholic Centre for Immigrants (established in 1976 due to need and become community-based non-profit organization in 1985.)
Housing for three to five weeks, orientation to Canada, and other related resettlement workshops	Health screening, outreach, and referral programs	Long-term resettlement support

Privately Sponsored Refugees

Refugees admitted under the PSR program require the support of sponsorships by permanent residents or Canadian citizens who are part of one of the following three streams:

(i) a sponsorship agreement holder;
(ii) a group of at least five Canadians or permanent residents who have proactively come together for this purpose; or
(iii) a community sponsor, such as a local organization, association, or corporation that is expected to apply for approval directly from the government.

Sponsors are legally obligated to provide financial support or a combination of financial and in-kind support to assist newcomers with their resettlement needs including housing, furniture, clothing, food, and connections to community programs for their resettlement and integration needs for a minimum of 12 months (Figure 3.1).

Syrian Refugees

Figure 3.1: Resettlement Phases of the PSR Program

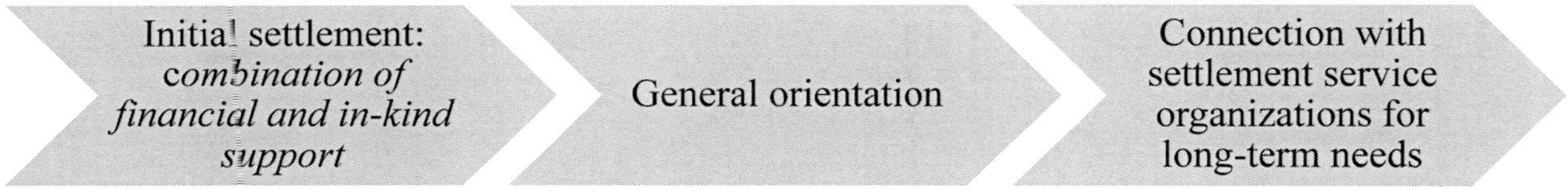

Initial settlement: *combination of financial and in-kind support*

General orientation

Connection with settlement service organizations for long-term needs

Blended Visa Office-Referred

The BVOR program was created with the objective of establishing a three-way partnership resettlement program involving the Government of Canada, UNHCR, and private sponsors. It is similar in some ways to the GAR and PSR programs; like the GAR, the BVOR is managed through refugee referrals from UNHCR or other designated agencies, which use specific criteria set by Canadian Visa officers (IRCC, 2018). To be eligible for the BVOR program, an individual or family must first be identified by UNHCR, which then matches the individual or family with private sponsors through IRCC. The individual or family must also be approved by a private sponsor who becomes a sponsorship agreement holder (SAH) with the federal government (Friesen, 2018). The agreement holder may be a private citizen and/or religious/ethnic organization that enters into this agreement to resettle refugees from abroad. Under the BVOR the government of Canada provides up to six months of income support with the sponsoring group providing an additional six months of financial support along with at least a year of social and emotional support (IRCC, 2018) (see Figure 3.2). The two separate phases of the BVOR are intended to facilitate faster resettlement and integration.

Syrian Refugees

Figure 3.2: The Two Resettlement Phases of the BVOR Program

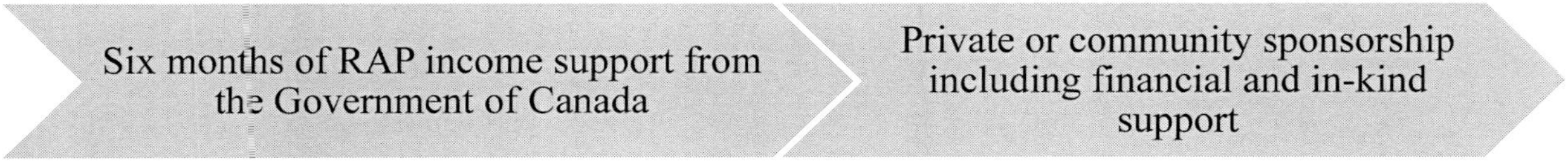

Six months of RAP income support from the Government of Canada

Private or community sponsorship including financial and in-kind support

Research Initiative Objectives

Although Canada has developed these three distinct refugee resettlement systems, few studies have focused on the system's overall effectiveness, specifically on each program's efficiency, relevance, or delivery of services. To address this research gap, the Emerging Voices project was conducted in 2016 to investigate the lived experiences of resettled Syrian refugees who arrived through the three sponsorship programs and resettled in Ottawa, Toronto, and London.

Method

The research team in the city of Ottawa was led by the chapter author and included a research assistant and two Arabic-speaking community informants. After obtaining research ethics approval from all participating universities, including Carleton University the team contacted resettlement agencies, and recruited 45 participants: 25 newcomers and 20 stakeholders working within the sponsorship programs. Two focus groups were held, the first consisting of 12 caseworkers, volunteers, and representatives of organizations and associations. The second focus group consisted of 25 refugees: 16 GARs, 5 BVORs, and 4 PSRs. Any study participants unable to attend the focus groups were invited to participate in individual interviews, and eight semi-structured individual interviews were conducted with stakeholders working within sponsorship programs.

Most interviews were completed in English, except one with a Syrian newcomer (BVOR). The focus groups were conducted in English or Arabic. All data were collected in the fall of 2017, and subjected to thematic analysis with a specific focus on participants' experiences within each program. Members of the Ottawa research team individually listened to the digital recordings on several occasions and reflected on the emerging stories, with the goal of bringing together the perspectives and (sub)themes among refugees and other stakeholders. This process helped identify some of the advantages and disadvantages of each sponsorship program and the resettlement process, which in turn helped clarify some of the gaps and barriers affecting the intended purpose of each program.

Findings

Participants from all stakeholder groups emphasized some of the highlights and the benefits of the PSR compared to the GAR or BVOR program. Newcomer participants emphasized their overall feelings of gratitude toward the programs and those who helped them. For example, most PSRs and BVORs saw their private sponsors and community volunteers as very helpful, referring to them as their second family or even literally calling them their *"families in Canada."* They mentioned the connections they had established with their sponsors and neighbours, explaining how that eased their integration process. However, they also identified disadvantages involved in each initiative, especially with the GAR, as did stakeholders. One participant said:

> Our settlement counsellors take two to three days to respond to our voice messages and sometimes we as newcomers have some emergencies that we really need immediate help with. Moreover, the settlement agencies have really big caseloads and not enough staff to serve a large number of refugees who came into the city. Compared to private sponsorship, as GARs we have no programs that enable us to integrate and share our values with the Canadian communities. (R10 newcomer focus group)

Newcomers also referred to feeling disappointed and not trusting some housing workers, noting that they often imposed on them or abused their power to deny them the choice of where to live. Some PSRs also described their sponsors in this way; one said, *"I feel like they own us"* (R8). Others felt that this kind of 'misunderstanding' was due to the lack of adequate orientation for both newcomers and sponsors.

Newcomers across all three programs referred to the barriers facing skilled workers due to a lack of accreditation or costly transition issues. Those seeking non-professional jobs felt that there was a lack of opportunity and options in Ottawa, and many referred to the language barrier as they tried to learn English and adjust to their new life in Canada. One said, *"if you miss classes they will not allow you to come back to school, even if you have a reason for your absence"* (R1 newcomer focus group). The transition to a new country is difficult, as is learning a new language in order to find a job and thereby integrate culturally and socially. Most newcomers questioned the need for such harsh restrictions. Table 3.2 summarizes how newcomers described the advantages and the disadvantages of each program.

Table 3.2: Newcomer Perceptions of Resettlement Programs

Program	Advantages	Disadvantages
GARs	• Initial housing and income support. • Faster health screenings and resettlement process. • Coordinated support systems during pre- and post-settlement. *"I find that the government sponsorship is the best for the refugees...they are more financially protected, more than anyone else."* (R2 newcomer focus group) *"Canada is a very welcoming country."*	• Language barriers. • Delayed responses for accommodation. • Lack of affordable housing or poor housing conditions. • Long waits for specialized health care. • Dissatisfaction with caseworkers regarding a lack of availability, and attention to specific needs. • Lack of employment opportunity for unskilled workers in Ottawa. • Delayed family reunification process. *"For government-assisted refugees, you have 12 families and one counselor; for privately sponsored refugees, you have 12 sponsors and one refugee. The amount of support that is available and the personal level is significantly different."* (R4 newcomer focus group)

	(R3 newcomer focus group)	
BVORs	• Having both GAR and PSR services (sponsor support for 6 months and government support for the remaining 6 months). • Better access to health specialists and better employment opportunities compared to GARs. *"For the half-government and half-private BVORs, I think they are the luckiest."* (S1 stakeholder focus group)	• Lack of freedom or personal choice about housing and other resettlement needs. • Isolation/delayed integration when sponsors also speak Arabic. • Reliance on personal connections when the sponsorship program ends. *"The downside of the BVOR is that only work for 6 months with a religious group or a counsellor – this is not enough to build a relationship."* (S2 stakeholder focus group) *"Private sponsors wouldn't attend any training sessions and do not know where the boundaries lie in a relationship over time and they are not connected to settlement agencies automatically."* (S3 stakeholder focus group)
PSRs	• Having an established pre-arrival connection with their sponsors that decreased their initial resettlement stressors such as fear	• Long wait for resettlement. • In some cases, feeling as if sponsors *"owned them"* or the lack of boundaries and

	of settling into a new place and orienting themselves with the people and culture.	lack of monitoring sponsorship outcomes.
	• Quick access to health care due to their connections.	• No guaranteed financial support during sponsorship or after sponsorship ends.
	• Personal and emotional support.	• Costly family reunification process.
	"If you're privately sponsored, you have that network from the moment you land." (R6 newcomer focus group)	*"There's a lot of waiting and anticipation."* (R7 newcomer focus group)
	"The private-sponsored refugees, they find jobs easily compared to GARs. The private sponsored tend to get more support – financially, emotionally. I think that PSRs take more benefits than GARs. Even at the airport, there are people to say hello, to get you to your home, to help you find all you need ready" (S4 stakeholders' group)	*"If you're sponsoring me, it doesn't mean you're owning me. I have my own freedom, family and rights."* (R8 newcomer focus group)

Discussion

Unlike other newcomers to Canada, refugees arrive after experiencing traumatic and life-changing events. Each responds differently; some experience little or no emotional disruption while others experience feelings of anxiety, terror, shock, shame, depression, intrusive thoughts, helplessness, powerlessness, or emotional numbness or disconnection (Evans andand Coccoma, 2014; Ehntholt and Yule, 2006; Han, 2015). For the latter group, added resettlement stressors diminish their sense of control, connection, and meaning-making processes, which in turn can affect their wellbeing and can even transfer to the next generation (Cozalino, 2010; Siegel, 2011).

Canada is a leading nation in establishing private sponsorship for refugees. Despite its reputation as one of the few countries that openly accepts refugees, there is much space for improvement. Each sponsorship program has challenges that need to be addressed. Successful adaptation to life in Canada is influenced by several factors, including life experiences prior to moving to Canada (e.g., level of violence committed against them and the effects on individuals and families) as well as support from sponsors, service providers, and communities during the post-migration process. Based on the input from study participants, positive changes could include making language training more accessible, having mandatory orientations and training sessions for private sponsors, and adding trauma-informed knowledge to training for service providers.

For decades, resettlement programs in Canada have been using an old model based on a one-size-fits-all approach, which ignores or minimizes post-resettlement needs that affect the emotional and physical wellbeing of refugees (Bokore, 2018; van der Kolk, 2014). With regard to Somali refugees in particular, previous research has identified long-term effects arising from unaddressed emotional issues and inadequate provision of services – even decades after their initial resettlement (Bokore, 2009, 2012, 2018; Danso, 2002; Warfa, 2002). Making changes to the current system will help prevent duplicating these negative experiences including prolonged poverty, health issues, and for the second generation, increased contact with the justice system including urban violence as well as high premature death rates (Bokore, 2009, 2012, 2018).

According to Bronfenbrenner's ecological systems theory (1977), successful integration requires identify issues and addressing needs related to:

i) the person's life in their country of origin;
ii) the pre-migration environment including life situations and experiences during displacement in neighbouring countries;
iii) their resettlement process, context, and the present situation in the resettlement country; and
iv) the post-migration environment (Anderson et al., 2004).

For a resettled refugee, the last stage – the post-migration environment – is critically important to ensure successful adaptation.

Policy discussions about resettlement must include a focus on pre-and post-migration gaps and disadvantages. In particular, it is vital to address post-resettlement service gaps and provide trauma-informed interventions for those who need it to promote the wellbeing of refugees and avoid the transference of trauma through generations (Bhui et al., 2006; Siegel, 2011).

Practice initiatives with refugee newcomers should begin during assessment and intervention planning, and should move beyond the elements of sponsorship, housing, healthcare, employment, and education. The key to a successful resettlement process is identification of each individual's responses to their past and present migration experiences. Therefore, helping professionals working with refugees need to learn how to conduct biopsychosocial assessments and have a basic working knowledge of neuroscience to help them understand the neurobiological responses to trauma experienced by refugees. Previous research has demonstrated that a neuroscience perspective can enhance assessment and intervention processes, especially in restorative and holistic practice with survivors (Cozolino, 2010; Farmer, 2009). This approach can prevent the current one-size-fits-all services provided for newcomers, and instead clarify how people respond to the same situations differently, for example how culture might influence brain activities (Aldwin &Levenson, 2004; Evans &Coccoma, 2014; van der Kolk, 2014). These additional data will help improve assessment and intervention processes, and can also help service providers and service users learn about trauma and how it can affect individuals mentally and physically.

Key Takeaway Points

1. Despite Canada's having developed three distinct routes to facilitate refugees settlement there remain numerous gaps in service and programming.

2. While GAR, PSR and BVOR all recognize the need for both financial and emotional support of refugees, most refugees in the study reported feelings of helplessness and disorientation, indicating the current resettlement efforts need to increase their emphasis on the psychosocial issues of resettlement.

References

Aldwin, C., & Levenson, M. (2004). Commentaries on "posttraumatic growth: Conceptual foundations and empirical evidence". *Psychological Inquiry,15*(1), 19-92.

Anderson, A., Hamilton, R., Moore, D., Loewen, S., & Frater-Mathieson, K. (2004). Education of refugee children: Theoretical perspectives and best practice. In R. Hamilton & D.

Moore (Eds.) *Educational interventions for refugee children: Theoretical perspectives and implementing best practices* (pp. 1-11). New-York: Routledge.

Bokore, N. (2009). Female survivors of African wars dealing with the past and present. *Journal of Sociological Research, 1*(1), E5, 1–13.

Bokore, N. (2012). Suffering in silence: A Somali Canadian case study. *Journal of Social Work Practice: Psychotherapeutic Approaches in Health, Welfare, and the Community, 27*(1), 95-113.

Bokore, N. (2018). Historical trauma, resettlement, and intervention strategies: An analysis of Somali-Canadians experiences. *Journal of International Migration, 56*(2), 146-162.

Bhui, K., Craig, T., Mohamud, S., Warfa, N., Stansfeld, S., Thornicroft, G., Curtis, S., & McCrone, P. (2006). Mental disorders among Somali refugees: Developing culturally appropriate measures and assessing socio-cultural risk factors. *Social Psychiatry and Psychiatric Epidemiology, 41*(5), 400–408.

Catholic Centre for Immigrants. (2019). *Syrian refugees*. Retrieved from http://cciottawa.ca/syrian-refugees/

Cozalino, L. (2010). *The neuroscience of psychotherapy: Healing the social brain.* New York: W.W. Norton and Company, Inc.

Danso, R. (2002). "From 'There' to 'Here': An Investigation of the Initial Settlement Experiences of Ethiopian and Somali Refugees in Toronto." *GeoJournal, 56* (1): 3–14.

Ehntholt, K., & Yule, W. (2006). Practitioner review: Assessment and treatment of refugee children and adolescents who have experienced war-related trauma: Practitioner review: Assessment and treatment of refugee children and adolescents. *Journal of Child Psychology and Psychiatry*, *47*(12), 1197-1210.

Evans, A., & Coccoma, P. (2014). *Trauma-informed care: How neuroscience influences practice*. New York: Routledge.

Friesen, J. (2018). Refugee sponsorship can be a long, complex process - here's how it works. *The Globe and Mail*. Retrieved from https://www.theglobeandmail.com/news/national/refugee-sponsorship-can-be-a-long-complex-process---here's-how-it-works/article26323043/

Farmer, R. (2009). *Neuroscience and social work practice*. Thousand Oaks: SAGE Publications.

Han, S., (2015). Understanding cultural differences in human behavior: a cultural neuroscience approach. *Current Opinion in Behavioral Sciences, 3*(1), 68–72.

Immigration, Refugees and Citizenship Canada. (2016). *Evaluation of the resettlement programs (GAR, PSR, BVOR, and RAP)*. Retrieved from https://www.canada.ca/en/immigration-refugees-citizenship/corporate/reports-statistics/evaluations/resettlement-programs.html

Immigration, Refugees and Citizenship Canada. (2017). *Canada's Syrian commitments*. Retrieved from https://www.canada.ca/en/immigration-refugees-citizenship/services/refugees/welcome-syrian-refugees/canada-commitment.html

Immigration, Refugees and Citizenship Canada. (2018). *Blended visa office-referred program: About the process*. Retrieved from https://www.canada.ca/en/immigration-refugees-citizenship/services/refugees/help-outside-Canada/private-sponsorship-program/blended-visa-office-program.html

McMurdo, A. (2016). Causes and consequences of Canada's resettlement of Syrian refugees. *Forced Migration Review, 52*(1), 82-84.

Siegel, D. (2011). *MindSight: The new science of personal transformation*. New York: Bantam.

van der Kolk, B.A (2014). *The body keeps the score: Brain, mind, and body in the healing of trauma*. New York: Viking.

Warfa, Nasir, et al. (2006). "Post-Migration Geographical Mobility, Mental Health and Health Service Utilisation Among Somali Refugees in the UK: A Qualitative Study." *Health & Place, 12* (4), 503-15.

CHAPTER FOUR

"WE ARE A GIFT TO CANADA": VOICES OF RESILIENCE AND RESETTLEMENT

BHARATI SETHI AND SNEŽANA OBRADOVIĆ-RATKOVIĆ

Introduction

Abundant research has focused on the resettlement experiences of women from refugee backgrounds in Canada, especially their experiences of trauma. Much less research has explored their resilience. One artist and writer struggled to name the quality that enables women from refugee backgrounds to transform horror into hope:

> I knew of one woman, a friend, with the quality that, for the sake of the work, I called 'fearlessness' but that I also sometimes referred to as 'resilience.' Neither of these words completely encompasses what I found, but I have never found the right word for the quality I recognize in all these women. (Wallworth, 2015, para. 3)

Resilience is a complex construct to define; the English language does not seem to have a single word that can fully express how someone can transform trauma into hope.

Some recent research has clarified the complex relationship between individual abilities or assets (e.g., positive attitude and perseverance) and the various contextual external factors (e.g., economic, social, political, environmental, and cultural) that can affect and contribute to resilience (Goodman, Vesely, Letiecq & Cleaveland, 2017; Pulvirenti & Mason, 2011; Ungar, 2012). By positioning resilience within a socio-ecological theoretical framework, scholars are able to explore a range of societal factors that promote or hinder women's resilience post-settlement (Ungar, 2012). However, to fully capture the resilience and vulnerability of women from refugee backgrounds, it is also important to consider the strategies and resources they use to function and make sense of life pre-migration and during transit, such as the time they spend living in refugee camps. By applying a strength-based approach, it is possible to incorporate – and honour – cultural, historic, and contextual elements and challenge the problematic dichotomy of a person being either "resilient" or "non-resilient" (Adamson, 2014; Pulvirenti & Mason, 2011). In this way, strength-based approaches are the key to understanding resilience among women and initiating effective interventions for their health and wellness. Based on our personal experiences as women from refugee backgrounds and migration researchers, we argue that a complete resilience framework must:

1. Challenge the individualistic deficit-based models that blame women from refugee backgrounds without considering how practices and policies influence resettlement at the individual, family, community, organizational, and government levels.
2. Move beyond the focus on trauma and shed light on women's assets and skills that help them cope and adapt to adverse circumstances.
3. Consider not only individual agency to navigate the post-migratory terrain, but also individual motivation toward a collective negotiation of assets and resources that are culturally meaningful (Atallah, 2017; Stainton et al., 2018).

Our work in the fields of resettlement and resilience research is framed from our perspectives as transnational feminist researchers and as migrant women who have experienced resettlement and resilience in our personal and professional lives. As a result, we work to scrutinize existing approaches to subalternity, voice, authorship, and representation, recognizing that it is impossible to describe an 'average' woman – either an average/typical Canadian woman or an average/typical woman from a refugee background. In this chapter, we explore resilience and agency among women with refugee backgrounds and honour the polyphonic voices of our research participants through photographs (Sethi, 2014; Wang, 1999) and poems (Glesne, 1997; Ratković, 2014). We identified emerging themes that reflected participants' perspectives and applied these themes to explore how women use resilience and agency as they adapt to myriad post-migration stressors including racialized and Othering discourses and family separation.[1]

---

[1] We are grateful to the women who shared with us their stories of resettlement and resilience.

Methods

This chapter draws from the findings of two different studies. We employed the principles of art-based research, including moral commitment to taking a stand and engaging with diverse audiences. We asked participants to choose their pseudonyms in order to build rapport, ensure confidentially, and honour heir voices.

A Photovoice Study of Women from Racialized Populations

In 2014, Sethi engaged in a Photovoice study[2] exploring the resettlement experiences of racialized women with immigrant and refugee backgrounds living in a mid-sized urban region in Ontario. In keeping with the tenets of Photovoice (Wang, 1999), participants recorded their post-migration work and health experiences using digital cameras. The following questions were used as prompts to facilitate discussion and dialogue about their self-generated photographs:

1. Choice: Why did you choose this photograph?
2. Theme: Tell me about the person, place, thing, colours, in the photograph;
3. Relationship: How does the photograph relate to you, your family, community, nation, work and health link?
4. Issues: What are the individual and societal issues your photograph addresses?
5. Message: What message do you want to give employers, healthcare practitioners, and policymakers through these images?

Data analysis was guided by constructivist grounded theory (Charmaz, 2006) and intersectionality (Bilge, 2009) methods. Constructivist grounded theory frames research as an interactive, intersubjective, and an interpretive process between researchers and participants. As Sethi coded data line by line into initial codes, focus codes, categories, and themes, she was vigilant in considering how various power relations such as race, class, and gender simultaneously intersected to influence the lives of participants. In this chapter, she discusses the experiences of six women with refugee

[2] Dr. Sethi's study was funded by the Ontario Women's Health Scholar's Award administered by the Ministry of Health and Long Term Care, and Vanier Canada Graduate Scholarship (VGS) funded by the Social Sciences and Humanities Research Council (SSHRC). The views expressed in this chapter are the views of the authors and do not necessarily reflect those of the funding agencies.

backgrounds from the total sample of 20 participants in the Photovoice study. Research ethics approval for the initial Photovoice study was provided by Wilfrid Laurier University, Waterloo, Ontario.

A Study of Women from Yugoslavia

In 2014, Ratković explored the experiences, transitions, and identities of 10 refugee women teachers from the former Yugoslavia who immigrated to Canada during or after the 1991–1995 war in that nation. She drew from narrative inquiry (Andrews, Squire, & Tambokou, 2008; Connelly & Clandinin, 1988), poetic transcription (Furman, Lietz, & Langer, 2006; Glesne, 1997), and transnational feminist methodologies (Alexander & Mohanty, 2010; Nagar & Lock Swarr, 2010) to represent the women's stories of resettling in Ontario and Québec. Her research was based on the following assumptions:

1. Human beings give meaning to their lives through story (Andrews et al., 2008).
2. Narrative inquirers make simultaneous connections between people's personal stories and the social structures the stories reflect and shape.
3. Teachers' knowledge is found in their past experiences, present minds and bodies, and future aspirations (Connelly & Clandinin, 1988).

To create poems from interview transcripts, Ratković identified the main stories in the transcript and condensed them into poems, retaining key words and phrases and omitting prepositions, adjectives, and adverbs. She reread and revised each poem several times to maintain the core meaning along with rhythm, rhyme, and metaphor. She also used a transnational feminist methodology to explore complexities and contradictions in the lives of participants, honouring their multiple voices and local knowledges (Nagar & Lock Swarr, 2010). She considered the social locations of herself and her participants and in order to practice self-reflexivity, work towards reciprocity and accountability, problematize research practices, and dismantle existing hierarchies of knowledge. In this chapter, we discuss the experiences of five women with refugee backgrounds from the total sample of 10 participants in the poetic inquiry study. Ratković's initial study received research ethics approval from Brock University, St. Catharines, Ontario. The following discussion draws from her findings and those of Sethi.

Women's Stories: Photographs and Poetry

Participants in both studies intricately weaved their resilience within their pre-migration and post-migration narratives. These stories provided insights into how they successfully navigated the post-settlement landscape and learned to adapt, thrive, and belong. Here, we bring together elements of resilience identified in both studies to challenge the media and societal portrayal of women from refugee backgrounds as weak, powerless, and unskilled while clarifying the systemic factors that hinder or promote resilience. We hope that the findings will help service providers and others who have the privilege to work with these fearless women to develop resilience-based models of service for this heterogeneous and growing population in Canada.

Overall, our integrated findings suggest that participants were not passive bystanders of oppression; they often actively resisted marginalization and dominant discourses of stereotypes through hard work, persistence, and/or education. Their resilience demonstrates their ability to cope and thrive despite structural barriers.

Resisting Racism and Discrimination

The first theme, resisting racism and discrimination, was a significant challenge faced by participants as they struggled to navigate the post-migration landscape. Most said they had experienced racism at the individual and societal level. Rudo, a participant in the Photovoice study, explained her experiences of racism as she worked in a nursing home: "White residents don't want you to touch them even when I am trying to help them. They call you nigger. They spit on you." Women's gender, race, and refugee/landed immigrant status often intersected, making the human capital obtained in their country of origin irrelevant and obsolete. For example, Arzoo, a participant from a Middle Eastern background, was employed as a teacher in her country of origin. In Canada, she worked as a customer service representative in a shopping mall. Other participants commented that they had experienced racism because of their names, an accent that was not desirable in the labour market, and their skin colour. Arzoo was the subject of social ridicule and exclusion for wearing a hijab. Similarly, women from Yugoslavia bore the burden of their South-Eastern European and Balkan origins, Slavic accents, and names – and the political stigma of being considered "bloody socialists," as Nina phrased it.

Some women from Yugoslavia, who identified as being White, felt that they fit seamlessly in the dominant Canadian society. Dana, who was completing a Ph.D. and teaching part-time at an Ontario university at the time of the interviews, argued that her teaching career and successful integration in the Canadian society was not the result of her White privilege, but rather her hard work. Others, when discussing their personal stories within their geographical, social, and political contexts, were more circumspect regarding their Whiteness. Nina argued that she lost her teaching position at an Ontario college because she was White but "not Anglo-Saxon-White." Snežana, who was completing her doctoral studies at the time of the interviews, reported negotiating an ambiguous racial identity. She noted that White middle-class Canadian-born women tended to consider her White and privileged while an Indigenous Ph.D. colleague described her as "olive." These complexities and contradictions of (not) being White made it difficult for Snežana to understand her location in Canadian society and increased her desire to engage with identity politics, intersectionality, and transnational feminist solidarity (Mohanty, 2003). Despite their different perspectives of resettlement in Ontario, the personal, political, and critical stories of Dana, Nina, and Snežana all reflect the importance of education and life-long learning during the resettlement process.

The racial identities assigned to racialized women, and the shades-of-White identities assigned to Yugoslav women, made participants' locations in Canadian society uncertain, vulnerable, and often challenged in different contexts, times, and places. However, the shades-of-White identities experienced by some of the Yugoslav women enabled them to demonstrate their agency by negotiating their racial locations on an ongoing basis and by recognizing or scrutinizing White privilege within Canadian society, their diasporic communities, and their personal and professional lives.

Enacting Resilience

The overarching and consistent theme of resilience shone through the stories of participants. They used their agency and found ways to lift their spirits and redefine their identity. Ruvashe's story is one excellent example of resilience. Her life was in danger and she was forced to flee Zimbabwe without her son. She took the photograph presented below for the Photovoice study and provided the following accompanying narrative:

The empty crib resembles the absence of my son in my life for the first 2 1/2 years of my time in Canada. I was very lonely and was not sure if I was ever going to see him again... I could not hang out at parties where their children or even went to any parks because everywhere I went, there was a constant reminder of my son.

Figure 4.1: Empty crib (photo by Ruvashe).

Despite experiencing pre-migration trauma of violence and post-migration poverty, racism, and loneliness, Ruvashe used her agency to make choices that enabled her to walk toward resilience: she completed her nursing degree in Canada, found a job in a local hospital, bought a home, and brought her son to Canada.

Maruška, one of the participants from Yugoslavia, shared another story of resilience related to obtaining Canadian credentials, as reflected in the following poem.

A Long Walk to Teaching

I was discriminated at my university

because I didn't speak the language well.

I get that, you know;

No English,

No courses,

No programs,

No degrees.

A counsellor said:

"Listen, considering your language incapabilities,

why do you even think about university?

Why don't you pick a vocational school?"

She literally said that!

Well, I thought,

and I thought,

and I chose university.

I completed a program for teaching English as a second language,

a master's degree in linguistics,

and a bridge-in program for internationally trained teachers.

I was a teaching assistant at the university.

I believed in myself.

My students believed in me.

I lined up my Canadian degrees.

I became a super occasional teacher.

Still walking towards my dream.

Maruška came to Ontario with her family in 1995 through a Government Assisted Refugees program. She and her husband left the program early because they believed that gaining Canadian work experience and contributing to the Canadian economy would enhance their resettlement process. Maruška was proud of her educational accomplishments in Canada but at the same time, she was aware that despite her Yugoslavian and Canadian degrees, she was unlikely to obtain a permanent full-time teaching position in Ontario. She referred to her teaching as "super occasional" but enjoyed her work with children. Despite facing discrimination and economic hardship, Maruška's strength, resilience, and love for teaching and learning helped her engage with the Canadian education system and society, albeit in a limited way.

Rudo, another participant in the Photoshop study, also exhibited resilience. She took the photo presented below and commented: "In life, I won't give up. Many times, I am just hanging. Even my legs hurt standing for hours. Even when I don't get enough sleep, I say I am not going to give up. I am going to hang on." She experienced vulnerability at the intersections of race (as a Black woman), age and gender (as an older woman), immigration status (as a refugee fleeing interpersonal and political violence from Africa), and socioeconomic class (employment working at several precarious jobs). The residents of a nursing home where she worked continually told her that her Black hands were not good enough to clean White faces. Still, Rudo held on – she phoned home every day and prayed with her children and other family members.

Figure 4.2: Hanging on (photo by Rudo).

By the end of the study, Rudo owned a home, had full-time employment, and was the recipient of the Employee of the Year award at the same nursing home where she was called a "nigger." She said proudly: "No matter what people call me, I am beautiful."

Jagoda, a teacher from Yugoslavia, also found that her refugee status, poverty, and vulnerability made her strong and fearless. She said that in 1992, during the wars, she confessed to her priest that she could not endure the poverty and despair anymore – she had arrived at the end of her journey and was done. The priest responded by telling her that yes, she was bearing the cross but that it was her own cross – one she could bear. Jagoda cherished these words, as well as a comforting comment from a neighbour, who said, "Jagoda, don't worry; God takes care of everything." Her new understanding and acceptance of adversity carried her through – and out of – war, poverty, and despair, as reflected in the following poem.

God Takes Care of Everything

In refuge,

I had a crisis,

I suffered many of them.

In refuge,

I met a priest and a neighbour;

Their words healed the pain.

In refuge,

I said: "I'm done.

I can't do this anymore."

In refuge,

My priest said: "Yes, you can.

God gave you the cross you can bear."

In refuge,

I told my neighbour: "I'm done.

I can't do this anymore."

In refuge,

My neighbour said: "Don't worry about a thing;

God takes care of everything."

In refuge,

I lost my hope, broke my wing;

My Lord took care of everything.

The study participants did not believe in retaliation and remained cheerful in the face of adversity. No matter how bleak their current prospects seemed, they persevered to focus on the light at the end of the tunnel. They were determined to face their adverse circumstances for the hope of a better life for their children. They praised their strong cultural roots and family relationships for responding to resettlement challenges. A previous study also reported that "deep faith practices such as prayer and meditation and congregational affiliation, can be wellsprings for resilience, particularly for families struggling to surmount barriers of poverty and racism" (Walsh, 2012, p. 181). Our findings relate to our earlier conceptualization of resilience as a dynamic process rather than a static individual trait (Pulvirenti & Mason, 2011) that is "not impenetrable" (Stainton et al., 2018, p. 3). Just as interactions between individuals and their environment are dynamic, flexible, and ongoing, people can and do change across space, time, and culture.

What We Learned

Women with refuge backgrounds who are resettling in Canada are a heterogeneous and resilient population. Their stories reflect courage and resilience. On an individual level, they are able to persevere and hang on to their dreams and their professional identities, actively resisting the label of Outsider. Enactment of their agency was central to their ability to be resourceful and steer their lives in a positive direction despite the individual and structural constraints and racialization they encountered during their migration journeys. Personal agency is considered an important asset and source of resilience. Liebenberg, Joubert, and Foucault expanded the understanding of agency "beyond its traditional definition as the 'capacity to act,' including additional capacities of meaning- and decision-making that is implied within individuals' capacity to act" (2017, p. 6). The study participants applied resilience resources including a sense of personal efficacy, active decision-making strategies, spiritual beliefs, family supports and relationships, transnational ties, and passion for life-long learning, all of which helped them thrive in Canada.

We discussed earlier the dangers of blaming individuals when we focus on resilience as an individual trait. The reality of resettlement is much more complex than a simplistic explanation that only those who are resilient can adapt and cope with resettlement challenges. For example, Maruška demonstrated her resilience by continuing her education in Canada, but her resettlement process was hindered due to her "super occasional" teaching; she was only able to partially reclaim her professional and Canadian status. If the credentials and work experiences of women with refugee backgrounds are discounted due to their accents, names, or skin shades, they are very unlikely to thrive. When resilience is framed as a dynamic, relational, and interactive process that involves an interplay between the individual and environment (Ungar, 2012; Walsh, 2012), we can see the need for support and collaboration between the government, local community, ethnic community, employers, service providers, and educational authorities to build resilience and foster adaptation (Fielding & Anderson, 2008). For example, Ruvashe received assistance from a social worker in navigating the Canadian social welfare, health, and education systems. Additionally, her employer provided her with flexible work hours also some financial assistance so that she was able to finish her nursing degree. When women from refugee backgrounds are supported, they are much more likely to "successfully navigate adversity, challenges or risks, to achieve and maintain positive mental health outcomes" (Liebenberg et al., 2017, p. 7)

As academics, our understanding of resilience is evolving, and we have much more to learn about the components that prevent, alleviate, or promote resilience, especially resilience among women with diverse historical, political, cultural, geographical, and economic backgrounds. We do know that because individual life experiences are unique, it is difficult to find a 'single pathway' that leads to resilience (Goodman et al., 2017). For the sake of our nation's prosperity and wellbeing, we must recognize and value women from refugee backgrounds. They are resilient, resourceful, and motivated to contribute to their new home. Nada called them "a gift to Canada."

Key Takeaway Points

1. Resilience frameworks should be used to develop strength-based models of refugee support services and design holistic pathways to resettlement.
2. Transnational feminist research methodology and art-based methods, such as Photovoice and poetic inquiry, can be utilized for social justice and advocacy to promote change at individual, family, and (local and global) community levels.
3. Women from refugee backgrounds are a gift to Canada.

References

Adamson, C., (2014). Stress, resilience, and responding to civil defence emergencies and natural disasters: An ecological framework. In L. Beddoe, & J. Maidment (2014). *Social work practice for promoting health and wellbeing: Critical issues* (63-75). New York: Routledge.

Alexander, M., & Mohanty, C. (2010). Cartographies of knowledge and power:Transnational feminism as transnational praxis. In A. Lock Swarr, & R. Nagar (Eds.), *Critical transnational feminist practice* (pp. 23-45). Albany: State University of New York Press.

Andrews, M., Squire, C., & Tambokou, M. (Eds.). (2008). *Doing narrative research.*London: Sage.

Atallah, D. G. (2017). A community-based qualitative study of intergenerational resilience with Palestinian refugee families facing structural violence and historical trauma. *Transcultural Psychiatry, 54*(3), 357-383. doi: 10.1177/1363461517706287

Bennett, K., Reyes-Rodriguez, M., Altamar, P., & Soulsby, L. (2016). Resilience amongst older Colombians living in poverty: An ecological approach. *Journal of Cross-Cultural Gerontology, 31*(4), 385-407. doi 10.1007/s10823-016-9303-3

Bilge, S. (2009). *Smuggling intersectionality into the study of masculinity: Some methodological challenges.* Paper presented at Feminist Research Methods: An International Conference, University of Stockholm. Retrieved from https://www.researchgate.net/publication/228998452_Smuggling_intersectionality_into_the_study_of_masculinity_some_methodologica l_challenges

Charmaz, K. (2006). *Constructing grounded theory: A practical guide through qualitative analysis.* London: Sage Publications.

Connelly, F., & Clandinin, D. (1988). T*eachers as curriculum planners: Narratives of experience.* New York: Teachers College.

Fielding, A., & Anderson, J. (2008). *Working with refugee communities to build collective resilience.* Perth: The Association for Services to Torture and Trauma Survivors.

Furman, R., Lietz, C., & Langer, C. (2006). The research poem in international social work: Innovations in qualitative methodology. *International Journal of Qualitative Methods, 5*(3), 24-34.

Glesne, C. (1997). That rare feeling: Re-presenting research through poetic transcription. *Qualitative Inquiry, 3*(2), 202-221.

Goodman, R., Vesely, C., Letiecq, B., & Cleaveland, C. (2017). Trauma and resilience among refugee and undocumented immigrant women. *Journal of Counseling & Development, 95*(3), 309-321.

Liebenberg, L., Joubert, N., & Foucalt, M. (2017). *Understanding core resilience elements and indicators: A comprehensive review of literature.* Retrieved from http://lindaliebenberg.com/wp-content/uploads/2017/11/PHAC-Resilience-Report-Final-Version-November-2017.pdf

Nagar, R., & Lock Swarr, A. (2010). Theorizing transnational feminist praxis. In A. Lock Swarr, & R. Nagar (Eds.), *Critical transnational feminist praxis* (pp. 1-20). Albany: State University of New York Press.

Pulvirenti, M., & Mason, G. (2011). Resilience and survival: Refugee women and violence. *Current Issues in Criminal Justice, 23*(1), 37-52.

Ratković, S. (2014). *Teachers without borders: Exploring experiences, transitions, and identities of refugee women teachers from Yugoslavia.* Doctoral thesis, Brock University, St. Catharines, Canada. Retrieved from https://dr.library.brocku.ca/handle/10464/5243

Ratković, S., & Sethi, B. (2017). Multisensory ethnography and a/r/tography: Mobilizing methodologies, disciplines, and knowledges. In S. Opić, B. Bognar, & S. Ratković (Eds.), *New approaches to research methodology in education* (pp. 167-189). Zagreb: Faculty of Teacher Education, University of Zagreb.

Stainton, A., Chisholm, K., Kaiser, N., Rosen, M., Upthegrove, R., Ruhrmann, S., & Wood, S. J. (2018). Resilience as a multimodal dynamic process. *Early Intervention in Psychiatry,* 1-8. https://doi.org/10.1111/eip.12726

Sethi, B. (2014). Intersectional exposures: Exploring the health effect of employment with KAAJAL Immigrant/Refugee women in Grand Erie through photovoice (Order No. 3662103). Available from ProQuest Dissertations & Theses Global. (1646467937). Retrieved from https://www-lib-uwo-ca.proxy1.lib.uwo.ca/cgi-bin/ezpauthn.cgi?url=http://search.proquest.com.proxy1.lib.uwo.ca/doc view/1646467937?accountid=15115

Ungar, M. (2012). *The social ecology of resilience: A handbook of theory and practice.* New York: Springer Science + Business Media.

Walsh, F. (2012). Facilitating family resilience: Relational resources for positive youth development in conditions of adversity. In M. Ungar (Ed.), *The social ecology of resilience: A handbook of theory and practice* (pp. 173-185). New York: Springer Science + Business Media.

Wallworth, L. (2015). *What refugee women teach us about resilience.* World Economic Forum. Retrieved from https://www.weforum.org/agenda/2015/01/refugee-women-resilience/

Wang, C. C. (1999). Photovoice: A participatory action research strategy applied to women's health. *Journal of Women's Health, 8*(2), 185-192.

CHAPTER FIVE

PARENTING IN CONTEXTS OF WAR, DISPLACEMENT, AND RESETTLEMENT: REFUGEE VOICES FROM THE SYRIAN CONFLICT

ABDELFETTAH ELKCHIRID AND BREE AKESSON

Today, one in four children live in a country that is affected by conflict or disaster, and 30 million children have been internally displaced by violence and conflict (United Nations Children's Fund [UNICEF], 2019). In addition to the obvious effects of physical harm, displacement and/or exposure to war-related stressors can affect children's development, cognitive capacity, self-esteem, positive coping mechanisms, and other life skills (Boothby, Strang, & Wessells, 2006). Parents may be able to minimize the effects of stress and trauma by providing children with consistent and responsive support (Barber, 1999; Garbarino & Kostelny, 1996; Miller & Jordans, 2016; Shonkoff et al., 2012; Thabet, Ibraheem, Shivram, Winter & Vostanis, 2009). However, in contexts of war, parenting roles may be severely challenged as families face violence and are forced to leave their homes in search of safety (Bradley, 2007; Williams, 2010). Challenges can include armed groups and violence, as well as political and socioeconomic factors such as lack of legal protection, poverty, instability, poor health, and lack of adequate housing – all of which can affect the psychological and emotional wellbeing of parents and in turn lead to negative outcomes among children (Miller & Jordans, 2016).

In this chapter, the authors draw from their previous research and experience working with Syrian refugee parents living in Lebanon and Canada (Akesson & Badawi, 2020; Akesson & Coupland, 2018a, 2018b; Akesson, Hoffman, El Joueidi & Badawi, 2018). The following discussion explores the challenges parents may face in the contexts of pre-flight (in

Syria), flight (from Syria to a neighbouring country), displacement (in Lebanon), and resettlement (in Canada). Specifically, it draws from Akesson's research involving 46 Syrian refugee families displaced and living in Lebanon, which received ethics approval from Wilfrid Laurier University's Research Ethics Board. It also draws from Elkchirid's direct practice experience working with 36 Syrian parents and 16 children in three different social service programs in Kitchener, Ontario. The findings illustrate the constantly shifting roles of parents during these difficult journeys, and how parents typically operate under the singular purpose of keeping their children safe and giving them a better life without the threat of war, despite the challenges they face.

Pre-Flight: Ensuring Children's Safety

During pre-flight, the period leading up to a family's decision to leave their home due to war, parenting tends to follow cultural and societal norms, with conflicts and issues handled from an intergenerational perspective. During this stage, parents benefit from support from extended family and community members. However, once war breaks out, families may not be able to rely on those forms of parenting support due to the instability of war. Parents may be personally targeted, experience physical violence, or witness the persecution, kidnapping, or murder of family and community members (Hopkins & Hill, 2008; Thomas, Nafees & Bhugra, 2004). Abu-Omar,[3] a 42-year-old father of five, said that Syrian forces would "shoot anyone they see. They would enter houses and slaughter the entire family at night."[4] War can also lead to other structural factors that affect families: poverty, poor economic or educational prospects, lack of access to health services, and environmental catastrophe such as famine. Within this context of violence, uncertainty, and fear, parents struggle to meet the needs of their children.

During this time, parents often make the decision to flee based on their children's safety. Umm-Iman, a 29-year-old mother of two, said: "It was for the children. They were in fear. Bombings were everywhere, so I told my husband we had to leave, for the sake of our children." Umm-Iman's words reiterate the importance of her children's safety and how this is a driving factor in her and her husband's decision to flee.

---

[3] All names are pseudonyms. In Arabic, Abu- indicates "father of" and Umm- indicates "mother of."

[4] Unless cited otherwise, all excerpts are from the authors' work with Syrian parents.

Flight: Fleeing for the Children

During flight, parents continue to focus on the safety of the family unit, especially during the harrowing journey(s) from their home to a safer place. Umm-Yousef, 36-year-old mother of five, described her family's difficult journey from Syria to neighbouring Lebanon:

> We came by car, but not legally. We needed to get many papers and it was not easy to get it. So we talked to a taxi driver and he drove us here. It was so hard. We walked so much and it was really tough and hard for us.

Parents, especially fathers, may be separated from their children to ensure the family's safe passage, especially in settings where fighting-age men are targeted by armed groups. As a result, journeys may be split into smaller segments to reduce risk. Abu-Omar, a 42-year-old father of nine, explained:

> From my house to the next village, it was difficult. There were many checkpoints. We left at night. Eventually I left them [my wife and children] with the driver, because I couldn't go with them. I left them before entering Damascus.

Separation of the family unit can be very traumatic for parents and children, and in some cases, Syrian parents forced to leave their families are never reunited with their families due to fear, refugee policies, and other barriers.

Displacement: Living in Limbo

Once the family reaches a safer (albeit possibly temporary) place, it no longer faces the constant threat of direct violence. However, in this context of displacement, parents often face structural factors in their new environments that challenge their capacities to adequately care for their children: poverty, un(der)employment and precarious work, and inadequate access to education and health care. Families also face uncertainty about whether and when they might be able to return to their country of origin or permanently resettle in another country.

A large majority (86%) of refugees worldwide are hosted by countries that are struggling economically (UNHCR, 2016). As a result, high rates of poverty, burdensome governmental policies and regulations, lack of affordable housing, food insecurity, decreased school attendance, and family violence increase vulnerability among refugee families. Among Syrian refugees, the effects of war and subsequent displacement along with these other factors have a destabilizing effect on parents as they struggle to meet the needs of their families in a low-resource and often unwelcoming environment (Akesson & Badawi, 2020). Some Syrian parents said that the conditions in Lebanon were so dire, they would rather return to Syria with their families and risk death. As 28-year-old, mother of four, Umm-Haytham explained:

> I'd rather live in the poorest areas of Syria than stay here [in Lebanon]. This place isn't safe. Here, I'm constantly worried about my children. I prefer to live with relatives in a locked room under the wreckage.

Economic precarity and the resultant inability to provide economically for children is a source of great frustration and hopelessness for parents. Abu-Farid, a 37-year-old father of seven, explained:

> It's affected us psychologically, because our kid comes to us saying he want 1000 Lebanese pounds [about CAD$1] and I can't provide it to him. He goes to school and tells me he wants a thousand… honestly, I feel frustrated, my heart feels chained, I don't have it to give it to him.

These feelings of parental inadequacy may lead parents to restrict their children's activities outside the home. Some parents said they never left home with their children because they were afraid the children would ask them to purchase something for which they did not have the money.

Resettlement

Shifts in Family Roles

Once settled in a new permanent country, refugee parents may face compounding challenges, such as financial, social, and environmental stressors. They also may experience shifts in family roles due to numerous other responsibilities. For example, in the post-migration context, mothers or fathers who worked in the home or on their farm in their country of origin may engage in work outside the home. Additionally, newly arrived refugees are often required to take language classes, which takes time away from parenting. Umm-Arij, 43-year-old mother of five, said:

> It is so difficult for me to keep up with my homework and also have enough play time with my children. I often find myself having to do less of both.

Many Syrian refugee parents also noted that they were more involved in certain aspects of their children's lives in the post-migration context, for example facilitating or controlling their children's socializing, than they would have been in their country of origin. Some said that to keep children safe and discourage negative behaviours, they felt they needed to be more engaged or more controlling. Some shifts in family roles were also related to parents' struggles with the new language. Abu-Bassem, a 47-year-old father of four, explained:

> I use to take them everywhere they need to go, and I use to help them with their school work. Now, they are the ones helping me understand what their teachers are writing in their agendas.

Another shift in parental role can occur when parents must learn a new language. For example, Umm-Arij, a 43-year-old mother of five, said:

> In Syria, and in Turkey, where we lived, I use to help them with their school work. Here, I have my own homework now. I would often ask them to help me do my ESL assignments.

Previous research has revealed that these kinds of role changes can threaten the authority of parents (Merry, Pelaez & Edwards, 2017), including refugee parents who have expressed the need to maintain authority over their children (Osman, Klingberg-Allvin, Flacking & Schön, 2016). Specifically, Osman et al. (2016) found that Somalian refugee parents wanted to be a role model, know the language well, and have a career, and that when they lacked these elements, their children had less respect for them and tended to ignore their requests and decisions.

Challenges to Authority, Culture, and Identity

Upon resettlement, many parents face a loss of cultural identity in terms of family structure and parenting methods (Alfadhli & Drury, 2018). Traditionally, many parents have wanted to have authority and command obedience are important to all parents, with a relatively authoritative and restrictive structure within the home (Smetana, Ahmad & Wray-Lake, 2015), However, more recently an individualistic model of behaviour has become more popular, especially in Western countries (Grant & Guerin, 2014). Kalliyvayalil (2004) conducted a study involving second-generation immigrants in Canada, and found that Canadian-born children of South Asian immigrants were torn between individualism and family obligation. This kind of contextual shift can cause stress and confusion, including among Syrian refugees. Abu-Omar, a 46-year-old father of three, commented:

> Since I came here [Canada] two years ago, I keep hearing about what parents are allowed to do, and what they are not allowed to do. To be honest, I am so confused about my authority, and what I can and cannot do.

Refugees also find it challenging to understand the new systems and the new culture in Canada, leading to difficulties in communication between parents and their children and a lack of social network support (Osman et al., 2016). This is also the case for Syrian refugees; Abu-Ali, a 39-year-old father of three, said:

> Things here are different. Back home if your neighbor sees your child doing something wrong, they would intervene and teach your kids good manners. Here, a neighbor is almost like a stranger. We hardly say anything to each other beyond hi.

As will all refugees, newcomer Syrian adults living in Canada usually feel culturally isolated as they have not had enough time to fully understand Canadian customs, including norms about parenting. They may also feel that their Arab and Muslim identities prevent them from easily integrating into their local communities (UNHCR, 2014). As a result, they typically seek to compensate for the loss of the neighbourhood support they were accustomed to in Syria by seeking support from the broader Syrian or Muslim communities. These communities can work in partnership with parents to foster positive outcomes for refugee families. Abu-Hafidh, a 48-year-old father of three, said:

> I found the Masjid to be really helpful. I have always gotten the information, and support I needed from people at the Masjid. They helped me get my driver's license and enroll in ESL classes.

Smetana et al. conducted a study involving Arab refugees; their findings also reflected the importance of community: "Loyalty and responsiveness to the extended family, along with conformity, community, and family honor, all are strongly emphasized" (2015, p. 2018).

Conclusion

Programs focused on refugee families need to also focus on the emotional health of parents, and the importance of a social support network cannot be overemphasized. Parenting processes should be supported by emphasizing what parents do well, and encouraging sharing among parents to develop and maintain social support networks in contexts of adversity.

Previous research has demonstrated that children and adolescents form and act on their own legitimacy beliefs within which authority, identity, and culture are framed; these beliefs are often individual, but contextual influences also play a part (Smetana, Crean, and Campione-Barr, 2003;

Smetana et al., 2015). Among Syrian refugee families, many contextual challenges influence children's legitimacy beliefs regarding their parents' capacity to parent. Their family's social isolation and their parents' inability to speak English intensifies the trauma children have experienced related to war, displacement, and immigration – all of which affect their legitimacy beliefs about effective parenting. Within this context, mental health practitioners need to focus on emotional and mental wellbeing among both parents and children. Measures to improve parenting experiences among refugee families should include trauma screening and referrals to counselling and therapy when needed.

Research has also demonstrated the importance of community participation and involvement within the context of resettlement (Alfadhli & Drury, 2018). Community involvement is particularly important for refugees, because sharing of parenting experiences among refugees has proven to be effective in identity building and achieving common goals. It also provides opportunities for in-community socializing for adults and children. Interactions with other families trying to instill similar cultural values in their children can also help Syrian refugee parents normalize, to their children, the transmission of cultural values and practices.

Key Takeaway Points

1. Refugee parents are most likely to receive the most help with parenting during the resettlement stage, in countries such as Canada with the capacity to support them and provide them with services. They have very limited access to educational, health, and legal services during the flight and displacement stages, which could last for months or even years.
2. While Syrian refugee families face similar challenges during their journeys to resettlement, they also face specific challenges applicable to each family, so it is up to the practitioners working with Syrian refugee families to become aware of their unique experiences. Most importantly, in designing support programs for these families, such services should be offered in a flexible enough way so as to respond to common challenges facing refugee populations, as well as more specific challenges facing parents and families.

References

Akesson, B., & Badawi, D. (2020). "My heart feels chained": The effects of economic precarity on Syrian refugee parents living in Lebanon. In C. W. Greenbaum, M. M. Haj-Yahia, & C. Hamilton (Eds.), *Handbook of political violence and children: Psychological effects, intervention and prevention policy.* Oxford, UK: Oxford University Press.

Akesson, B., & Coupland, K. (2018). Seeking safety, finding fear: Syrian families' experiences of (im)mobility and the implications for children's rights. *Canadian Journal of Children's Rights, 5*(1), 6–29.

Akesson, B., & Coupland, K. (2018b). Without choice?: Understanding Syrian refugee families' decisions to flee. *International Organization for Migration (IOM) Migration Research Series, 54.*

Akesson, B., Hoffman, D. A. T., El Joueidi, S., & Badawi, D. (2018). "So the world will know our story": Ethical reflections on research with families displaced by war. *Forum Qualitative Sozialforschung / Forum: Qualitative Social Research, 19*(3).

Alfadhli, K., & Drury, J. (2018). The role of shared social identity in mutual support among refugees of conflict: An ethnographic study of Syrian refugees in Jordan. *Journal of Community & Applied Social Psychology, 28*(3), 142–155.

Barber, B. K. (1999). Political violence, family relations, and Palestinian youth functioning. *Journal of Adolescent Research, 14*(2), 206–230.

Boothby, N., Strang, A., & Wessells, M. G. (Eds.). (2006). *A world turned upside down: Social ecological approaches to children in war zones.* Bloomfield, CT: Kumarian Press.

Bradley, R. H. (2007). Parenting in the breach: How parents help children cope with developmentally challenging circumstances. *Parenting, 7*(2), 99–148.

Garbarino, J., & Kostelny, K. (1996). The effects of political violence on Palestinian children's behavior problems: A risk accumulation model. *Child Development, 67*(1), 33–45.

Grant, J., & Guerin, P. B. (2014). Applying ecological modeling to parenting for Australian refugee families. *Journal of Transcultural Nursing: Official Journal of the Transcultural Nursing Society, 25*(4), 325–333.

Hopkins, P. E., & Hill, M. (2008). Pre-flight experiences and migration stories: The accounts of unaccompanied asylum-seeking children. *Children's Geographies, 6*(3), 257–268.

Kallivayalil, D. (2004). Gender and cultural socialization in Indian immigrant families in the United States. *Feminism & Psychology, 14*(4), 535–559.

Merry, L., Pelaez, S., & Edwards, N. C. (2017). Refugees, asylum-seekers and undocumented migrants and the experience of parenthood: A synthesis of the qualitative literature. *Globalization and Health, 13*(1), 75.

Miller, K. E., & Jordans, M. J. D. (2016). Determinants of children's mental Health in war-torn settings: Translating research into action. *Current Psychiatry Reports, 18*(6), 58.

Osman, F., Klingberg-Allvin, M., Flacking, R., & Schön, U.-K. (2016). Parenthood in transition: Somali-born parents' experiences of and needs for parenting support programmes. *BMC International Health and Human Rights, 16*, 7.

Shonkoff, J. P., Garner, A. S., Siegel, B. S., Dobbins, M. I., Earls, M. F., McGuinn, L., ... Wood, D. L. (2012). The lifelong effects of early childhood adversity and toxic stress. *Pediatrics, 129*(1), e232–e246.

Smetana, J. G., Ahmad, I., & Wray-Lake, L. (2015). Iraqi, Syrian, and Palestinian refugee adolescents' beliefs about parental authority legitimacy and its correlates. *Child Development, 86*(6), 2017–2033.

Smetana, J. G., Crean, H. F., and Campione-Barr, N. "African American Middle Class Families' Changing Conceptions of Parental Authority." Paper presented at the Biennial Meetings of the Society for Research in Child Development, Tampa, Fla., Apr. 2003.

Thabet, A. A., Ibraheem, A. N., Shivram, R., Winter, E. A., & Vostanis, P. (2009). Parenting support and PTSD in children of a war zone. *The International Journal of Social Psychiatry, 55*(3), 226–237.

Thomas, S., Nafees, B., & Bhugra, D. (2004). "I was running away from death" - the pre-flight experiences of unaccompanied asylum seeking children in the UK. *Child: Care, Health and Development, 30*(2), 113–122.

United Nations High Commissioner for Refugees. Syria regional response plan (RRP6) annual report; 2014. Retrieved from https://data2.unhcr.org/en/documents/download/45922

United Nations Children's Fund. (2019). *UNICEF Humanitarian Action for Children: Overview.* New York, NY: UNICEF. Retrieved from https://www.unicef.org/sites/default/files/2019-01/Humanitarian-action-for-children-2019-eng.pdf

United Nations High Commissioner for Refugees. (2016). *Global trends: Forced displacement in 2015.* Geneva, Switzerland: UNHCR. Retrieved from   https://s3.amazonaws.com/unhcrsharedmedia/2016/2016-06-20-global-trends/2016-06-14-Global-Trends-2015.pdf

Williams, N. (2010). Establishing the boundaries and building bridges: A literature review on ecological theory: implications for research into the refugee parenting experience. *Journal of Child Health Care, 14*(1), 35–51.

CHAPTER SIX

LISTENING TO INNOCENCE: EFFECTS OF ISLAMOPHOBIA ON MUSLIM CHILDREN

SIHAM ELKASSEM, RICK CSIERNIK, ANDREW MANTULAK, GINA KAYSSI YASMINE HUSSAIN, KATHRYN LAMBERT, PAMELA BAILEY AND ASAD CHOUDHARY

Introduction

Muslims worldwide are becoming the focus of more negative attention fueled by Islamophobia (Baljit, 2018; Beydoun, 2016; 2018; Council for Arab Islamic Relations-California (CAIR-California), 2015; Lean, 2012; Wilkins-LaFlamme, 2018). This is also the case in Canada, as illustrated by recent media reports:

> 6 dead, 8 injured in terrorist attack at Quebec City mosque
> Montreal Gazette, January 30, 2017

> Protesters outside Masjid Toronto call for ban on Islam as Muslims pray inside
> CBC News, February 17, 2017

> Arrest made after Muslim family threatened, assaulted at ferry terminal
> CP24 (Toronto), July 27, 2018

> Attacks against Canadian Muslims and other hate crimes are surging
> National Observer, November 29, 2018

Hamilton (Ontario) mosque plans for worst-case scenarios after terrorist attacks in New Zealand Hamilton Spectator, March 15, 2019

"I became very paranoid": Muslim Canadian explains why she stopped wearing the hijab
Global News, April 10, 2019

Islamophobia can be defined as the fear or hatred of all Muslim people, and is deeply interconnected with racism, xenophobia, and other forms of dehumanization that lead to discrimination, exclusion, and violence against individuals and communities (Beydoun, 2016; Garner & Selod, 2015). Islamophobia also entails anti-Muslim or anti-Islamic attitudes or emotions. The concept of Islamophobia became more recognized in the late 1990s and early 2000s – especially after 9/11 and the current crisis in the Middle East – with the intent of addressing the harmful rhetoric and actions directed at Muslims and Islam in Western liberal democracies (Bleich, 2011; Disha, Cavendish & King, 2011; Poynting & Perry, 2007). However, Islamophobia has had a long history, with the earliest use of the term dating to 1923 in the Oxford Journal for Theological Studies (Mrazek, 2017).

Within Canada, social and healthcare professionals are obligated to address the needs of their service users. Unfortunately, these helping professionals have failed to address systemic discrimination and oppression caused by Islamophobia (Lundy, 2011; Raczak, 2008; Verkuyten, 2013). This has had particularly important consequences for children, who are always among the most vulnerable populations.

Background

A computerized literature search of Google Scholar, JSTOR, ProQuest, SAGE, and Social Work Abstracts was conducted, using the keywords anti-Muslim bigotry, bullying, discrimination, Islamophobia, Muslim, and school-aged children. This search yielded few studies focusing on how Islamophobia affects Muslim children (Aroian, 2012; CAIR-California, 2015). The limited body of research that does exist suggests that Muslim children, in both public and non-Islamic private schools, regularly encounter discrimination from school administrators, teachers, and peers (Arioan, 2012; CAIR-California, 2015; Hwang & Pang, 2017; Maes, Stevens & Verkuyten, 2014; Welply, 2018).

The contemporary definition of Islamophobia is connected to the idea of Orientalism, a term coined by scholar Edward Said to describe the Western perspective of Eastern societies as exotic, primitive, and/or inferior (Said, 1979; Poynting & Mason, 2007). Westerners tend to associate Islam and Arabs with negative images, stereotypes, and sentiments, despite the fact that not all Muslims are from the Middle East or South Asia; they can be found in all parts of the world and are from a variety of racial and ethnic backgrounds (Samari, Alcalá & Sharif, 2018). Additionally, despite the increasing interest in Islamophobia, scholars have not even yet reached a consensus on a definition because the issue is so complex (Beydoun, 2016). The California branch of the Council on Arab Islamic Relations (CAIR-California), a civil liberties and advocacy organization, defines Islamophobia as a prejudice against or hatred of Islam and Muslims (CAIR-California, 2015). Beydoun (2016) developed a more comprehensive definition, according to which Islamophobia operates along three dimensions:

1. Structural policy: a process by which governmental bodies perpetuate suspicion and fear of Muslims through establishment of formal profiling, surveillance, and immigration policy.
2. Dialectical process: whereby policy and political rhetoric shapes and endorses negative stereotypes of Islam and Muslim people, promoting initiatives such as the "War on Terror," and thereby emboldening violence within society.
3. Private Islamophobia: whereby fear, suspicion, and violence against Muslims are conveyed by individuals through religious or racial slurs, overt discrimination, rallies, hate speech, and public protests.

Beydoun's dimensions move beyond simply defining Islamophobia as 'fear' or dislike' of Islam and Muslims and can allow a much richer understanding of the term. They can be applied to move beyond simplistic understandings of Islamophobia as hate crimes or micro-aggressions against refugees, and also help clarify the institutional structures that shape racism and discrimination.

Anti-Muslim sentiments have been increasing in the Western world since the early 21st century, and have been intensified by the humanitarian crisis created by the civil war in Syria. Anti-Muslim prejudice continues to be much more prevalent than prejudice against European refugees (Hellwig & Sinno, 2017; Savelkoul, Scheepers, Tolsma & Hagendoorn, 2011; Strabac & Lishtaug, 2008). Additionally, in 2017 the Angus Reid Institute released the findings of a survey on faith and religion in public life: respondents (a random sample of 1972 Canadians) indicated that the faiths most beneficial to Canadian society were Catholicism (35%), Protestantism

(26%), and Evangelical Christianity (24%); the religion identified as most damaging – with double the scores for any other faith – was Islam (46%).

Regular discourse among politicians and the media tends to fuel discrimination and to legitimize anti-Muslim fearmongering and Islamophobia. CAIR-California (2015) reported that Islam is the most frequently mentioned religion in television news in the United States and also receives the most negative news coverage. Gallup (2010) reported that in the United States, media coverage of Islam had a negative tone 40% of the time, and 67% of the time it was associated it with extremism by Muslims. A national online survey conducted by the Canadian Muslim Forum and Canadians for Justice and Peace in the Middle East in 2017 confirmed that Islamophobia and religious discrimination is a problem in Canada and also that it is politically polarizing: 50% of Liberal, NDP, and Green party supporters consider religious discrimination against Muslim citizens to be a significant issue, compared with only 14% of Conservative supporters. Politicians in the United States and Canada use Islamophobic speech and legislation to advance their own agenda; for example, American President Donald Trump (2016) and Quebec Premier Francois Legault (2018) both used anti-Muslim refugee rhetoric in their successful electoral campaigns.

Islamophobia can fuel hate crimes against any person associated with Islam, as well as anyone who looks like or fits the stereotype of being of Arab ancestry or following Islam by dressing other than in traditional Western fashion. This could include dark-skinned, bearded men who wear turbans or women who wear a head covering. As a result, a number of the victims of anti-Muslim violence have been Sikhs and individuals of Indian, Lebanese Christian, and Greek descent (Poynting & Perry, 2007), and a Sikh temple in Hamilton, Ontario was burned down in response to the 9/11 attacks.

In 2014, two Canadian soldiers were tragically killed by individuals linking themselves to violent extremism, which led to an immediate increase in anti-Muslim incidents and hate crimes reported to the National Council of Canadian Muslims ([NCCM], 2014). The NCCM received reports of 48 different hate crime incidents after that event: 11 physical attacks on individuals or groups of individuals; 34 property attacks on Muslim institutions; and 3 direct threats against Muslim institutions. The Environics Institute (2016) found that one in three Canadian Muslims report having experienced discrimination in public spaces, the workplace, or educational settings within the previous five years, primarily based on their religion or ethnicity.

Islamophobia can have particularly severe consequences for Muslim children, who frequently encounter discrimination in public and at school (Arioan, 2012; CAIR-California, 2015; Zinn, 2001). Additionally, Mae et al. (2013) found that in almost all cities worldwide, children from refugee groups are confronted with stigmatization, discrimination, and unfavourable images of their own group. Another study involving 621 Muslim students enrolled in public and non-Muslim private schools in California found these children routinely faced verbal assaults, specifically references to bombs or being called terrorists; it also found that 55% of Muslim students had been bullied, 19% had experienced cyberbullying because of their religion, and 29% of hijab-wearing students had experienced offensive touching or pulling of their hijab (CAIR-California, 2015). Muslim girls are also known to be at risk for harassment by strangers because of headscarves and other traditional clothing (CAIR-California, 2015). Within the school context – the first point of Western socialization for refugee children – Islamophobia manifests in the form of teasing, bullying, name-calling, taunting, as well as physical confrontations and assaults. Additionally, discriminatory incidents within school settings are not only perpetrated by students – but also by teachers (Arioan, 2012; Maes, Stevens & Verkuyten, 2013). However, to date few studies have focused on these issues in the Canadian context. We addressed this research gap by connecting directly with youth to explore their experiences of being Muslim in Canada.

Methodology

In total, 13 female and 12 male students from grades six, seven, and eight attending a Muslim day school in southwestern Ontario participated in three focus groups over a period of two weeks. Their parents had been born in countries including Afghanistan, Algeria, Egypt, Eritrea, Lebanon, Libya, Pakistan, Palestine, Sudan, and Syria. Each focus group had two facilitators, including at least one research team member self-identifying as Muslim. Focus group discussions were audio-recorded and transcribed verbatim. Transcripts were reviewed for themes by members of the research team (four Muslim and four non-Muslim). Themes were then compared, using exemplars supporting each theme as a cross-referencing mechanism. Ethics approval for the study was granted by the Research Ethics Review Committee at King's University College (London, Ontario).

Findings

Three prominent themes emerged from the children's responses to how they are treated in Canadian society:

1. How others saw them, including being subjected to stereotyping and experiencing discrimination.
2. How this made them feel, primarily fear and powerlessness, especially about the future.
3. How they viewed themselves and their faith, where themes of hopefulness also emerged.

How Others See Us: Stereotypes and Discrimination

The experiences described by focus group participants reflected oppressive Orientalist stereotypes about Muslims. Despite their young age, many referred to being labelled as terrorists.

> One really difficult thing is, like being judged by a lot of people. I've been, like called a terrorist before. I was walking into, like a basketball game and everyone's like whoa, look, they're going to bomb the school now. It was, like very ... it hurt a lot, but there's nothing I can do about it. (8FV4)[5]

> Like, in the media, if you hear terrorist you don't think of a Mexican or a Canadian, you just ... you automatically think of a Muslim. (7MV1)

As is the case with most stereotypes, participants felt these misrepresentations were entirely negative:

> I can count so many different...people from different races that have done so many bad things, yet nobody's going to go and say oh, you did this and then all of your race is bad, but one Muslim goes and does something and they're like, oh, this person did this now all Muslims are bad. (7FV1)

They also felt that these negative stereotypes led to discrimination and being treated differently because they did not look 'Canadian' and described various situations ranging from subtle micro-aggressions and name-calling to more overt verbal and physical confrontations.

---

[5] This represents the individual code given to each respondent. Individual codes were used to support credibility and dependability during the thematic analysis.

Whenever we're walking around, like me and my mom, you can see people's eyes on us.Like, it's so obvious, the way people look at us sometimes, and they might not come up   to us and say anything but just the dirty looks. (8FV4)

We sat down somewhere and there were people there they would go and move away because we sat there (6FV3).

I was at Victoria Park and then some guy came by and he started swearing at us…and saying your guys are horrible, get out of here, you suck. (6FV5)

We were driving…there was this one guy…and he started screaming at us…Muslims don't know how to drive, go back to your own country. (8MV2)

These excerpts are representative of the discrimination faced by all participants on an ongoing basis – during crucial stages of their psychological development.

How We Are Made to Feel: Fear and Powerlessness

A common theme among participants in all three grades was fear of retribution for practicing their faith. They expressed feeling great vulnerability, with many constantly anticipating that something negative could happen to them at any time and that they could not fight back in any way without furthering the negative stereotypes. Additionally, many were aware that females wearing hijabs may be a target due to their visible affiliation with Islam. According to a Statistics Canada (2015) report on hate crimes in Canada, Muslim populations have the highest percentage of hate crime victims who are female (Leber, 2017). The realization that females (participants themselves and/or female family members) are often the primary targets of Islamophobic violence led to increased vulnerability and fear among both male and female participants, in turn eliciting feelings of helplessness and hopelessness.

It was St. Patrick's Day and we were in downtown so it was really crowded and my mom was driving and these two people were walking by, they were wearing St. Patrick's… they had those hats, and one of them threw it at my mom's window and the other person threw it on the hood of the car and they just left and my mom started crying. She felt so hurt. (8MV2)

During the basketball season for school, we all went to a tournament and we had to go pray […] I hear a bunch of guys start coming up and I just remember being so scared. Like, I was just, like please don't do anything, please just leave. (7FV2)

There was an incident... there was a shooting at the Mosque in Quebec and our school's right beside a Mosque. Then I was scared. I didn't want to go to the Mosque. I was scared because they killed so many people in the Mosque and they were praying. (8MV4)

I keep a metal stick under my bed. (7FV5)

These excerpts illustrate the ongoing fear within these students as they entered adolescence and began to create self-images that would be the foundation for their future – within a nation that was intended to be a safe haven.

How We See Ourselves: Images of Hope

Despite all the negative experiences, themes of hope emerged. The study participants were all attending a full-time Islamic day school with a stated vision to provide high quality learning combined with Islamic teachings to promote a positive Muslim identity. Scholars have identified this technique as one way to foster safe environments where Muslim children can cultivate and maintain a positive sense of self and identity (Seddon & Ahmad, 2011; Zine, 2007). Healthy maintenance of self-definition and identity has been identified as one of the primary challenges facing Muslim communities in North America (Alvi, Hoodfar & McDonough, 2003; Zine, 2007).

I think, as somebody that grew up in this school, as part of the Muslim community, I'm just so proud to see such smart young people that are so knowledgeable, and I think, if anything, you guys are going to be the leaders of tomorrow and today, so I think you all should be very, very proud and you have such great insights. (7FV4)

Importantly, despite the discrimination and the fear that was experienced by all participants, a distinct theme of hope emerged throughout focus groups. Participants commented that their faith brought them feelings of connectedness and unity, along with a sense of purpose and meaning.

There was actually some [support] provided. Like, after that day [of the Quebec shooting], lots of people in London, like from all ethnicities, they came out to the Mosque and they started, like protesting and they all helped and everything...and I just felt that was, like really nice. (8FV5)

They say behind every shadow there's light. The Quebec shooting may have seemed like a terrible event, you might find no good from it, but you could see that people sympathized for us after that. They were kinder to us. It shows us that there are still people who care. *Not everything is dark.* (8MV3)

Previous research has demonstrated that helping professionals can play an important role as hope bringers, especially when working with distressed, traumatized, and oppressed populations (Hubble, Duncan, Miller & Wampold, 2010; Jeyne, 2005; Larsen, Edey & Lemay, 2007). Strength-based practice is likely to be much easier when the target population already has a foundation of hope, as illustrated by the above excerpts.

Discussion

The Muslim children participating in this study had already been exposed to discrimination and micro- and macro-level aggressions. They had developed to varying degrees a sense of fear related to being different: being the Other. Islamophobia was a constant companion during their daily lives and had direct effects in every facet of their lives. However, the focus group discussions revealed a substantive difference between how the Muslim participants saw their faith versus how they perceived non-Muslims as viewing Islam. The barrage of negativity left participants feeling marginalized and disempowered, but at the same time their faith served as a major support in their lives by creating a sense of community.

Research has consistently demonstrated that bigotry and ignorance breed fear and hate, especially when individuals in positions of power and dominance are the ones perpetuating ignorance and fear (Beydoun, 2018; Faisal, 2017; Macedo & Bartolomé, 2016). Under these conditions, a larger proportion of society is likely to follow and become emboldened in their actions. Anti-discrimination strategies and interventions are needed at micro-, mezzo-, and macro-levels of society. They will require willingness and concerted effort to speak out against discrimination at all levels of society: within the school environment, the community, and the larger political arena.

Oppression of any group should be a concern for all of society; "Islamophobia is not a Muslim problem, but an affront to our common humanity. It is a fundamental violation of human rights and human dignity" (Carter Centre, 2018, p. 2). Islamophobia is known to be both a social and public health issue; evidence has demonstrated that it is associated with poor mental health and healthcare seeking behaviours regardless of the country it occurs in or the ethnic background or citizenship status of the individual (Samari et al., 2018). The Muslim community needs allies from outside the Muslim community who will listen and learn from the experiences of Muslims and leverage their own privilege to counter Islamophobia. This kind of collective responsibility and solidarity is essential, and may involve interreligious collaboration with groups that may have experienced racism and discrimination based on faith. In addition to this kind of advocacy, educational and social justice initiatives will be critically important in finding pragmatic and long-term solutions to all forms of religious discrimination. Within the Muslim community, it will be necessary to openly discuss how Islamophobia affects children and provide parents with opportunities to discuss the concerns they have about their children and themselves.

At the micro level, school-aged children who are Muslim would benefit from opportunities to have ongoing conversations about their experiences outside of their family unit; some study participants indicated reluctance to ask family members certain questions or to tell them about their negative experiences. Among focus group participants, spiritual practice, community, and family served as sources of hope in the face of difficulty, and standard counselling interventions may not be adequate or culturally suitable for working with this population. Effective interventions must incorporate the positive contributions made by these practices; previous research has demonstrated that strong faith practices and beliefs are associated with less depression, less anxiety, faster recovery from depression, and a better overall sense of wellness (Abu-Raiya & Pargament, 2010; Adams & Csiernik, 2014; Csiernik, 2012; Koenig, 2008). Therefore, Islamic faith practices associated with healing and wellness can serve as important protective factors for Muslim children and should be included in any strengths-based assessments.

Helping professionals within Canada pride themselves on their levels of commitment to diversity, but many scholars have identified how academic disciplines continue to be affected by colonialism and Christian values, norms, and practices (Canda 1990; Doe 2004; Hodge & Horvath, 2011; Ingersoll 1998; Koenig & Spano 2007; Kriegelstein 2006; Murdock 2005). Helping professionals tend to lack knowledge about the difficulties faced by Muslim clients, so there is a need for more collaboration with the Muslim community to help them understand issues related to Islamophobia, racism, and discrimination (Ahmed & Amer, 2012; Ahmed & Hashem, 2016). Many of the facilitators who participated in this study had never engaged with members of the Muslim community before; helping professionals should immerse themselves in racialized and refugee communities to understand their challenges and work toward authentic alliances. Teachers, school staff, and other caregivers would all benefit from training related to how to support and respond to children experiencing Islamaphobia and its effects-aggressions and discrimination they currently endure. Overall, more engagement at the community level is needed to explore the effects of Islamophobia, especially on children, and how support the Muslim community.

The main challenge for helping professionals will be finding ways to address the fear of this specific refugee group among the broader Canadian population. They need to find ways to navigate tensions related to differences in faith; as they engage in this important work, it is vital that they are aware of the additional trauma associated with being young and Muslim in Canada. Effective strengths-based programming can build on hope ... *for not everything is dark.*

Key Takeaway Points

1. Islamophobia has significant effects on Muslim children, who regularly encounter discrimination and micro-aggressions directed at themselves and their family members. It is critical that they have space to safely share their experiences, both within and outside the family unit.
2. Children who are supported often know what they need to feel safe and secure. They have the skills, knowledge, and values to navigate difficult times, especially if they receive emotional support. Helping professionals need to include them in dialogue when developing responses to critical incidents in a child- and family-centred manner.
3. Anti-oppressive community approaches based on participatory models may be effective in addressing group-based marginalization. Strengths, knowledge, and traditions among communities and families can help individuals, including children, who are subjected to ongoing oppression and difficulty, so these should be recognized and incorporated into programs to address Islamophobia. While it is important to focus on struggles, opportunities for conversations around hopes, dreams, and possibilities are especially vital.

References

Abu-Raiya, H. & Pargament, K. (2010). Empirically based psychology of Islam: Summary and critique of the literature. *Mental Health, Religion & Culture 14*(2), 93-115.

Adams, D. & Csiernik, R. (2014). Spirituality and the workplace. In R. Csiernik (Ed.). *Workplace wellness: Issues and responses.* (pp. 153-166). Toronto: Canadian Scholars Press.

Ahmed, S. & Amer, M. (2012). *Counseling Muslims: Handbook of mental health issues and interventions.* New York: Routledge.

Ahmed, S. & Hashem, H. (2016). A decade of Muslim youth: Global trends in research. *Journal of Muslim Mental Health, 10*(1). doi: http://dx.doi.org/10.3998/jmmh.10381607.0010.104

Alvi, S., Hoodfar, H. & McDonough, S. (Eds.). (2003). *The Muslim veil in North America: Issues and debates.* Toronto: Canadian Scholar's Press.

Angus Reid Institute. (2017). *Faith and religion in public life.* Retrieved from http://angusreid.org/faith-public-square/

Aroian, K. (2012). Discrimination against Muslim American adolescents. *The Journal of School Nursing, 28*(3), 206-213.

Baljit, N. (2018). Cultural explanations of patriarchy, race, and everyday lives: Marginalizing and "othering" Muslim women in Canada, *Journal of Muslim Minority Affairs, 38*(2), 263-279.

Beydoun, K. (2016). Islamaphobia: Toward a legal definition and framework. *Columbia Law Review, 116*(7), 108-125.

Beydoun, K. (2018). *American Islamophobia: Understanding the roots and rise of fear.* Berkley: University of California Press.

Bleich, E. (2011). What is Islamophobia and how much is there? Theorizing and measuring an emerging comparative concept. *American Behavioral Scientist, 55*(12), 1581–1600.

Canda, E. (1990). Afterword: Spirituality re-examined. *Spirituality and Social Work Communicator, 1,* 13–14.

Canadian Muslim Forum & Canadians for Justice and Peace in the Middle East. (2017). *A grave problem: EKOS Survey on Islamophobia in Canada.* Retrieved from https://d3n8a8pro7vhmx.cloudfront.net/cjpme/pages/4101/attachments/original/1517850987/CJPME-CMF_Survey_on_Islamophobia_-_2018-02-06-FINAL.pdf?1517850987

Carter Centre (May 2018). *Countering the Islamophobia industry: Toward more effective strategies.* Retrieved from: https://www.cartercenter.org/resources/pdfs/peace/conflict_resolution/countering-isis/cr-countering-the-islamophobia-industry.pdf

CBC News. (2017). *Protesters outside Masjid Toronto call for ban on Islam as Muslims pray inside.* Retrieved from https://www.cbc.ca/news/canada/toronto/anti-muslim-protest-masjid-toronto-1.3988906

Csiernik, R. (2012). The role of spirituality in mediating the trauma of social work internships. In J. Groen, D. Coholic & J. Graham (Eds.). *Spirituality in social work and education: Theory, practice and pedagogies.* Waterloo: Wilfrid Laurier Press.

Council for Arab Islamic Relations- California. (2015). *Mislabelled: The impact of school bullying and discrimination on California Muslim students.* Retrieved from https://youthlaw.org/wp-content/uploads/2017/03/CAIR-CA-2015-Bullying-Report-Web.pdf

CP24. (2018). *Arrest made after Muslim family threatened, assaulted at ferry terminal.* Retrieved from https://www.cp24.com/news/arrest-made-after-muslim-family-threatened-assaulted-at-ferry-terminal-1.4030478

Disha, I., Cavendish, J. & King, R. (2011). Historical events and spaces of hate: Hate crimes against Arabs and Muslims in post-9/11 America. *Social Problems, 58*(1), 21–46.

Doe, S. (2004). Spirituality-based social work values for empowering human service organizations. *Journal of Religion and Spirituality in Social Work, 23*(3), 45–65.

Environics Institute for Survey Research. (2016). *Survey of Muslims in Canada.* Retrieved from https://www.environicsinstitute.org/docs/default-source/project-documents/survey-of-muslims-in-canada-2016/final-report.pdf?sfvrsn=fbb85533_2o .

Faisal, K. (2017). Canada not immune from a legacy of fear-mongering. *The Washington Report on Middle East Affairs, 36*(2), 40-41.

Gallup (2010). *Islamophobia: Understanding anti-Muslim sentiment in the west.* Retrieved from http://www.gallup.com/poll/157082/islamophobia-understanding-anti-muslim-sentiment-west.aspx

Garner, S. & Selod, S. (2015). The racialization of Muslims: *Empirical studies of Islamophobia. Critical Sociology, 41*(1), 9-19.

Global News. (2019). *'I became very paranoid': Muslim Canadian explains why she stopped wearing the hijab.* Retrieved from https://globalnews.ca/video/5150814/i-became-very-paranoid-muslim-canadian-explains-why-she-stopped-wearing-the-hijab

Hamilton Spectator. (2019). *Hamilton mosque plans for worst-case scenarios after terrorist attacks in New Zealand.* Retrieved from https://www.thespec.com/news-story/9224021-hamilton-mosque-plans-for-worst-case-scenarios-after-terrorist-attacks-in-new-zealand/

Hellwig, T. & Sinno, A. (2017). Different groups, different threats: Public attitudes towards immigrants. *Journal of Ethnic and Migration Studies, 43*(3), 339-358.

Hodge, D. & Horvath, V. (2011). Spiritual needs in health care settings: A qualitative meta-analysis of clients' perspectives. *Social Work, 56*(4), 306–316.

Hubble, M., Duncan, B., Miller, S. & Wampold, B. (2010). Introduction. In B. Duncan, S., Miller, B., Wampold & M. Hubble (Eds). *The heart and soul of change: Delivering what works in therapy, second edition.* (pp. 23-46). Washington: American Psychological Association.

Hwang, B. & Pang, K. (2017). An era of Islamaphobia: The Muslim immigrant experience in America. *Pepperdine Journal of Communication Research, 5*(11). Retrieved from http://digitalcommons.pepperdine.edu/pjcr/vol5/iss1/11

Ingersoll, E. (1998). Refining dimensions of spiritual wellness: A cross-traditional approach. *Counselling and Values, 42*(3), 156–166.

Jevne, R. (2005). Hope: The simplicity and complexity. In J. A. Eliott (Ed.), *Interdisciplinary perspectives on hope.* (pp. 259-289). Hauppauge: Nova Science Publishers.

Koenig, H. (2008). *Medicine, religion, and health: Where science and spirituality meet.* West Conshohocken: Templeton Foundation Press.

Koenig, T. & Spano, R. (2007). The cultivation of social workers' hope in personal life and professional Practice. *Journal of Religion and Spirituality in Social Work, 26*(3), 45–61.

Krieglstein, M. (2006). Spirituality and social work. *Dialogue and Universalism, 16* (5–6), 21–29.

Larsen, D., Edey, W. & Lemay, L. (2007) Understanding the role of hope in counselling: Exploring the intentional uses of hope. *Counselling Psychology Quarterly, 20*(4), 401-416.

Lean, N. (2012). *The Islamophobia industry: How the right manufactures fear of Muslims.* London: Pluto Press.

Leber, B. (2017). Police-reported hate crime in Canada, 2015. Juristat (Statistics Canada), Catalogue no. 85-002-X.

Lundy, C. (2011). *Social work, social justice & human rights: A structural approach to practice* (2nd ed.). Toronto: University of Toronto Press.

Maes, M., Stevens, G. & Verkuyten, M. (2014). Perceived ethnic discrimination and problem behaviours in Muslim immigrant early adolescents: Moderating effects of ethnic, religious, and national group identification. *The Journal of Early Adolescence, 34*(7), 940-966.

Macedo, N. & Bartolomé, L. (2016). *Dancing with bigotry: Beyond the politics of tolerance.* New York: Palgrave MacMillan

Montreal Gazette. (2017). *6 dead, 8 injured in terrorist attack at Quebec City mosque.* Retrieved from http://montrealgazette.com/news/quebec/4-reported-dead-in-shooting-at-quebec-city-mosque

Mrázek, M. (2017). The Word "Islamophobia" As a terminus technicus of social sciences? *Central European Journal for Contemporary Religion, 2*(1), 19-28.

Murdock, V. (2005). Guided by ethics: Religion and spirituality in gerontological social work practice. *Journal of Gerontological Social Work, 45*(1/2), 131–154.

National Council of Canadian Muslims. (2014). *ODIHR hate crime report.* Retrieved from http://www.nccm.ca/wp-content/uploads/2015/11/Hate-Crime-Report-2014-National-Council-of-Canadian-Muslims.pdf

National Observer. (2008). *Attacks against Canadian Muslims and other hate crimes are surging.* Retrieved from https://www.nationalobserver.com/2018/11/29/news/attacks-against-canadian-muslims-and-other-hate-crimes-are-surging

Poynting, S. & Mason, V. (2007). The resistible rise of Islamophobia: Anti-Muslim racism in the UK and Australia before 11 September 2001, *Journal of Sociology, 43*(1), 61–86.

Poynting, S. & Perry, B. (2007). Climates of hate: Media and state inspired victimization of Muslims in Canada and Australia since 9/11. *Current Issues in Criminal Justice, 19*(2), 150-171.

Raczak, S. (2008). *Casting out: The eviction of Muslims from western law and politics.* Toronto: University of Toronto Press.

Said, E. (1979). *Orientalism.* New York: Vintage.

Samari, G., Alcalá, H. & Sharif, M. (2018). Islamophobia, health, and public health: A systematic literature review. *American Journal of Public Health, 108*(6), e1-e9

Savelkoul, M., Scheepers, P., Tolsma, J. & Hagendoorn, L. (2011). Anti-Muslim attitudes in the Netherlands: Tests of contradictory hypotheses derived from ethnic competition theory and intergroup contact theory. *European Sociological Review*, *27*(6), 741–758.

Seddon, M. & Ahmad, F. (Eds.). (2011). *Muslim youth: Challenges, opportunities and expectations.* London: Bloomsbury Academic

Strabac, Z. & Listhaug, O. (2008). Anti-Muslim prejudice in Europe: A multilevel analysis of survey data from 30 countries. *Social Science Research, 37*(1), 268-286.

Verkuyten, M. (2013). Justifying discrimination of Muslim immigrants: Outgroup ideology and the five-step social identity model. *British Journal of Social Psychology*, *52*(2), 345-360.

Welply, O. (2018). 'I'm not being offensive but…': intersecting discourses of discrimination towards Muslim children in school. *Race Ethnicity and Education, 21*(3), 370-389.

Wilkins-Laflamme, S. (2018). Islamophobia in Canada: Measuring the realities of negative attitudes toward Muslims and religious discrimination. *Canadian Review of Sociology, 55*(1), 86-110.

Zinn, J. (2001). Muslim youth in Canadian schools: Education and the politics of religious identity. *Anthropology and Education Quarterly*, *32*(4), 399-423.

Zine, J. (2007). Safe havens or religious 'ghettos'? Narratives of Islamic schooling in Canada. *Race, Ethnicity and Education, 10*(1), 71-92.

CHAPTER SEVEN

QUEER AND TRANS MIGRANTS WITH PRECARIOUS STATUS LIVING IN CANADA: POLICIES, IDEOLOGIES, REALITIES, AND PRACTICES

EDWARD LEE

Canada has positioned itself as a leader in lesbian, gay, bisexual, trans, queer, and intersex (LGBTQI) human rights, notably through recent announcements of international development funding and the implementation of a 'queer and trans friendly refugee claim process. However, a more in-depth examination reveals a complex reality for queer and trans migrants with precarious status living in Canada, including refugee claimants, visitors, international students, temporary workers, sponsored family members, protected persons, undocumented individuals, and those living in detention. A paradox has emerged within Canadian policy and practice relating to LGBTQI human rights leadership and Canada promoting itself as a safe haven. In June 2018, the Québec government publicly announced granting four million dollars toward the creation of an international francophone network aimed at defending the human rights of French-speaking LGBTQI people across the globe. According to then *Minister of International Relations and La Francophonie*, Christine St-Pierre:

> The creation of the new network underscores the province's commitment and will help vulnerable people break their isolation and overcome the discrimination they face because of their sexual orientation, gender identity or gender expression. (MI, 2018, para 5)

Soon after that announcement, the federal government allocated 30 million dollars of funding to advance LGBTQI human rights in the Global South and to help build a national platform for collaboration and exchange among Canadian-specific groups (Global Affairs Canada, 2018). Additionally, Canada and Chile have co-chaired the *Equal Rights Coalition* since June 2017; this initiative brings together approximately 40 nation-states to advance LGBTQI human rights (Government of Canada [GOC], 2017). These announcements position Canada as a key state leader in a global struggle for LGBTQI human rights, including its stance on protecting refugees. However, the Canadian government has simultaneously implemented policies designed to block LGBTQI people from the Global South from accessing improved sexual orientation and gender identity and expression (SOGIE)-based refugee claims in Canada (Lee, 2018; 2019). These policies affect temporary resident visa (TRV) and permit eligibility, and ultimately operate "as a tool of migrant exclusion that is ultimately disinterested in the realities of (in particular poor and working-class) queer and trans people from the Global South… marking them as almost always ineligible" (Lee, 2018, p. 67).

Further, in 2012 the Canadian government passed Bill C-31, despite opposition from refugee advocacy and migrant justice groups, who have called it an 'anti-refugee law.' It facilitates removal procedures, lengthier detention stays, and the creation of a differential refugee claim process for those from designated countries of origin (DCOs), so-called 'safe countries' (Canadian Council for Refugees [CCR], 2017, Lee & Brotman, 2013). As a result, refugee claimants from DCOs – including LGBTQI claimants – were forced to adhere to a more rapid timeline without access to appeal. In 2015, the Canadian Association of Refugee Lawyers won a decision in federal court to ensure that all refugee claimants from DCOs would be able to access to appeal after a negative ruling in a refugee hearing (CCR, 2015).

In May 2017, after many months of consultations with community groups, lawyers, researchers, and related stakeholder groups, the Immigration and Refugee Board (IRB) implemented guidelines for SOGIE-based refugee claims (IRB, 2017). Section 6 of these guidelines, titled *Avoiding stereotyping when making findings of fact*, states that "decision-makers should not rely on stereotypes or inappropriate assumptions in adjudicating cases involving SOGIE as they derogate from the essential human dignity of an individual" (IRB, 2017, section 6). This includes, for example, not presuming that trans people will always seek to have surgical or physiological treatment if they have access to that treatment.

Perhaps the most innovative aspect of these guidelines is Section 8, in which intersectionality is explicitly referenced and applied so that analysis of refugee claims based on SOGIE must account for inter-related factors related to disability, religion, race, ethnicity, and age (IRB, 2017, Section 8). Section 8 requires IRB adjudicators to consider how SOGIE-based discrimination and persecution may interact for some individuals, along with other factors that result in increased and differential risk. Although these guidelines were informed by an extensive consultation process with the goal of addressing the multi-faceted barriers experienced by LGBTQI refugee claimants (LaViolette, 2007, 2009; Lee & Brotman, 2013), it is still unclear to what extent they will actually improve the refugee process. For example, they do not address the specific barriers faced by LGBTQI individuals during the refugee claim process, including exposure to homophobia and transphobia and difficulty in accessing LGBTQI competent and financially accessible legal assistance (Lee & Brotman, 2011, 2013).

This chapter explores the disconnect between how the Canadian government positions itself with regard to LGBTQI human rights and providing a safe haven for LGBTQI migrants, versus how individuals actually navigate the Canadian immigration regime, including the refugee claim process. Ruling regimes operate through text-mediated processes and practices that are driven by real people and are organized at administrative and political levels (Ng, 2006; Smith, 1990), and this chapter presents some key results from my doctoral research and their implications for how service providers should engage in anti-oppressive practice with LGBTQI migrants.

First, it is important to clarify the key terms used here to describe sexuality and gender. The acronym LGBTQI is often used to describe the complex range of sexual orientation and gender identity and expression (Cantu, 2009; Lee & Brotman, 2011). This complexity is furthered by colonial histories that have erased non-Western ways of knowing and situating sexualities and genders within Indigenous social organization (Bleys, 1995; Dutta, 2012; Lee & Brotman, 2011). Within the Canadian context, Indigenous scholars and activists have mobilized the term 'Two-Spirit' as a political identity – beyond the notion of sexual orientation or gender identity – to signal the ways in which Indigenous people with diverse sexual and gender identities and expressions were often accepted within their Nation/community and also played valuable social roles (Meyer Cook, 2008; Meyer Cook & Labelle, 2004). Various Indigenous terms related to sexuality and gender were used in complex ways prior to, during, and after colonial eras across Africa, Asia, and the Americas, further complicating the ways in which LGBTQI migrants from the Global South take up these terms (Dutta, 2012; Ekine, 2013; Ekine & Abbas, 2013; Lee; 2018).

The terms 'queer' and 'trans' are also used in this chapter to signal theories and politics that challenge heteronormativity, cisnormativity, normative sexual practices, and dominant social norms (De Genova, 2010;

Lee & Brotman, 2011). Cisnormativity refers to how social institutions, processes, and practices reproduce the gender binary and the erasure of trans people while heteronormativity refers to how these institutions, processes and practices presume heterosexuality (Cohen, 1997; Stryker, 2008). Throughout this chapter, these terms are mobilized in different ways to allow for both critical structural analysis and the development of strategies for political resistance.

Queer and Trans Migrants as 'Non-Genuine'

Background

My doctoral study (with research ethics approval from McGill University) explored how the everyday lives of queer and trans migrants with precarious status are socially organized by the Canadian immigration regime. I drew from written reflections of my own experiences, primary data from five interviews that I completed with LGBTQI migrants living in Ontario and Quebec, secondary data from eight previous interviews with LGBTQI migrants conducted for the Speak Out! LGBTQ refugee research project, and 49 policy and media texts.

I will begin by providing a brief description of three migrants and their migration paths as they relate to the Canadian immigration regime. Anthony (pseudonym) self-identifies as a Muslim gay man from Asia and described his sexual orientation and gender expression as follows: "I'm a male, right, but I attract to male and I dress as a male… but if I do cross-dressing, then in certain situation, maybe I do filming, I will take the role easily… or may(be) I could go to the club and cross-dress and that will not bother me at all." His migration path included travelling back and forth from Asia to the United States and eventually to Canada, where he transitioned from having student status, and then visitor status, to being a refugee claimant and a protected person.

Emma migrated from Mexico to Canada; she self-identifies as a woman who critiques notions of gender and the gender binary. She is involved in the trans community and described herself in relation to her family, community, and heritage: "I'm a woman of colour, proud of my Mexican roots and who came from a matriarchy and I'm very proud of this, because there were a lot of strong women around me all my whole life… I consider myself a responsible and conscientious person who has… the capacity to support in different ways." After experiencing violence in Mexico, she migrated to Canada and applied for refugee status upon arrival.

Daniela was a make-up artist who owned a beauty salon in Mexico before being forced to flee due to experiencing violence as a trans woman. She described herself as follows: "I'm a strong person, I never feel…like a victim, no. Even if I had a history in Mexico [that is] very, very sad, very hard… Maybe I'm not the perfect person, but I'm strong and I need to be stronger for other generations." She had traveled back and forth from Mexico to the United States prior to migrating to Canada and then applying for refugee status and becoming a protected person.

Making the Distinction

One feature of the Canadian immigration regime is the ideological production of a set of supposed facts about refugees that actually obscure their actual experiences (Smith, 2005), including those of queer and trans migrants with precarious status like Anthony, Emma, and Daniela. This disconnect between ideology and real experience is reflected in its mobilization of the term 'genuine' as an ideological code. The term 'genuine' is used across various texts linked to the *Immigration and Refugee Protection Act* regulations as well as the government website. A 'genuine' student, visitor, or refugee is framed – implicitly or explicitly – in comparison to those who are fraudulent or abusing the system. The government website states, "finding who needs Canada's protection is a process that must take into consideration the responsibility of helping those in genuine need while protecting the system against those who seek to abuse it. The health and safety of Canadians must also be ensured" (Citizenship and Immigration Canada (CIC) – Refugee System in Canada (RSC), 2014, para 4). The following discussion explores how the application of this term is problematic, based on the experiences of Anthony, Emma, and Daniela.

Anthony entered Canada with a study permit and an employment agreement with a Canadian couple who covered the costs of his tuition and accommodations. As part of their agreement, Anthony attended language classes but also worked full time during the week, making him a 'non-genuine' student. The Canadian couple had initially agreed to sponsor Anthony so that he could become a permanent resident. However, when this did not happen and Anthony's study permit expired, he shifted to a tourist visa while continuing to work for this couple, thus shifting from a 'non-genuine student' to a 'non-genuine visitor.' After finally realizing that they were not going to follow through on the agreement, Anthony searched for another way to remain in Canada.

I'm starting to find the information and then I, my resource (is) only internet... so I check internet, how to get to re-establish my status... it's between combination of (government) website and then other resources and then, like, how to connect to...start the process? And then what kind of ground that we base on qualify as person who need protection...I never think that I would end up to the process, so I don't learn it.

He learned about how to apply for refugee status and possibly shifting from being framed as a 'non-genuine visitor' to a 'non-genuine refugee.' Within Canada, refugee claimants tend to be framed as possible 'abusers of the system,' until they are determined to be a 'genuine refugee.' The textual separation of the temporary and refugee categories within immigration law, and the omission of a temporary resident pathway to filing an in-land refugee claim – operated in concert with the ideological code of 'genuine' – make it very difficult for someone in Anthony's situation to apply for refugee status.

For the most part, this textually mediated process is implicit and therefore difficult to map out in a precise manner. However, some texts explicitly contrast 'genuine' and 'non-genuine' visitors, students, or refugees. For example, a document titled *Business Visitors from China to Canada: Applying for a Temporary Resident Visa,* states "Canadian companies will not be held responsible for applicants found to be non-genuine visitors after their arrival in Canada. It is an unfortunate fact that some Chinese nationals invited to Canada for business purposes make refugee claims after arrival" (CIC - BVCC, 2006, p. 9). This example illustrates a direct link between being identified as a 'non-genuine visitor' and filing a refugee claim: a 'non-genuine' Chinese visitor who files a refugee claim becomes a 'non-genuine' refugee. When Anthony had visitor status and decided to apply for refugee status, the Canadian immigration regime would classify him as a 'non-genuine visitor' – and as a refugee claimant, he would be considered a 'non-genuine refugee' until he was accorded refugee status.

Emma's refugee claim process serves as another example of how queer and trans refugees are ideologically coded as 'non-genuine.' She migrated to Canada just a few months prior to the government's imposition of a temporary resident visa (TRV) from Mexican nationals (CIC – ACIVM, 2014; Canadian Press, 2014). The decision to impose a TRV requirement for Mexican visitors was directly linked to the number of people arriving from Mexico who made refugee claims upon arrival (Jenicek et al., 2009). Again, the ideological code of 'genuine' was used as a device to justify the removal of 'non-genuine' visitors, and thus 'bogus' refugee claimants from Mexico. Emma said that after filing a refugee claim, she was met with 'rude,' 'discriminatory.' and 'disgusting' responses from immigration authorities. She sat in a room for 12 hours, had her fingerprints taken, and was told she would have to return to the airport a few days later to process her request. She described her encounters with more immigration authorities when she returned to the airport:

> I have an agent who was very rude with me. She saw my papers, and she said '…this is not working…all what you're saying here, is nothing that Canada can protect you for, because you…obviously had a problem of… family (interpersonal) violence'…I was like, 'but why do you tell me that?'…I was so frustrated…I don't want to go back, I feel so unsafe…and there is no place for me there' and she gets upset, she throws the papers…

She also referred to another immigration agent was frustrated with her: he told her that he was a gay man with gay friends in Mexico, and that his friends felt safe there, so she should go back. Finally, after being pressured by two immigration agents to drop her refugee claim and return to Mexico, Emma spoke to a third officer who processed her claim. The actions of the first two immigration agents were not consistent with Canadian refugee law, but they illustrate how evaluations of Emma's refugee claim were affected by the socially sanctioned perception of the 'non-genuine' and 'bogus' Mexican refugee claimant. Emma's experience suggests a socially organized process against Mexican refugee claimants in the months leading up to the imposition of the TRV requirement.

For example, the ideological code of 'genuine' was circulated and replicated throughout government websites and mainstream media to justify the exclusion of Mexican refugee claimants, including LGBTQI individuals. One government press release referred to stopping those who 'jump the immigration queue' in order to better process 'genuine' refugee claims (CIC – ACIVM, 2014). The public scrutiny on 'bogus' Mexican refugees also obscured the realities of thousands of temporary workers from Mexico who enter Canada (Villegas, 2013). Overall, the ideological framing of 'non-genuine' Mexican refugees was used to justify both the imposition of the TRV and socially sanctioned racism among immigration authorities – labelling individuals as 'non-genuine' is not just about their actions; it is also about their personhood.

Additionally, North American media articles consistently identify certain tourist areas as safe for gays and lesbians, including gay and lesbian Mexicans (Jenicek et al., 2009) – but the experiences of trans Mexicans are conspicuously absent. Moreover, media coverage often omits the state violence and corruption that exists within Mexico, as demonstrated by the deaths of a number of refused refugees who were forced to return to Mexico (Martin & Lapalme, 2012). Daniela spoke about a trans woman she knew who was refused refugee status and was murdered upon going back to Mexico:

> I'm in shock…it's very violent, it's very traumatic for me… I accept when somebody die, but somebody killed you…it's too much… I can not sleep these days, like how is (this) possible? I talk to you and I see her… no I can't believe it…But this happen, sadly. But she died.

Both Emma and Daniela were eventually accepted as refugees, but their process of becoming 'genuine' refugees was made invisible by the ideological code that initially renders all Mexican refugee claimants as 'non-genuine.'

Anthony, Emma, and Daniela's experiences navigating the Canadian immigration regime reveal the need for those working within the settlement sector to pay close attention to how socially constructed categories shape how migrants will be deemed eligible or not eligible for services and resources. The experiences of these three refugees also illustrate how cisnormativity and heteronormativity are embedded within various immigration and refugee policies and practices, which presume that migrants are cisgender and heterosexual. For example, immigration forms require checking either a 'male' or 'female' box, thereby preventing dialogue with queer and trans migrants who may have a more complex gender identity. This kind of presumption also prevents certain migrants with precarious status, such as visitors, students, or temporary workers, from making a refugee claim based on gender identity-based persecution.

It is also important to be aware that trans migrants with precarious status from the Global South may explore other viable pathways to gaining permanent residency. Many of the queer and trans migrants I have met did not apply for refugee status because they were aware of the challenges and structural violence embedded within the process – instead, they found ways to gain permanent residency through student, work, and humanitarian-related pathways. The following section explores how practitioners may engage in anti-oppressive practice with all queer and trans migrants in ways that attend to these nuances and complexities.

Implications for Anti-Oppressive Practice with Queer and Trans Migrants

As demonstrated in this chapter, ideology regarding precarious status differs from real experiences. By closely listening to those directly affected, practitioners can learn about specific ways in which policies and practices organize everyday lives and psyches. By engaging in critical dialogue with queer and trans refugees positioned as experts in their own lives, practitioners can help these individuals think about the existing structures (Bishop, 2005; Lee & Miller, 2014) and ways to better navigate the policies and processes related to their precarious status. By being aware of structural barriers, practitioner can also help minimize the effects of internalized oppression (Lee & Brotman, 2015).

The settlement sector been shifting toward a neo-liberal managerialism (Baines, 2011), with business-oriented management solutions, state funding tied to efficiency-based measures, and client targets (Clarke, 2012). This kind of workplace managerialism can be navigated and resisted using micro-level strategies such as 'widening the gates' of access to social welfare (Ross, 2011). Moreover, practitioners can apply situational ethics whereby decisions are informed by a core set of social justice-oriented principles, rather than assuming an inherent neutrality or goodness in laws and policies (Mullaly, 2010). This kind of critical ethical practice can support queer and trans refugees in ways that identify and respond to oppressive policies and practices. However, it is important to note that this may lead to conflict due to the institutional limitations placed on social workers and other helping professionals as they try to treat all human beings with dignity, regardless of status. This could involve some risk for individual workers, especially considering the increasing criminalization of migrants with precarious status.

However, even direct service activism may not challenge the broader social relations that reproduce inequities (Chatterjee, 2013; Ross, 2011). Certain policies in Canada, like those related to precarious status, are historically informed by colonization and White settler society (Pon, 2009; Razack, 2002; Thobani, 2007). In its present form, settlement work reproduces "historical and structural practices of neo-colonialism and essentialism, which impose false binaries on the identities of LGBTQ people, intersect(ing) with immigration and integration experiences" (Yee et al., 2014, p.98).

Ideally, social service delivery would incorporate intersectionality and hybridity (Yee et al., 2014). When working toward this kind of transformative social change, it will be important to consider how settlement processes could actively recognize how interlinked processes of gendered racialization and heterocisnormativity shape the everyday lives of queer and trans migrants with precarious status. Another important issue to consider is how this kind of critical analysis could be fostered in conjunction with collective empowerment within queer and trans migrant communities. Developing innovative and community-driven practices can increase access and foster empowerment among the communities that are directly affected: in this case, trans and queer migrants with precarious status. Ultimately, transformative social change will require political and economic action that makes visible historical conditions while also addressing structural concerns and everyday survival (Wilson, Calhoun & Whitmore, 2011).

Key Takeaway Points

1. Although Canada has made many legal advancements in relation to LGBTQI human rights, many types of social and structural inequalities continue to affect this population, especially queer and trans migrants with precarious status, including those going through the refugee claims process.
2. Dialogue with queer and trans migrants reveals the disconnect between government ideology versus how individuals actually experience the often heteronormative and cisnormative discourses, policies, and practices applied in Canada.
3. Many immigration and refugee programs and services are exclusionary to queer and trans migrants due to structural barriers that result from intersecting forms of racism, sexism, homophobia, transphobia, classism, and ableism, and the type of precarious status that these individuals have upon arrival in Canada. Anti-oppressive practice with will require critical reflection on how to help these individuals navigate these structural barriers; it will also require advocating for improved services and resources.

References

Aiken, S. J. (2001). Of gods and monsters: National security and Canadian refugee policy. *Revue québécoise de droit international*, *14*(1), 7-36.

Baines, D. (2011). An overview of anti-oppressive practice: Neoliberalism, inequality and change. In D. Baines (Ed.). *Doing anti-oppressive practice: Social justice social work*, 2nd edition. (pp. 22 - 48). Halifax: Fernwood Publishing.

Bishop, A. (2005). *Beyond token change: Breaking the cycle of oppression in institutions.* Halifax: Fernwood Publishing.

Bleys, R. (1995). *The geography of perversion: Male to male sexual behaviour outside the west and the ethnographic imagination, 1750-1918.* New York: New York University Press.

Canadian Press. (2014). Mexican travel to Canada plummets after Ottawa imposes visa restrictions. *The Guardian.* Retrieved from http://www.theguardian.pe.ca/Travel/2009-12-17/article-1291880/Mexican-travel-to-Canada-plummets-after-Ottawa-imposes-visa-restrictions/1

Cantu, L (2009). *The sexuality of migration: Border crossings and Mexican immigrant men.* New York: New York University Press.

Canadian Council for Refugees. (2015). *Court strikes down appeal bar for nationals of Designated Countries of Origin.* Retrieved from https://ccrweb.ca/en/court-strikes-down-RAD-bar-DCOs

Canadian Council for Refugees. (2017). *Five years later, refugees are suffering the consequences of unfair and inefficient changes to the refugee system.* Retrieved from https://ccrweb.ca/en/media/five-years-later-refugee-system

Chatterjee, S. (2013). Rethinking skill in anti-oppressive social work practice with skilled immigrant professionals. *British Journal of Social Work, 45*(1), 363-377.

Citizenship and Immigration Canada (CIC) – Archived Canada Imposes a Visa on Mexico (ACIVM) News Release. Retrieved from the Department of Citizenship and Immigration Canada: http://news.gc.ca/web/article- en.do?m=/index&nid=466839

Citizenship and Immigration Canada (CIC) – Business Visitors from China to Canada: Applying for a Temporary Resident Visa (BVCC) (2006). Ottawa: Minister of Public Works and Government Services Canada.

Citizenship and Immigration Canada (CIC) - The Refugee System in Canada (RSC) (2014). Retrieved from http://www.cic.gc.ca/english/refugees/canada.asp

Clarke, J. (2012). Doing anti-oppressive settlement work: A critical framework for practice. In S. Pashang (Ed.). *Unsettled settlers: Barriers to integration* (pp. 79 – 101). Toronto: De Sitter Publications.

De Genova, N. (2010). The queer politics of migration: Reflections on "illegality" and incorrigibility. *Studies in Social Justice, 4*(2), 101–126.

Dutta, A. (2012). An Epistemology of Collusion: Hijras, Kothis and the Historical (Discontinuity of Gender/Sexual Identities in Eastern India. *Gender & History,* 24(3), 825-849.

Ekine, S. (2013). Contesting narratives of queer Africa. In S. Ekine & Abbas, H. (Eds.). *Queer African reader.* (pp. 78 - 91). Dakar: Pambazuka Press.

Ekine, S. & Abbas, H. (eds.). (2013). *Queer African reader.* Dakar: Pambazula Press.

Fitzgerald, D.S. (2019). *Refuge beyond reach: How rich democracies repel asylum seekers.* Oxford: Oxford University Press.

Global Affairs Canada. (2018). Canada announces new funds in support of LGBTQ2 rights. Retrieved from https://www.canada.ca/en/global-affairs/news/2019/02/canada-announces-new-funds-in-support-of-lgbtq2-rights.html

Government of Canada. (2019). *The human rights of LGBTI persons.* Retrieved from https://international.gc.ca/world-monde/issues_development-enjeux_developpement/human_rights-droits_homme/rights_lgbti-droits_lgbti.aspx?lang=eng

Government of Canada. (2016). *Equal rights coalition.* Retrieved from https://international.gc.ca/world-monde/issues_development-enjeux_developpement/human_rights-droits_homme/coalition-equal-rights-droits-egaux.aspx?lang=eng

Immigration and Refugee Board. (2017). *Chairperson's Guideline 9: Proceedings before the IRB involving Sexual Orientation and Gender Identity and Expression.* Retrieved from https://irb-cisr.gc.ca/en/legal-policy/policies/Pages/GuideDir09.aspx#a8_5_2

Jenicek, A., Lee, E., & Wong, A. (2009). "Dangerous shortcuts": Media representations of sexual minority refugees in the post-9/11 Canadian press. *Canadian Journal of Communications,* 34(4), 635–658.

LaViolette, N. (2007). Gender-related refugee claims: Expanding the scope of the Canadian guidelines. *International Journal of Refugee Law,* 19(2), 169–214.

LaViolette, N. (2009). Independent human rights documentation and sexual minorities: An ongoing challenge for the Canadian refugee determination process. *International Journal of Human Rights,* 13(2-3), 437–476.

Lee, E. O. (2018). Tracing the coloniality of queer and trans migrations: Resituating heterocisnormative violence in the Global South and encounters with migrant visa ineligibility to Canada. *Refuge: Canada's Journal on Refugees,* 34(1), 60–74.

Lee, E. O. (2019). Responses to structural violence: The everyday ways in which queer and trans migrants with precarious status respond to and resist the Canadian immigration regime. *International Journal of Child, Youth & Family Studies, 10*(1), 70 – 94.

Lee, E. O., & Brotman, S. (2011). Identity, refugeeness, belonging: Experiences of sexual minority refugees in Canada. *Canadian Review of Sociology, 48*(3), 241–274.

Lee, E. O., & Brotman, S. (2013). Speak Out! Structural intersectionality and anti-oppressive practice with sexual minority refugees in Canada. *Canadian Social Work Review, 30*(2), 157 - 183.

Lee, E. O., & Brotman, S. (2015). Social work and sexual and gender diversity. In N. Ives, M.

Denov & T. Sussman (Eds.). *Social work histories, contexts and practices: A Canadian perspective.* (p. 259 - 287) Don Mills: Oxford University Press.

Lee, E. O., & Miller, L. (2014). Collaborative media making with queer and trans refugees:

Social locations, competing agendas and thinking structurally. In H.M. Pleasants & D. E.

Salter (Eds.). *Community-based multiliteracies and digital media projects: Questioning assumptions and exploring realities.* (p.47 - 61) New York: Peter Lang Publishing.

Lee, E. O., Hafford-Letchfield, T., Pullen Sansfaçon, A., Kamgain, O., & Gleeson, H. (2017). *The state of knowledge about LGBTQI migrants living in Canada in relation to the global LGBTQI rights agenda.* Montréal: Université de Montréal.

Martin, P., & Lapalme, A. (2012). *Mexican mobility and Canada: Hardening boundaries and growing resistance. NACLA: Reporting on the Americas since 1967.* Retrieved from https://nacla.org/blog/2012/8/8/mexican-mobility-and-canada-hardening-boundaries-and-growing-resistance

Meyer-Cook, F (2008). Two-spirit people: Traditional pluralism and human rights. In S.Brotman & J. J. Levy. (Eds). *Homosexualités: variations linguistiques et culturelles.* (pp.245-280). Québec: Presses de l'Université du Québec, Coll. Santé et Société.

Meyer-Cook, F. & Labelle, D. (2004). Namaji: Two-Spirit Organizing in Montreal, Canada. *Journal of Gay and Lesbian Social Services, 16*(1), 29-51.

Montreal International (2018). *Creation of an international francophone LGBTQI network.* Retrieved from https://www.montrealinternational.com/en/news/creation-of-an-international-francophone-lgbtqi-network/

Mullaly, B. (2010). *Challenging oppression and confronting privilege* (2nd ed.). Don Mills: Oxford University Press.

Murray, D. A. B. (2016). *Real queer? Sexual orientation and gender identity refugees in the Canadian refugee apparatus.* London: Rowman & Littlefield.

Ng, R. (2006). Exploring the globalized regime of ruling from the standpoint of immigrant workers. In C. Frampton, G. Kinsman, A.K. Thompson & K. Tilleczek. (eds.). (p.174-188). *Sociology for changing the world: Social movements/social research.* Fernwood publishing: Halifax.

Pon, G. (2009). Cultural competency as new racism: An ontology of forgetting. *Journal of Progressive Human Services, 20*(1), 59-71.

Razack, S. H. (2002). *Race, space and the law: Unmapping a white settler society.* Toronto: Between the Lines.

Ross, M. (2011). Social work activism amidst neoliberalism: A big, broad tent of activism. In D. Baines (ed.). *Doing Anti-Oppressive Practice: Social Justice Social Work.2ⁿᵈ edition.* (pp. 250-264). Halifax: Fernwood Publishing.

Smith, D. E. (2005). *Institutional ethnography: A sociology for people.* Lanham: AltaMira.

Smith, G. W. (1990). Political activist as ethnographer. *Social Problems, 37*(4), 629–648.

Stryker, S. (2008). *Transgender history.* Berkeley: Seal.

Thobani, S. (2007). *Exalted subjects: Studies in the making of race and nation in Canada.* Toronto: University of Toronto Press.

Villegas, P. (2013). Negotiating the boundaries of membership: Health care providers, access to social goods and immigration status. In L. Goldring & P. Landolt (eds.). *Production and negotiating non-citizenship: Precarious legal status in Canada.* (pp. 221 – 237). Toronto: University of Toronto Press.

Wilson, M., Calhoun, A., & Whitmore, E. (2011). Contesting the neoliberal agenda: Lessons from Canadian activists. *Canadian Social Work Review/Revue canadienne de service social, 28*(1), 25-48.

Yee, J.Y., Marshall, Z., & Vo, T. (2014). Challenging neo-colonialism and essentialism: Incorporating hybridity into new conceptualizations of settlement service delivery with lesbian, gay, bisexual, trans, and queer immigrant young people. *Critical Social Work, 15* (1), 88 – 103.

CHAPTER EIGHT

GROUP REFUGEE RESETTLEMENT IN CANADA: LEARNING FROM THE KAREN

EI PHYU SMITH, SHEILA HTOO, MICHAELA HYNIE AND SUSAN MCGRATH

Introduction

In 2005, the United Nations High Commissioner for Refugees (UNHCR) and the government of Thailand agreed that the 140,000 refugees from Myanmar (known as Burma prior to 1989) who had been living in remote camps along the Thai border for more than 20 years should be resettled to other countries because local integration or return was no longer considered feasible. Canada was one of 10 nations that participated in the group resettlement of Karen refugees, members of an ethnic minority community that had long faced persecution in Myanmar. Canada has a long history of resettling refugees, but planned group resettlement is not common. However, this initiative was viewed as a process that would allow for the efficient resettlement of large numbers of refugees from one specific group. In 2006, Canada offered to accept 3900 Karen refugees, 95% of whom came as government assisted refugees (GAR) and 5% as privately sponsored refugees (PSR) (Citizenship and Immigration Canada [CIC], 2009).

Research Approach

Our study of the group settlement experiences of the Karen in Canada used a holistic social integration model (Hynie et al., 2016). The term 'integration' is contested, but scholars in the area of forced migration are increasingly defining it in terms of participation in social institutions and the activities, and economic, political, and social life of communities (Ager & Strang, 2008; Smith, 2008; Strang & Ager, 2010). According to Hynie's holistic integration model, integration occurs across three spheres: subjective individual elements (e.g., a sense of belonging and security), objective individual characteristics (e.g., language, employment, and housing) and the social and institutional environment (e.g., social connections, institutional adaptation, and welcoming communities), all of which reinforce and influence one another (Hynie et al., 2016).

This chapter draws from three research initiatives as well as the personal experiences of one of the authors. First, it draws from a project involving all four authors, funded by an internal grant from York University, which also provided research ethics approval. In that study, we interviewed 14 Karen refugees from across Canada and conducted a focus group with four settlement workers who were themselves Karen and working with this community. Most quotes come from this project. Two of the authors have also focused on the Karen people in their doctoral dissertations. Ei Phyu Smith (2015; 2016) explored how the material cultures of Karen refugees influence their conceptualization of the tangible and imagined meanings of home and everyday life, from the refugee encampments in Thailand to being resettled in Canada. Quotes drawn from her dissertation cite that work. Sheila Htoo is a Karen refugee and community leader who has provided support and guidance to her community as they settle in Canada. Her ongoing doctoral thesis explores how the Salween Peace Park, an Indigenous Karen conservation initiative, has emerged as one solution to the complex and long-standing political conflicts in Karen State in Myanmar. Htoo's work is demonstrating the historically strong social and political ties among the Karen people, an important factor in their process of resettlement in Canada. She also adds her personal experiences and direct observations to this work.

History of the Karen

The Mae La Oon and Mae Ra Maung refugee camps are located in a very remote area of northwestern Thailand along the Myanmar border. The Karen refugees living in these camps had been systematically persecuted and internally displaced for decades by successive military regimes in Myanmar. In 1975, the military carried out its infamous Four Cut Policy, a scorched-earth military campaign against ethnic populations in an area controlled by an armed resistance, the Karen National Union (KNU), in the southeast region of the country. The military campaign was launched as a counter-insurgency strategy to completely cut off the armed resistance from its ethnic population. As a result, ethnic populations were forced from their villages; some were placed under the control of the military government and most were permanently displaced and forced to flee to refugee camps in neighbouring Thailand (Smith, 1991).

In addition to brutal mass killings, forced labour, and torture of their loved ones by military troops, Karen refugees witnessed their villages and farmlands burned to the ground; they were forced to live in multiple refugee camps in Thailand for decades with no access to formal schooling and limited opportunities for skill development and employment. The refugee camps in Thailand were not only isolated but also physically unsafe; some were affected by flooding and landslides, with dozens of refugees killed during each incident (Htoo's personal experience of flooding in Mae Kong Kah, 2002; Saw Thein Myint, 2011). Karen refugees sponsored by the Canadian government were chosen from the Mae La Oon and Mae Ra Maung camps as priority applicants with the greatest humanitarian needs such as physical and mental disabilities, families with young children, and families headed by a widowed parent (CIC, 2009).

Settlement in Canada

The Karen were resettled throughout Canada, with most sent to Ontario (40%) and the Prairies (38%) (CIC, 2009). The government resettled them in groups at each site to allow them to maintain their close-knit community ties. However, there was no consultation with the Karen refugees either in Thailand or in Canada about where they would be located. The few who spoke English were among the first cohort resettled so they could support the settlement process of others (CIC, 2009). Htoo was one of these, and she notes that this had the potential to place a large burden of resettlement responsibility on those who arrived first, without their participation in planning for this expectation. As GARs, the Karen were provided with financial support for one year, after which they were eligible to apply for social assistance if they had not found employment. Slightly more than half of those settled were male (53%), and many were children or youth (CIC, 2009).

The Karen could not rely on a pre-existing population in the host country to provide informal settlement support. Prior to 2006, a handful of Karen and Karenni (a related ethnic group that also experienced oppression) refugee students had studied in Canadian universities through the World University Service of Canada (WUSC) program. Although the former Karen students reached out to the government prior to the planned group settlement, they were not consulted. One former WUSC student who we interviewed in Ottawa commented:

> When you're talking about the policy when the Canadian government are planning to bring in a large group of refugees from a specific country, I have a feeling that they should at least consult with the community representative from that country and get the opinion or suggestion or work closely with them along the way in order to make it successful for both the Canadian government and for the newcomer (KM3).

Although the Karen refugees received the standard pre-arrival cultural orientations and trainings, these programs were far from adequate in meeting their high level of settlement support needs. Lack of pre-arrival orientation is a common concern for refugee groups in general (Korn et al., 2014), but it was particularly problematic for the Karen. Being resettled from a remote and closed refugee camp to a large urban centre in a developed country is a shocking experience that comes with unimaginable challenges (Guruge et al., 2015; Htoo's personal experience, 2004). The Karen refugees needed to acquire basic life skills, ranging from using stoves and public transportation, before they could consider accessing formal services such as immigration, legal, education, and healthcare.

Engagement of Settlement Institutions

The unique experiences of this new and underserved refugee population created opportunities as well as challenges for frontline settlement service agencies to be proactive, innovative, and responsive in their approaches and models of delivering settlement, primary healthcare, and educational services efficiently and effectively. While some organizations were able to change, adapt, and become flexible and innovative in their service provision approaches, others struggled to adjust and some failed to appropriately adapt their models of service delivery to their Karen clients, with serious implications for their work with clients. One example of good practice was observed in Toronto, where several settlement and service agencies collaborated with Karen leaders to establish the Karen Partnership Group to better coordinate services for the Karen community (Shakya et al., 2014).

Language was the most critical challenge, and was interwoven with other settlement issues at multiple levels including subjective experiences of belonging and security, institutional barriers, and community attitudes, as well as more functional elements such as accessing employment, housing, and education, consistent with Hynie's holistic integration model

(Hynie et al., 2016). The newcomers were offered English language learning classes, but literacy in their own language was not necessarily considered as a prerequisite. A vast majority (80–90%) spoke little or no English, which posed challenges not only for language instructors but also for settlement and healthcare agencies seeking to provide services to this population (CIC, 2009).

The difficulties the Karen experienced in learning the English language had implications for their access to employment. One Ottawa settlement worker spoke about the kind of work that the Karen were finding, commenting, "Yeah it's still low-wage job of course because the language ability is an issue it's a big problem." A Karen refugee we interviewed in Toronto told us about the difficulties of finding a job and the lack of recognition of skills.

> We wait, wait, wait for the phone call but they never call. We have to find another job, another job every day. For me, a very upset when I stay home because I need a job, I need a job, I need, everyday I'm looking for a job, any kind of job, like a precarious job, no matter what my skill back home, they said okay that is not recognized here, so when we come here we have to start at the beginning, everything at the beginning. (KF1)

All refugees from protracted situations need additional health support; as with other refugee populations, Karen refugees had health problems including chronic conditions such as asthma and diabetes as well as more treatable ones including dental problems, malnutrition, and parasites (Kenny & Lockwood-Kenny, 2011; Pottie et al., 2011). Their treatment required both short-term assistance and long-term care through a family physician, but the language barrier and lack of interpreters made it challenging to provide any kind of services, although access to health care was much better in more urban regions. Many of the refugees also had mental health issues due to their exposure to violence and trauma prior to migrating to Canada, and diagnoses of these conditions were complicated by both the language barrier and unwillingness to share personal details with a healthcare professional. In research conducted by Smith, one Karen community member commented:

> When they provided counseling to the Karen there was a kind of culture clash, between the Karen clients and the service providers because the service provider tried to ask them something which they cannot conceptualize like the service provider ask them 'okay, tomorrow when you wake up and if you had a chance to change something in your life what

would it be?' That kind of thing the Karen cannot conceptualize. (Smith, 2015: p. 26)

Advocacy and Resistance

Strong social bonds and committed leaders were key to how the Karen as a community responded to the barriers they faced. For example, some found work with community members, thereby navigating around the challenges they faced in terms of learning English and finding employment. However, this kind of employment also limited language learning. Still, many preferred employment to school because it provided a better return. Additionally, some Karen refugees felt that they were being harassed by teachers in language classes because of their lack of education and literacy. Although this experience may not be unique to the Karen community, Karen community leaders met with a coalition of healthcare and settlement workers to call for accountability and better training for language instructors. This critical feedback from a refugee community was not well received by the professional workers (Htoo's personal experience in the Karen Project Partnership, 2012).

A similar kind of group advocacy occurred in response to concerns about language learning for Karen students in the school system. One Karen community leader in Toronto spoke about working to engage the schools:

> We talked about that with the school because the LEAP class is not very, we don't think it's very effective 'cause the teachers are not doing, I don't want to say that they're not doing a great job, they are doing a good job, but at the same time you know we can do better. You know what I mean, we can do better for these kids … we started a meeting with teachers and school principal last year, so hopefully we will have that again in February. So, I'm going, and a lot of Karen parents are going so hopefully we can discuss about that issue …we want them to at least finish high school. (KF10)

The Karen parents in Toronto developed a clear agenda and asked for a special meeting of school officials. Simultaneous translation was arranged using equipment from York University. School officials wanted to focus on orienting the parents to the school, but the parents quickly changed the focus to their list of concerns about their children's experiences in school, with recommendations for changes, and requested a follow-up meeting to check on progress.

One Karen settlement worker in Ottawa, who had originally come to Canada as a WUSC student, spoke about working hard to get the attention of the broader community about the newcomer Karen refugees and their needs:

> We face a lot of challenges but at the same time we outreach, media cover
> our story, the school board met with us, the community had a meeting even
> the politicians involved. So, I mean we make a lot of noise in order to get
> attention and we were small; we were small, but we want to make sure that
> as I said they get some help. (KM3)

Gender Roles

Traditional gendered relationships in the home are mainly framed through the undertaking of masculinized and feminized roles that are embedded within a culture and affect the management of the household (Dudley, 2010). Prior to settlement in Canada, many Karen men had a more prominent role in the family, but Karen gender relations cannot be easily defined as being patriarchal. Additionally, gender relations have continued to evolve after arrival in Canada, depending on specific family circumstances. In some families, blurring of gender roles continues in the post-migration context, with men helping out with domestic duties and ongoing potential for more collaboration around household responsibilities. Some parents took employment that involved irregular hours, so household duties had to be shared with other family members. In other families, male members of the household have never engaged in domestic duties and expect female members to continue with these duties in addition to their paid work. We asked a prominent community leader to reflect on the reconfiguration of gender roles during the various stages of displacement; he told us about changes in expectations about women working outside the home:

> In terms of the men and women I mean I don't see a lot of barrier but one
> thing that what we used to have is the man is the one that look for job and
> bread winners and the women is still home taking care of the kids right. So
> that is something that my wife and I have to challenge them if you want to
> support yourself or support your family you cannot rely so much on your
> husband to just work alone and support you at least your wife has to work
> part-time or do something in order to be able to bring in enough money for
> your family. (KM3)

This excerpt offers some insight into the intricate nature of gender relations within the Karen community. Although women have had more opportunities to adopt different roles in Canada, social and cultural factors still have the potential to constrain their aspirations and change may be undertaken reluctantly and minimally. Resettlement may shift gender roles but does not change the basic communal strategies used to ensure the wellbeing of the family – and these strategies become even more critical when a family must confront challenges such as paying high rents and buying food and clothing within modest incomes, especially after previously having basics such as food and shelter provided in a refugee camp. The financial wellbeing of families may depend on several family members having jobs, including youth who may work part-time jobs while completing high school and university. Not every family is fortunate in finding suitable work, so some might rely on social assistance. Overall, just as families faced challenges at refugee camps, they faced both similar and new stresses in Canada, including limited finances, lack of meaningful employment, or feelings of alienation from living in a foreign culture. All of these factors can destabilize homes and shift the political terrain of the family.

Important Role of Community Leaders

Although the Karen refugee community faced many resettlement challenges, the strength of their close-knit and highly organized community structures, headed by a handful of highly connected regional and national community leaders, contributed significantly to positive settlement experiences and successful integration into Canadian society. These leaders, including young leaders such as Sheila Htoo, were instrumental in facilitating the resettlement process and services: they served as interpreters, life skill workers, settlement workers/counsellors, as well as community leaders and volunteers meeting the basic needs of newcomers that are often unmet by formal settlement, social, and healthcare services.

Previous research has demonstrated that community leaders, including youth leaders, play an important and instrumental role in bridging the gap between service providers and refugee clients (Shakya et al., 2014). Although these community leaders may also be recent refugees with families, full-time work, and school responsibilities, they draw from their own means and resources to fill important service gaps for their fellow newcomers, often at great personal cost (Lee et al., 2002; Shakya et al., 2014). One example is the challenge to keep strict professional and personal boundaries. Because of the nature of frontline work as an interpreter and outreach worker, Karen newcomers would call outside of regular (9-5) office hours as they did not necessarily understand this work policy, and they would misunderstand and react negatively when calls were not answered. Sheila Htoo also observed how professional and personal boundaries became blurred when she was expected to go above and beyond the roles of interpretation and accompaniment, for example in complex medical cases. When one arose that led to an emergency room visit and hospitalization, she felt that, as a member of this community, she could not leave the hospital at the end of her interpretation assignment and had to remain in a voluntary capacity to meet the needs of newcomer clients. Communities that have access to strong and educated leaders upon arrival tend to have a better chance of connecting with settlement and healthcare service providers. They are able to organize themselves and advocate collectively for what they needed: for the Karen, this was collective integration.

Conclusion

Efforts at integration often emphasize changes at the individual level, rather than how both host and newcomer communities support and adapt. As evidenced by the Karen community, successful social integration reflects the agency of newcomers across multiple levels as they navigate barriers and build on their strengths. The Karen were active agents shaping their settlement experience: they were highly motivated to settle, seeking the security that they had never had. One young woman was optimistic about their future of the Karen as citizens of Canada:

> I'm free, I'm free from all kinds of persecution and all kinds of, you know, you don't have to worry about, you know, for your children for the next generation because they have a place to live, they have a place to call home and I think I can experience, I would be, I think I will be citizen next year cause I'm in the process of (laughs) applying for my citizenship so it's going to be my first time having, you know, becoming citizen, something I never had and I think, you know, that experience will change everything. (KF10)

Community self-organizing is a potentially powerful integration strategy with varying success; it depends greatly on collaboration and working relationships between community leaders and a network of service providers in their respective cities and neighbourhoods. Previous research has demonstrated that refugee youth, in particular, have been instrumental in the resettlement of Karen, Afghan, and Sudanese communities in Toronto (Shakya et al., 2014). The Karen refugee community faced many challenges and had difficult pre-settlement experiences, but it also had unique post-settlement capabilities as a close-knit and highly organized community. The community leveraged innovative models of community organizing to aid integration into Canadian society.

Overall, the experiences of Karen refugees in Canada reveal that the resettlement of large groups of refugees from the same country can moderate elements of the holistic integration process in four main ways. First, social connections within the community, including strong bonds and leadership, can facilitate the strengthening of social links, such as developing connections to institutions and access to social capital. Large refugee communities are more likely to have access to a strong leader or to be able to identify leaders and organize around them.

Second, large refugee communities demand more institutional adaptation in terms of education, settlement services, and health care. A certain minimum size is needed to ensure sufficient political pressure and awareness for these changes to be made, although too large a group can overwhelm the ability of institutions to adapt.

Third, members of large refugee communities can rely on each other to create employment opportunities in the face of employment-related barriers such as language. Networks are the main way newcomers find jobs, so newcomers with access to a large and well-connected network, including some people with good social links to resources, have a better chance of finding employment.

Finally, the resettlement of large refugee communities can also reduce the likelihood of forming social bridges with the host community; this can have benefits as well as drawbacks. For older adults, having a large co-ethnic community may be a protective factor with few negative consequences. However, it can also slow language learning and thus access to education and secure employment, which be more of an issue for youth who could learn more quickly with stronger bridges to other communities.

Key Takeaway Points

1. Agencies can build on strong community ties and committed leaders within refugee populations to engage the community in controlling and shaping their resettlement pathways.
2. Language learning programs need to address the challenges of diversity, including different levels of literacy and education among students. Adopting an anti-oppressive approach to practice is recommended.
3. Strong community leaders who are working in bridging roles and are often employed by settlement agencies require support to manage the

demands upon them. It is important to engage with community members already in Canada, as well those who will be arriving, about the timing and location of migration.

References

Ager, A., & Strang, A. (2008). Understanding integration: A conceptual framework. *Journal of Refugee Studies, 21*(2), 166-191.

Citizenship and Immigration Canada. (2009). *Assessment of the Karen refugee resettlement initiative in 2006 and 2007.* Prepared by Resettlement Division (Refugees Branch) and Refugee Program Delivery Unit (Operational Management and Coordination Branch). Ottawa, Canada.

Dudley, S. (2010) Feeling at home: Producing and consuming things in Karenni refugee camps on the Thai-Burma border. *Population, Space and Place 17*(6), 742-755.

Guruge, S., Shakya, Y., & Hynie, M. (2015) Refugee youth and migration: Using arts-informed research to understand changes in roles and responsibilities. *Forum: Qualitative Social Research, 16*(3), 1-36.

Hynie, M., Korn, A., & Tao, D. (2016). Social context and social integration for Government Assisted Refugees in Ontario, Canada. In M. Poteet & S. Nourpanah (Eds.), *After the flight: The dynamics of refugee settlement and integration* (pp. 183-228). Newcastle upon Tyne: Cambridge Scholars Publishing.

Kenny, P., & Lockwood-Kenny, K. (2011). A mixed blessing: Karen resettlement to the United States. *Journal of Refugee Studies 24*(2), 217-238.

Korn, A., Manks M., & Strecker, J. (2014). Managing expectations through building cultural capital: The student refugee program experience. In C.A. Brewer & M. McCabe (Eds.), *Immigrant and refugee students in Canada* (pp. 249-260). Edmonton: Brush Education Inc.

Lee, B., McGrath, S., Moffatt, K., & George, U. (2002). Exploring the insider role in community work practice within diverse communities. *Critical Social Work, 2*(2), 69-78.

Myint, S. (2011). Heavy floods battered refugee camps. *Karen News*, August 9. Retrieved from http://karennews.org/2011/08/heavy-floods-battered-refugee-camps/

Pottie, K., Greenaway, C., Feightner, J., Welch, V., Swinkels, H., Rashid, M., Narasiah, L., Kirmayer, L., Ueffing, E., MacDonald, N., Hassan, G., McNally, M., Khan, K., Buhrmann, R., Dunn, S., Dominic, A., McCarthy, A., Gagnon, A., Rousseau, C., & Tugwell, P. (2011). The

Canadian collaboration for immigrant and refugee health. *Canadian Medical Association Journal, 183* (12), E824-E925.

Shakya, Y., Guruge, S., Hynie, M., Htoo, S., Akbari, A., Jandu, B., Spasevksi, M., Berhane, N., & Forster, J. (2014). Newcomer refugee youth as 'Resettlement Champions' for their families: Vulnerability, resilience and empowerment. In: L. Simich & L. Andermann (Eds.), *Refuge and resilience: International Perspectives on Migration, volume 7* (pp. 131-154). New York: Springer, Dordrecht.

Smith, E. (2015) *To build a home: The material cultures, gender relations and the cultivation of meanings by Karen refugees from Burma.* Toronto: York University

Smith, E. (2016) To build a home: The material cultural practices of Karen refugees across borders. *Area, 48*(3), 278-284.

Smith, M. (1991) *Burma: Insurgency and the politics of ethnicity.* London: Zed Books.

Smith, R. (2008). The case of a city where 1 in 6 residents is a refugee: Ecological factors and host community adaptation in successful resettlement. *American Journal of Community Psychology, 42*(3/4), 328-342.

Strang, A., & Ager, A. (2010). Refugee integration: emerging trends and remaining agendas. *Journal of Refugee Studies, 23*(4), 589-607.

SECTION III

THE PROMISE OF EDUCATION

Chapter Nine

Educating Refugee Students in Canada: Toward a Pedagogy of Healing

Snežana Obradović-Ratković, Dragana Kovačević, Neelofar Ahmed and Claire Ellis

Introduction

Canada received nearly 30,000 refugees in 2018 (Falconer, 2019; Yousif, 2019), more than half of whom were under the age of 18 (United Nations High Commission for Refugees Canada, 2019). Canadian educators are expected to respond appropriately to the needs of refugee students and increasingly diverse student populations. Although such work can be complex and demanding (Dufresne, 2015; Ryeburn, 2016), refugee students bring a wealth of life skills, perspectives, survival skills, and motivation to Canadian classrooms (Travers, 2012). To adopt an asset-based approach to education, educators and policymakers must understand students' backgrounds and trauma-informed pedagogies.

Recognizing that education can be a healing process for refugee and war-affected children, we argue that teachers can facilitate healing, peace, and community building (Travers, 2012), all essential components to refugee students' resettlement and wellbeing. We conducted a scoping review (Arksey & O'Malley, 2005; Levac, Colquhoun, & O'Brien, 2010) of the national and cross-sectoral literature and policies addressing refugee student inclusion, education, and wellbeing in Canada. We analyzed the literature using a transformative cross-cultural leadership lens to chart a pedagogy of healing that is rooted in "liberation, emancipation, democracy, equity, and justice" (Shields, 2010, p. 6). In Canada, few studies have focused on refugee students' transition to Canadian schools (Ratković et al., 2017). Our findings will be of interest to educators by identifying the socio-psychological challenges faced by refugee students in Canadian K–12 classrooms and by proposing asset-based pedagogies.

Theoretical Framework

With increasing migration and globalization, the world is simultaneously becoming more cohesive and more fragmented. Shields (2002) described this paradox as the driving force of accelerating diversity:

> Some nations are breaking up; others are forming. New interpretations of history, tradition, and cultural identity are exacerbating existing tensions. New economic and political alliances and tensions are resulting in changing patterns of mobility and immigration, sometimes even dislocation. Increasingly, people are confronted with diversity, not only in the global community, but also locally. (p. 209)

Due to this rapid diversification of communities, there has been little consistency within educational praxis and policy. Stakeholders in education must develop new competences and approaches that are rooted in asset-based pedagogies, social justice, and cross-cultural leadership. The goal of transformative cross-cultural leadership is to build respectful and just communities of difference by addressing power, class, and social and ethnic constructs (Shields, 2003). This leadership approach requires that teachers and school administrators acknowledge systematic discrimination and develop cultural competences; they must shift away from tolerating difference to encouraging and celebrating difference within schools and communities.

Shields (2003) also urged educators to engage with questions of justice and democracy to promote individual and public good. Cross-culturally competent teachers regularly identify, reflect on, and address advantage and disadvantage, inclusion and exclusion, privilege and marginalization, recognition and ignorance, voice and silence, and informed and biased decision-making. Such educators are concerned with "moral questions of goodness, righteousness, duty, and obligation" (Sergiovanni, 1990, p. 23), decreasing the probability of stereotyping, categorizing, stigmatizing, or excluding refugee students.

To transform schools into sites of social justice, equity, and wellbeing, educators must use their knowledge and power to transform social relationships (Quantz, Rogers, & Dantley, 1991). Furman and Shields stressed (2005) the importance of self-reflection in teaching and educational leadership:

> Leadership for social justice requires a careful examination of one's own
> beliefs and practices and those of the institution within which one works, for
> justice is played out in both individual relationships and systemically, in
> policies that assume that any single approach to curriculum, programming,
> resource allocations, or accountability is appropriate for children. (p. 126).

According to Shields (2010), effective educators implement transformative practices in their classrooms by adopting critical theories, social and cultural reproduction theories, and social justice leadership. They acknowledge, deconstruct, and critique "social/cultural knowledge frameworks that generate inequity" (p. 6). Such educators live and teach with tension, moral courage, and commitment to activism. Their main pedagogical goal is individual, organizational, and societal transformation. To meet the diverse needs of refugee and other students with diverse backgrounds including students with immigrant and Indigenous backgrounds, students living in poverty, and racialized students, educators must "promote collective interest of the school and the community" (Nur & Nur-Awaleh, 2013, p. 10).

Methodology

We conducted a scoping review of peer-reviewed articles published in the English language between 1997 and 2017. To explore the experiences of refugee students in the context of their childhood developmental stages, we restricted the search to literature and policy pertaining to K-12 education in Canada. We used a six-stage methodological framework (Arksey & O'Malley, 2005; Levac et al., 2010) to:

1. Identify research questions.
2. Identify relevant studies and policies.
3. Select studies.
4. Chart data.
5. Collect, summarize, and report results.
6. Consult with experts in the field.

We searched three well-known databases: ERIC, Google Scholar, and the University of Toronto Library search interface (UofTLI). After conducting three rounds of database searches combining the subject terms "Canada," "migrant," "refugee," "school," "strategies," and "teachers," we retrieved 82 relevant articles (UofTLI = 46; ERIC = 20; Google Scholar = 16) and completed bibliographic branching of the retrieved articles, which involved scanning the titles and abstracts of the references cited in these 82 articles to expand relevant search results. This process yielded an additional

42 sources, for a total of 124 identified sources. After individually reading the 124 sources for eligibility, making notes, and discussing our individual decisions, 52 sources were selected for analysis. We eventually included seven additional sources, for a total of 59 included documents. The seven additional sources were not identified through database searches; they were published or recommended by our research team members. We selected the literature including any of the following subject terms: "migrant," "newcomer," or "refugee" while excluding the sources that exclusively discussed English as Second Language (ESL) learners and English Language Learners (ELLs). We used Moher, Liberati, Tetzlaff, and Altman's (2009) Preferred Reporting Items for Systematic Reviews and Meta-Analyses (PRISMA) flow diagram to provide a visual representation of the literature search and selection process (Figure 9.1).

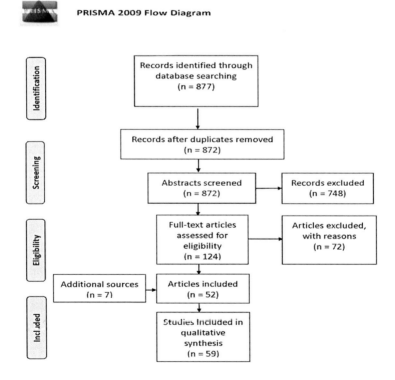

Figure 9.1. Scoping review PRISMA flow diagram. Adapted from Moher, Liberati, Tetzlaff, and Altman (2009).

Once the literature review was completed, we reviewed Canadian education policy using search terms identical to those search terms used in the literature search for the term "refugee." The literature search using the keyword "refugee" had yielded limited results; therefore, we began policy search by using the phrase "teaching strategies migrant students [name of province/territory] school" to search Ministry and Department of Education websites across Canada to find educational policies focusing on immigrant, refugee, or newcomer students. We then read the list of results and determined the relevance of each document based on its title or by searching the whole document for the word "refugee," followed by "immigrant," followed by "migrant."

We found that some Ministry and Department of Education websites provide complete information, from curriculum documents and policies to memoranda and minutes of meetings while others offer a limited selection of publicly available content, making their policies and curricula difficult to access, assess, and implement.

Results of the Scoping Review

Our scoping review yielded a limited number of studies and educational policies focusing on refugee students and their transition to Canadian schools. We identified a substantive gap pertaining to kindergarten to Grade 12 (K-12) education for refugee students: only 23 of 59 selected sources published between 1997 and 2017 explored education for these students. More sources were published in 1998 (n= 9) and 2014 (n= 8); these sources may have been published in response to terrorism (after the 9/11 terrorist attack) or a refugee influx (e.g., from Yugoslavia and Syria), rather than as proactive commitments to the inclusion, success, and wellbeing of refugee students. Canadian educators, policymakers, and other stakeholders in education may find it difficult to access information about effective strategies and policies to support refugee students during and after the resettlement process.

Challenges Refugee Students Face in the Canadian Classroom

Children and youth who have experienced the violence and dangers of war are at high risk of experiencing post-traumatic stress disorder (PTSD), a condition "characterized by intrusive memories of the past, sleep disturbances, nightmares, hyper-arousal, affective numbing and emotional withdrawal" (Rummens & Sea, 2002, p. 6). Additionally, bullying and psychological isolation by peers and apathetic teachers may jeopardize refugee students' sense of worth and belonging (Shakya et al., 2010). A lack of trust between the host society and newcomers also hinders the settlement process for refugee students and families. Kondic (2011) found that refugee students are cautious about trusting the new society, which further hinders their integration process. Ratković et al. reported that, "psychological isolation at school and discriminatory attitudes from some teachers place refugee students' self-esteem, social competence, and academic achievements at risk, hindering the student's social, economic, and political integration in the receiving society" (2017, p. 3).

Two of the greatest challenges refugee students face in the resettlement process are coping with the loss of pre-exile friendships and a lack of post-exile peer support. Research has demonstrated that establishing friendships in the host country has highly significant effects on refugee students' sense of belonging (Kondic, 2011; Kovačević, 2016), and that social support is one of the most important mediators in facilitating a smooth transition process for refugee children and adolescents (Gagné, Shapka, Law, & Coll, 2012) .

During the resettlement process, refugee students may also face additional family responsibilities. Family stressors can include translating for parents, babysitting siblings, cooking, cleaning, and continuously running errands (Omidvar & Richmond, 2003). Parents often work precarious contract positions and overnight shifts, contributing to displacement or precarious housing. Familial obligations may force children to spend time completing chores and parental duties, leaving them little to no time to complete homework, socialize, or make friends (Guruge et al., 2015). Additionally, the religious and cultural norms of minority groups are sometimes in conflict with Canadian educational policies and practices, including religious holidays and gender roles (Lang-Gould, Rahman, & Halward, 2007). In this context, refugee children may feel torn between their families and the need to "fit in" with their peers (Campey, 2002).

Psychological and social challenges decrease academic performance and overall achievement among refugee students. The skill assessments, tests, and practices currently used in Canadian K-12 classrooms can also act as a barrier for refugee students; Tong, Huang, and McIntyre (2006) argued that "culturally and linguistically different children are frequently misclassified as having disabilities when none actually exists" (p. 203). Lack of resources and time constraints have been cited as the greatest challenges for educators working with refugee students. Moreover, refugee youth who have encountered challenges, such as disrupted schooling, are likely to remain unsupported in the classroom (Kovačević, 2016).

Promising Pedagogical Approaches

Schools that have adopted an asset-based approach to education have improved the experience of refugee students in Canadian classrooms (MacNevin, 2011; Rossiter & Rossiter, 2009; Rummens & Dei, 2010). Asset-based approaches emphasize the resources, strengths, and talents of communities and individuals, rather than problems or deficits that need to be resolved (Kramer et al., 2012). Lopes and Louis (2009) identified five main principles of asset-based pedagogy:

1. Identifying student strengths.
2. Offering personalized learning options.
3. Enhancing student strengths through networking.
4. Utilizing knowledge about student strengths in and beyond the classroom.
5. Developing student strengths in diverse settings.

Through such pedagogy, students learn that their experiences, culture, race, and gender are assets to the classroom and the learning process (Morison, 2017). Classroom exercises such as multicultural story sharing and arts-based school programs can help refugee students' bond with their peers and gain a sense of belonging, which are critical mediators in easing the transition to Canadian schools (Tavares, 2012b). Fostering intensive language and differentiated instruction has also been recommended to assist with the transitioning process (Ontario Ministry of Education, 2013). Furthermore, bilingual education helps children value each other's knowledge and experience, fostering respect and collaboration (Nowak-Fabrykowski & Shkandrij, 2004).

This type of education also helps refugee children stay connected with their parents and relatives, and feel safe and accepted, because "each language employs the semantic connotations and cultural signifiers prevalent in a given society" (Nowak-Fabrykowski & Shkandrij, 2004, pp. 287–288). In other words, different languages describe reality and relationships in different, or even opposing, ways. To bridge gaps between the different realities of languages, cultures, and traditions, education should focus on two main areas:

c) The development of respect for the child's parents, his or her own cultural identity, language and values, for the national values of the country in which the child is living, the country from which he or she may originate, and for civilizations different from his or her own.

d) The preparation of the child for responsible life in a free society, in the spirit of understanding, peace, tolerance, equality of sexes, and friendship among all peoples, ethnic, national and religious groups and persons of indigenous origin. (United Nations Convention on the Rights of the Child, 1989, Article 29, c & d)

Setting high expectations for all students and ensuring that communication between teacher and student is clear and consistent are simple yet effective strategies for supporting refugee student education, resettlement, and wellbeing (Stewart, 2011).

Schools can create inclusive, safe, and healing spaces where refugee children can discuss their experiences and express their concerns and feelings. This can be facilitated by adopting a cross-cultural transformative leadership approach that promotes "a more inclusive, equitable, and deeply democratic conception of education" (Shields, 2010, p. 2) in diverse contexts. Effective transformative educational leader ask questions such as: What is the purpose of schooling? Whose knowledge counts? Who succeeds in the system? (Shields, 2003). Cross-culturally competent teachers identify, reflect on, and challenge disadvantage, exclusion, marginalization, and ignorance, decreasing the probability of stereotyping, stigmatizing, or excluding refugee students. This kind of approach to education is "anti-racist, anti-sexist, anti-homophobic, and responsive to class exploitation" (Weiner, 2003, p. 100).

Transformative cross-cultural leaders (Shields, 2002, 2003, 2010) can help refugee students strengthen their agency, academic achievements, social integration, and individual and collective wellbeing. They can use their knowledge and power to develop relationships with partners in education—school administrators, student parents, student communities, and resettlement agencies—to transform social relationships (Quantz, Rogers, & Dantley, 1991) within schools and communities. The establishment of resettlement programs within and outside of schools can foster such partnerships and help transform social relationships. School-based prevention programs can foster solidarity, tolerance, and resilience as well as represent an alternative to health services often underused by refugee children and youth (Beauregard, Gauthier, & Rousseau, 2014). Therefore, promotion of these programs among refugee students and their communities must be cross-sectoral, intentional, and systematic.

Policy Directions

This scoping review has revealed a shortage of direct policy solutions to support refugee children and their families as they navigate resettlement in the Canadian educational context. Provincial variances revealed knowledge and policy gaps that impede the development of holistic and multi-level approaches to supporting refugee students. However, promising directions for policy learning and innovation have been recognized in the literature and are included in the policy documents available in some provinces (Appendix 9).

The wellbeing of a child is an important focus in practice and policy. Asset-based approaches have gained traction in some provinces including British Columbia and Manitoba, but educators in most provinces and territories lack knowledge about the diverse needs and experiences of refugee students. Schools are more prone to deficit-based approaches that frame marginalized students such as refugees based on needs and challenges, rather than focusing on their strengths and opportunities for growth (Kovačević, 2016; MacDonald, 2015; Roy & Roxas, 2011). Sharing resources and best practices in asset-based pedagogy would strengthen the national educational fabric.

More training and support for teachers, cultural brokers, and administrators is needed to ease the transition for refugee students in new schools and promote a productive and healing learning environment. For example, the Manitoba Ministry of Education has developed resources for teacher education related to refugee learners and resettlement support resources (Tavares, 2012a), the psychosocial and educational realities facing refugee students, and practical strategies to support refugee students (Tavares, 2012b). All school districts should provide training and professional development opportunities for teachers and other stakeholders on refugee resettlement, cross-cultural communication, and the needs of refugee students in the classroom. Developing cross-sector partnerships between resettlement programs, schools, and refugee student communities can also promote awareness of services available for refugee students and their families. By engaging in these cross-sector partnerships, school boards can support refugee student transition in Canadian schools and promote a productive and healing learning environment.

Additionally, by acknowledging both the power of storytelling and the importance of silence and choice in their classroom, teachers can create safe and empowering spaces for refugee students. Play and creative activities can foster safe and healing school environments. Such pedagogy (Richman, 1998 as cited in Travers, 2012b, p. 47):

- Enables relaxation and enjoyment and improves motivation to learn;
- Encourages integration into a group;
- Develops social skills and friendships;
- Enables success even among students with poor English-language skills;
- Raises self-esteem and does not overemphasize academic skills;
- Affirms a positive identity through activities related to the child's culture;
- Explores sensitive issues such as anger and bullying;
- Allows expression of feelings in a safe way.

In sum, cultural mediators play a critical role in refugee students' education, resettlement, and wellbeing. Teachers with refugee background can act as critical cultural mediators and agents of change in schools and communities (Block, 2012; Ratković & Pietka-Nykaza, 2015). Canadian teachers must be equipped with different teaching methods and styles to provide opportunities for all students to succeed (Kovačević, 2016). They can learn from the cultural, pedagogical, and personal experience of refugee teachers (Ratković, 2015). Streamlining the existing recertification process for refugee teachers is one critical step to support this goal.

Toward a Pedagogy of Healing

Our review revealed significant gaps in the Canadian educational literature and policy as they relate to refugee student support and education. Canadian educators, resettlement officers, and policymakers tend to lack cross-cultural competence, a social justice focus, transformative leadership skills, and policy guidance. Asset-based pedagogies, including arts-based school programs and bilingual education, have been instrumental in fostering refugee student transition, resilience, and wellbeing in some jurisdictions. Research methods such as arts-informed or arts-based research, narrative inquiry, or participatory action research may be useful (Bharati, 2019) in identifying strategies teachers, policymakers, refugee families, and communities can use to ease the transition, empower students, and inform policy. Additionally, hiring refugee teachers and incorporating their knowledge into Canadian curricula would improve education not only for refugee children but also for other marginalized youth (Ratković et al., 2017).

Policymakers and educational authorities in Canada must seek and mobilize knowledge about the impact of resettlement on the social, psychological, and academic wellbeing of refugee students as well as promote safe learning environments and asset-based approaches to education. Canadian provincial and federal governments can support refugee student education and resettlement by funding research studies that investigate the ways in which teachers, policymakers, refugee families, and the community facilitate refugee student resettlement, academic success, resilience, and wellbeing.

National and transnational policy exchange would further strengthen Canadian education systems. Within Canada, inter-provincial exchange would help mobilize existing educational policies and resources; provinces lacking educational policies about refugee students would benefit from exchanging resources with British Colombia, Manitoba, and Ontario. Transnational policy exchange with other countries could also be beneficia. Some collaboration has already begun using Australian resources related to asset-based approaches. Further dialogue and knowledge exchange with other countries will provide new ideas and best practices. Overall, researchers and policymakers should engage with the education, resettlement, and wellbeing of refugee students in proactive, rather than reactive, ways. Proactive engagement has the potential to generate timely knowledge and sustainable practices that foster effective teaching, learning, and resilience in Canada's diverse classrooms.

Key Takeaway Points

1. Stakeholders in education should adopt asset-based approaches to education by building on the resources, strengths, and talents of refugee students.
2. Cross-culturally competent teachers identify, reflect on, and challenge disadvantage, exclusion, marginalization, and ignorance, decreasing the probability of stereotyping, stigmatizing, or marginalizing refugee students.
3. Educators, refugee serving agencies, healthcare practitioners, policymakers, and refugee families must develop cross-sector

partnerships to create and sustain a supportive learning environment for refugee children.

Acknowledgements

This research was supported by the Social Sciences and Humanities Research Council of Canada, the ESPMI Network, and the Faculty of Education, Brock University. We are also grateful to Courtney A. Brewer and Janelle Baptiste-Brady for their contributions to the project and their ongoing support.

References

Arksey, H., & O'Malley, L. (2005). Scoping studies: Towards a methodological framework. *International Journal of Social Research Methodology, 8*(1), 19–32.

Block, L. A. (2012). Re-positioning: Internationally educated teachers in Manitoba school

communities. *Canadian Journal of Education, 35*(3), 85–100.

Bonnis, B. (2005*). Canada: Multiculturalism, religion, and accommodation.* Electronic Thesis and Dissertation Repository. 3278. https://ir.lib.uwo.ca/etd/3278

Campey, J. (2002). Immigrant children in our classrooms: Beyond ESL. *Education Canada, 42*(3), 44–47.

Furman, G., & Shields, C. (2005). How can educational leaders promote and support social justice and democracy community in schools? In W. Riehl (Ed.), *A new agenda for research in educational leadership* (pp. 119–137). New York, NY: Teachers College Press.

Dufresne, S. (2015). *Canadian researcher worries teachers unprepared for Syrian students.* CBC News. Retrieved from http://www.cbc.ca/news/canada/manitoba/teachers-unprepared-syrian-refugees-1.3345253

Falconer, R. (2019). Social policy trends: Global refugee resettlement and Canada. *The School of Public Policy publications, 12.* https://doi.org/10.11575/sppp.v12i0.61854

Gagné, M., Shapka, J., Law, D., & Coll, C. (2012). *The impact of immigration on children's development.* Contributions to Human Development. Basel: Karger.

Immigration, Refugees and Citizenship Canada (2017). *Canada — Admissions of resettled refugees by province/territory of intended destination, gender, age group and immigration category.* Retrieved from http://open.canada.ca/data/en/dataset/4a1b260a-7ac4-4985-80a0-603bfe4aec11

Guruge, S., Hynie, M., Shakya, Y., Akbari, A., Htoo, S., & Abiyo, S. (2015). Refugee youth and migration: Using arts-informed research to understand changes in their roles and responsibilities. *Forum Qualitative Sozialforschung /Forum: Qualitative Social Research, 16*(3), Art. 15. http://dx.doi.org/10.17169/fqs-16.3.2278

Kondic, R. (2011). *Yugoslavian immigrant youth and the negotiation of their identity within the Canadian context: The effects of post-traumatic stress disorder* (Unpublished master's thesis). Ryerson University, Toronto, ON. Retrieved from https://digital.library.ryerson. ca/islandora/object/RULA:1660

Kovačević, D. (2016). *Yugoslavian refugee children in Canadian schools: The role of transformative leadership in overcoming the social, psychological, and academic barriers to successful integration* (Unpublished master's research paper). Brock University, St. Catharines, ON. Retrieved from https://dr.library.brocku.ca/handle/10464/10821

Kramer, S., Amos, T., Lazarus, S., & Seedat, M. (2012). The philosophical assumptions, utility and challenges of asset mapping approaches to community engagement. *Journal of Psychology in Africa, 22*(4), 537–544.

Levac, D., Colquhoun, H., & O'Brien, K. K. (2010). Scoping studies: Advancing the methodology. *Implementation Science, 5*(69), 1–9.

Lopez, S., & Louis, M. (2009). The principles of strengths-based education. *Journal of College and Character, 10*(4), 1–8.

MacDonald, M. T. (2015). EMERGING VOICES: Emissaries of literacy: Representations of sponsorship and refugee experience in the stories of the lost boys of Sudan. *College English, 77*(5), 408–428.

MacNevin, J. (2011). *Feeling our way in the dark: Educational directions for students from refugee backgrounds* (Unpublished master's thesis). University of Prince Edward Island, University of Prince Edward Island, PEI. Retrieved from https://islandpines.roblib.upei.ca/eg/opac/record/884931

Morrison, K. (2017). Informed asset-based pedagogy: Coming correct, counter-stories from an information literacy classroom. *Library Trends, 6*(2), 176–218.

Nur, S., & Nur-Awaleh, M. (2013). Exploring school principals' responses to the needs of Somali immigrant students. *Cultural and Pedagogical Inquiry, 5*(2), 4–24.

Omidvar, R., & Richmond, T. (2003). Immigrant settlement and social inclusion in Canada. *Working Paper Series, 9*(2), 1–22. Retrieved from

http://accessalliance.ca/wpcontent/uploads/2015/03/SummaryImmigra
ntSettlementAndSocialInclusion2003.pdf

Ontario Ministry of Education. (2013). *Policy/Program memorandum No.
119. Developing an implementing equity and inclusive education
policies in Ontario schools.* Retrieved from
http://www.edu.gov.on.ca/extra/eng/ppm/119.pdf

Quantz, R. A., Rogers, J., & Dantley, M. (1991). Rethinking transformative
leadership: Toward democratic reform of schools. *Journal of Education,
173*(3), 96–118.

Ratković, S., Kovačević, D., Brewer, C. A., Ellis, C., Ahmed, N., &
Baptiste-Brady, J. (2017). *Supporting refugee students in Canada:
Building on what we have learned in the past 20 years.* Report to Social
Sciences and Humanities Research Council of Canada, Brock
University, St. Catharines, ON. Retrieved from
https://espminetwork.com/new-report-supporting-refugee-students-in-
canada-building-on-what-we-have-learned-in-the-past-20-years/

Ratković, S., & Pietka-Nykaza, E. (2016). Forced migration and education:
Refugee women teachers' trajectories in Canada and the UK. In C.
Schmidt & J. Schneider (Eds.), *Diversifying the teaching force in
transnational contexts: Critical perspectives* (pp. 179–200). Rotterdam:
Sense Publishers.

Rossiter, M., & Rossiter, K. (2009). Diamonds in the rough: Bridging gaps
in supports for at-risk immigrant and refugee youth. *Journal of
International Migration and Integration, 10*(4), 409–429.

Roy, L., & Roxas, K. C. (2011). "Whose deficit is this anyhow?" Exploring
counter-stories of Somali Bantu refugees' experiences in "doing
school." Harvard Educational Review, *81*(3), 521–541.
doi:10.17763/haer.81.3.w441553876k24413

Rummens, J., & Dei, G. (2010). Including the excluded: De-marginalizing
immigrant/refugee and racialized students. *Education Canada, 50*(5),
48–53.

Rummens, J., & Seat, E. (2002). *Assessing the impact of the Kosovo conflict
on the mental health and well-being of newcomer Serbian children and
youth in the Greater Toronto Area - Summary research report (2000-
2002).* Joint Centre of Excellence for Research on Immigration and
Settlement (CERIS), Toronto. ON. Retrieved from
http://ceris.ca/wp-content/uploads/virtual-library/Doucet.2003.pdf

Ryeburn, B. (2016). Stepping up to support refugee students. *Teacher
Magazine, 28*(3). Retrieved from
http://www.bctf.ca/publications/TeacherArticle.aspx?id=39095

Sergiovanni, T. J. (1990). Adding value to leadership gets extraordinary results. *Educational Leadership, 47*(8), 23–27.

Shakya, Y., Guruge, S., Hynie, M., Akbari, A., Malik, M., Htoo, S., Khogali, A., Mona, A., Murtaza, R., & Alley, S. (2010). Aspirations for higher education among newcomer refugee youth in Toronto: Expectations, challenges, and strategies. *Refuge, 27*(2), 65–78.

Shields, C. M. (2002). Cross-cultural leadership and communities of difference: Thinking about leading in diverse schools. In Leithwood K. et al. (Eds.), *Second international handbook of educational leadership and administration* (pp. 209–244). Dordrecht: Springer.

Shields, C. M. (2003). *Good intentions are not enough: Transformative leadership for communities of difference.* Lanham: Scarecrow Press.

Shields, C. M. (2010). Transformative leadership: Working for equity in diverse contexts. *Educational Administration Quarterly, 46*(4), 558–589.

Stewart, J. (2011). *Supporting refugee children: Strategies for educators.* Toronto: University of Toronto Press.

Tavares, T. (2012a). *Life after war: Professional learning, agencies, and community supports.* Winnipeg, MB: Manitoba Education. Retrieved from https://www.edu.gov.mb.ca/k12/docs/support/law/community_supports.pdf

Tavares, T. (2012b). *Life after war: Education as a healing process for refugee and war-affected children.* Winnipeg, MB: Manitoba Education. Retrieved from https://www.edu.gov.mb.ca/k12/docs/support/law/full_doc.pdf

Tong, V., Huang, C., & McIntyre, T. (2006). Promoting a positive cross-cultural identity: Reaching immigrant students. *Reclaiming Children and Youth, 14*(4), 203–208.

United Nations High Commission for Refugees. (2018). *Figures at a glance: Statistical yearbooks.* Geneva: UNHCR.

United Nations High Commission for Refugees Canada. (2019). *Rebuilding lives.* Ottawa: UNHCR. Retrieved from https://www.unhcr.ca/what-we-do/rebuilding-lives/

Weiner, E. J. (2003). Secretary Paulo Freire and the democratization of power: Toward a theory of transformative leadership. *Educational Philosophy and Theory, 35*(1), 89–106.

Yousif, N. (2019). *Canada's resettlement of refugees highest in the world for first time in 72 years, new data shows.* Retrieved from https://www.thestar.com/edmonton/2019/01/23/canadas-resettlement-of-refugees-highest-in-the-world-for-first-time-in-72-years-new-data-shows.html

Appendix 1

Resources for Teacher Training, Policy Learning, and Development

Canada
Title: Capacity Building K-12: Supporting Students with Refugee Backgrounds, Special Edition # 45 **Type:** Resource **Author (Year):** Ontario Ministry of Education (2016) **Link:** http://www.edu.gov.on.ca/eng/literacynumeracy/inspire/research/cbs_refugees.html
Title: Building Hope: Refugee Learner Narratives **Type:** Report **Author (Year):** Manitoba Education and Advanced Learning (2015) **Link:** https://www.edu.gov.mb.ca/k12/docs/support/building_hope/index.html
Title: Students from Refugee Backgrounds – A Guide for Teachers and Schools **Type:** Guide **Author (Year):** British Columbia Ministry of Education (2015) **Link:** www2.gov.bc.ca/gov/content/education-training/k-12/administration/program-management/refugee-students
Title: Life after war: Professional Learning, Agencies, and Community Supports **Type:** Guide

Author (Year): Tavares/Manitoba Education. (2012) **Link:** https://www.edu.gov.mb.ca/k12/docs/support/law/community_supports.pdf
Title: Life After War: Education as a Healing Process for Refugee and War-Affected Children **Type:** Guide **Author (Year):** Tavares /Manitoba Education and Training (2012, updated 2014) **Link:** https://www.edu.gov.mb.ca/k12/docs/support/law/index.html
Title: Supporting Refugee Children: Strategies for Educators **Type:** Paperback book **Author (Year):** Jan Stewart (2011) **Link:** https://utorontopress.com/ca/supporting-refugee-children-2
Australia
Title: Calmer Classrooms: A Guide to Working with Traumatized Children **Type:** Resource **Author (Year):** Department of Communities, Child Safety and Disability Services & Department of Education, Training and Employment, State of Victoria and State of Queensland (2013) **Link:** http://earlytraumagrief.anu.edu.au/files/calmer_classrooms.pdf
Title: Strengthening Outcomes: Refugee Students in Government Schools **Type:** Policy **Author (Year):** Victoria Department of Education and Early Childhood

Development (2007)

Link: https://docplayer.net/16955363-Strengthening-outcomes-refugee-students-in-government-schools.html

Title: Opening the Door: Provision for Refugee Youth with Minimal/No Schooling in the Adult Migrant English program

Type: Project Report

Author (Year): Moore, H., Nicholas, H., & Deblaquiere, J. (2008)

Link:
http://www.ameprc.mq.edu.au/docs/research_reports/research_report_series/Opening_the_door.pdf

Title: Count Me In! A Resource to Support ESL Students With Refugee Experience in Schools

Type: Resource

Author (Year): Government of South Australia. Department of Education and Children's Services (2007)

Link:
https://dlb.sa.edu.au/mentmoodle/pluginfile.php/166/course/section/45/Count_me_in.pdf

Title: The Education Needs of Young Refugees in Victoria

Type: Resource

Author (Year): Victorian Foundation for Survivors of Torture (2007)

Link: https://www.cmy.net.au/publications/education-needs-young-refugees-victoria

Title: A School Counselling Guide to Working with Students From Refugee and Displaced Backgrounds.

Type: Resource

Author (Year): Queensland Program of Assistance to Survivors of
Torture and Trauma (QPASTT) (2007)

Link: https://qpastt.org.au/wordpress/wp-
content/uploads/2014/05/School-counselling-2007-updated-2014.pdf

CHAPTER TEN

AIMING HIGHER: THE CASE FOR REFUGEE ACCESS TO TERTIARY EDUCATION IN CANADA

CLAIRE ELLIS, COURTNEY OREJA AND EMMA JANKOWSKI

Introduction

Globally, students with refugee backgrounds have scarce access to post-secondary education opportunities. According to the United Nations High Commissioner for Refugees (UNHCR), only 1% of refugees are enrolled in tertiary education, in comparison to the global enrollment rate of 36% (UNHCR, 2017a). UNESCO (1998) defines tertiary education (also known as post-secondary and higher education) as any type of study, training, or training for research at the post-secondary level that is provided by colleges, universities, or other educational establishments approved as institutions of tertiary education by a government authority. The gap in access to education for refugees has significant consequences, as tertiary education provides individuals with the potential to increase their skills, confidence, knowledge, and resources for personal development, as well as economic and social prosperity and mobility. The positive effects of tertiary education transcend social, economic, and political spheres, with the potential to foster leadership, support, and conflict resolution, and aid in the assistance of conflict-affected societies

Despite advances in programming and increased international attention, the provision of tertiary education for refugees has largely remained in the shadows of primary and secondary education, with inherent limits as explored in Chapter 9. Basic education is established through a human rights perspective, acknowledged in the Declaration of Human Rights and the 1989 Convention on the Rights of the Child (Dryden-Peterson, 2012), and in principle afforded to refugees through Article 22 of the 1951 Refugee Convention. In comparison, access to tertiary education is often justified through a human resource lens, based on the assumption that tertiary education can increase adaptation, integration, and self-reliance of refugees once in a resettlement situation (Zeus, 2011). As with non-refugee students, tertiary education is seen as providing a path to upward economic and social mobility, increasing earnings and expanding social networks (Ferede, 2010). However, the barriers facing students with refugee backgrounds can restrict their participation and lead to additional challenges during their settlement experience.

We conducted a literature and policy review of post-secondary education and displacement, and found that education is an important element of resettlement. The following discussion is intended to foster further discussion on this potentially scalable policy direction in Canada. We begin by reviewing global initiatives to address disrupted post-secondary education and identifying the key barriers students face as they navigate post-secondary education in the context of forced migration and resettlement. We then examine the benefits of increasing access to tertiary education for refugee students and outline the resettlement process of the World University Service of Canada's (WUSC) Student Refugee Program (SRP), exploring the nuances of this education-centric refugee resettlement sponsorship model in Canada. Finally, we discuss the research and policy implications for post-secondary educational access for refugees and conclude with recommendations for practice and policy development.

Global Trends in Policy Responses to Post-Secondary Education for Refugees

As of December 2017, more than 71.4 million people were of concern to UNHCR (2017b), including 39.1 million internally displaced persons, 19.9 million refugees, and 3.9 million stateless persons. Of these, slightly more than 65,000 were permanently resettled to other countries, with the majority of refugees remaining in neighbouring asylum countries and camp situations. Widening access to postsecondary education for students with refugee backgrounds has been an increasing focus of the UNHCR since the 1960s and is still considered a durable solution to displacement (Dryden-Peterson, 2011). As part of its 2017–2021 Strategic Directions, UNHCR engaged a three-pronged approach that included connected learning initiatives, scholarship programs in countries of asylum, and linking countries of resettlement to education opportunities for refugees (UNHCR,

2019). These pathways involve collaborations with states, international and local NGOs, and post-secondary institutions to provide funding, develop technology-based learning programs, and expand access to national education systems. For example, the UNHCR DAFI (Albert Einstein German Academic Refugee Initiative, funded by the government of Germany) program has provided scholarships to more than 14,000 students since 1992 (UNHCR, 2017a).

In response to ongoing and large-scale conflicts that produce refugee migrations, there have been calls for tertiary education institutions to respond to the increasing need for resettlement and education opportunities (Goodman, 2016). A review of policy interventions in North America and Europe revealed a wide variety of approaches including accredited on-site or blended learning programs, international online learning programs, scholarships, information sharing platforms, assessment of credentials and qualifications, and efforts to address other access barriers (Streitwieser, Loo, Ohorodnik & Jeong, 2018). The Council of Europe's European Qualifications Passport for Refugees is a pilot project aimed at providing an education qualification assessment scheme for refugees, including those without access to verified documents (Streitwieser et al., 2018). The governments of some refugee-receiving countries, such as Scotland, have implemented more inclusive policies for refugee students, such as waiving fees so that refugee students pay domestic rather than international fees (University and College Union, 2007).

Dryden-Peterson (2016) noted that the experiences of refugee students attempting to access education in neighbouring asylum countries versus resettlement countries can differ greatly, as resettlement generally involves a more permanent solution and access to citizenship. However, local and international action to increase access to tertiary education in protracted and temporary refugee situations has recently gained traction. For example, in the Borderless Higher Education for Refugees (BHER) Project, two Kenyan universities and two Canadian universities have collaborated to provide funded in-camp university courses to refugee students living in the Kenyan Dadaab camps (Giles, 2018). Another significant trend has been the development of technology-driven initiatives that supply tertiary education through open and online courses and apps, allowing students to continue learning in spaces of displacement and using technology to link exiled teachers and students (Crea & Sparnon, 2017; Dahya & Dryden-Peterson, 2017). Despite the reality that more refugees are living in urban areas and refugee camps in the Global South, most research and policy responses to tertiary education for refugees have focused on resettlement contexts in the

Global North; Ramsay and Baker (2019) argued that this disparity illustrates the global imbalance of power between North and South.

Barriers to Post-Secondary Education for Refugees

Refugees share many of the same settlement challenges experienced by immigrant newcomers, but they often face additional constraints due to the largely abrupt and complex experiences of forced migration (Bajwa et al., 2017). Despite their high aspirations for advanced study, refugee students who begin tertiary studies face unique circumstances that affect their ability to succeed academically (Lenette, 2016). These can include limited opportunities to access early education in displacement and/or refugee camp situations, informational and support barriers in the post-secondary environment and at home, and wellness factors that are specific to students with refugee backgrounds.

Dryden-Peterson and Giles (2010) described disrupted primary and secondary education for refugees as a 'broken pipeline.' The compounding issues of protracted conflict and consequent displacement to neighbouring countries or a refugee camp can lead to progressively narrowed schooling opportunities as refugee children become youth (Dryden-Peterson & Giles, 2010). This process disproportionately affects the participation of girls and young women, who are less likely to have access to education in refugee situations (Plasterer, 2010). Thus, the inconsistent availability of primary and secondary education is a significant barrier to accessing tertiary education.

However, the refugee students who succeed in accessing and completing secondary studies often have limited financial opportunities to pursue further education, as well as unclear information regarding tertiary financial student support. Few scholarships are available for refugee students, and even these may involve difficult-to-navigate and complex bureaucratic processes related to bursaries, loans, and scholarships. Shakya et al. (2010) investigated the core systemic barriers experienced by newcomer refugee youth and concluded that the main barriers are access to information, credential recognition, language, finance, and discrimination. Bajwa et al. (2017) also found that informational barriers led to misinformation about financial aid, credential recognition, study permits, and educational and professional supports. These factors, coupled with the aforementioned broken pipeline, have resulted in minute representation of the refugee population at the tertiary education level (Dryden-Peterson & Giles, 2010).

During tertiary education, academic support is an important factor in successful transitions between levels of study for students of all backgrounds. For refugee students who have resettled in societies where the language of education differs from their home or native language, this type of support, typically provided by family, is often in short supply. In most cases, this is due to limited language and literacy skills in the dominant or official language in the country of resettlement within many refugee communities, a barrier especially common for older refugees, including the parents of refugee students (Dryden-Peterson, 2017). In these situations, it is vital to bridge social capital; refugees who build relationships with individuals who have tertiary education and advanced language skills in the dominant language of the resettlement country are more likely to succeed academically. Bridging social capital is a daunting task unless some commonalities are present, such as country of origin or gender (Dryden-Peterson, 2017). However, the support-seeking process can be facilitated by incorporating refugee experiences into service models and ensuring the availability of culturally appropriate relationship-building opportunities (Lenette, 2016).

Finally, personal wellbeing, or wellness, strongly affects the ability of refugees to access and succeed in tertiary education. Myers, Sweeney, and Witmer described wellness as "a way of life oriented toward optimal health and well-being, in which body, mind, and spirit are integrated by the individual to live life more fully within the [...] community" (2000, p. 252). Among refugee populations, experiences of forced migration and resettlement create challenges in achieving a healthy and satisfied life (Blount & Acquaye, 2017). These problems are compounded by social inequalities in education, as well as in other key areas such as housing, employment, and monetary resources, thereby impeding emotional, spiritual, and intellectual elements that can contribute to overall wellbeing (Hess et al., 2014). Moreover, although participation in education is an enabling and protective factor in the refugee trajectory, the adjustment process and stressors of tertiary education can actually further increase mental health challenges for the population (Jack et al., 2019). Despite awareness of these interrelated concerns, colleges and universities have been slow to respond to the needs of refugee students (Lenette, 2016).

Tertiary Education: A Pathway to Social and Economic Inclusion

Social Capital Through Education

Social capital theory is abundant in the body of literature about newcomer integration (Aizlewood & Pendakur, 2005; Brubaker, 2002; Pendakur & Mata, 2012; Putnam, 2007). On one hand, bonding social capital provides opportunities to strengthen in-group social ties (Brubaker, 2002) and offers tangible (albeit limited) benefits including childcare, shared housing, and small loans (Dryden-Peterson, 2017). On the other hand, bridging social capital involves connections between groups, and can require overcoming social hierarchies. Although social capital can offer benefits including employment and academic opportunities, this kind of bridging social capital is more difficult to access and maintain (Putnam, 2007). According to Ryan (2011), bridging social capital first involves horizontal social capital, i.e., relationships between members of different groups who occupy similar social locations, followed by vertical social capital, i.e., relationships between members of different social groups. Because these contacts occupy different social locations, these relationships can result in more beneficial outcomes due to access to valuable resources and specialized knowledge (Gericke et al, 2018).

For refugee students, both vertical and horizontal bridging social capital can take the form of structured relationships offered through mentorship or scholarship programs, or more informally through peer-to-peer support offered by post-secondary institutions. Dryden-Peterson (2017) noted that these types of relationships can help refugee students understand the 'rules of the game.' Peer-to-peer support serves as an important opportunity for refugee students to begin making out-group connections and build bridging social capital; this issue will be explored in more depth later in this chapter.

Access to Employment

Obtaining employment in the country of settlement is a major obstacle for many refugees. Unsurprisingly, research shows that when compared with their counterparts with access only to primary or secondary education, refugees who have engaged with tertiary education are more likely to obtain employment and participate meaningfully in the local economy (Ramsay & Baker, 2019). An analysis of the economic returns of investment in post-secondary education of government-assisted and privately sponsored refugees arriving in Canada from 2002–2005 revealed that participation in education within the initial seven years after arrival had positive effects on employment and income levels (Prokopenko, 2018). These findings point to the critical success factor of tertiary education for refugee newcomers, and the need to improve access and support for refugee tertiary education.

Post-secondary education can reverse the disempowering processes experienced throughout the refugee trajectory, and can initiate a process of self-sufficiency, increased access to opportunities, and linkages to a local community (Dryden-Petersen & Giles, 2010). Facilitating the educational journeys of refugee students – in terms of access, in the classroom, and through tailored student supports – simply makes economic sense (Lenette, 2016). Further, beyond the economic value of continued education, access to post-secondary education provides a catalyst for personal growth and social inclusion. From an employment perspective, refugees' creation and use of bridging social capital is closely associated with their educational backgrounds: refugees who have attended tertiary education have social locations that provide opportunities to access groups with stronger labour market connections (Gericke et al., 2018).

Post-Secondary Education as a Gateway to Resettlement in Canada

In 1978, the World University Service of Canada (WUSC) identified a gap in refugee access to tertiary education and took action by connecting third-country refugee resettlement with access to postsecondary education. This resulted in the creation of the Student Refugee Program (SRP), which has enabled more than 1700 refugee youth from 39 countries to resettle and access post-secondary education in Canada since its inception (WUSC, 2017a).

The SRP is unique on the global scale: it brings together resettlement and tertiary education by leveraging a non-traditional partnership with postsecondary institutions (WUSC, 2017a). It differs significantly from scholarship programs because it offers a durable, long-term solution to displacement instead of taking a short-term approach that focuses solely on attaining education. Students selected through the SRP become permanent residents upon their arrival in Canada. The SRP operates under Canada's Private Sponsorship of Refugees (PSR) program through the auspices of Immigration, Refugees and Citizenships Canada (IRCC). WUSC acts as a Sponsorship Agreement Holder (SAH): a humanitarian, religious, or community organization that has an agreement with the Government of Canada to sponsor convention refugees or any member of the country of asylum class. Students are selected via a competitive process through the collaboration of several key stakeholders who organize their travel documents, required tests, and pre-arrival orientation (Plasterer, 2010; Shankar et al., 2016).

In addition to WUSC's government designation, the organization has developed strong relationships with Canadian postsecondary institutions to deliver the program on campuses across Canada. The PSR program mandates a sponsorship undertaking period wherein all persons sponsored must be provided with housing, settlement assistance, and support for their first 12 months in Canada or until they become self-sufficient (IRCC, 2019). Each year, colleges, universities, and CEGEPs[1] across the country take on the responsibilities of sponsoring one or more students by providing the institutional, social, and financial support for their first year in Canada, and often beyond this mandatory time frame. Interest and commitment to sponsoring student refugees has ballooned over the years from Canada's tertiary education community. In 2016 alone, the SRP grew by 63% due to a sense of urgency among post-secondary education partners to respond to the global refugee crisis (WUSC, 2017b). Funding for the SRP can involve any combination of student and/or faculty levies, institutional waivers and bursaries, external donations, and fundraising (WUSC, 2017a). Some post-secondary institutions decide to extend this undertaking period and provide funding to students beyond their first year in Canada to relieve additional financial burden.

The SRP's continued growth would not be possible without the ongoing support of Canadian postsecondary students; it employs a youth-to-youth sponsorship model in which Canadian postsecondary students play an active role in the sponsorship of refugee students. Each participating campus hosts a Local Committee (a student group supported by a staff or faculty advisor) to facilitate the settlement and institutional aspects of the sponsorship, such as finances, social participation, academic advising, and accessing on-campus housing. This approach to sponsorship provides an unparalleled opportunity for Canadian youth to play a direct and tangible role in responding to the global refugee crisis.

---

[1] CEGEP (Collège d'enseignement général et professionnel) is a transitional education program equivalent to a general or vocational college. The vast majority of Quebec students start CEGEP at age 17 and attend for two years.

Despite support from the SRP, refugee students face hardships in navigating their new lives in Canada. One study involving SRP students at the University of British Columbia revealed that short orientation periods, a lack of social inclusion, and pressures to support families overseas hampered their settlement and wellbeing (Plasterer, 2010). Still, by incorporating ongoing student feedback, including the active engagement of SRP students in the local committees, program evaluation, and responsive local program reforms, the SRP can serve as a helpful platform for finding new ways to better support refugee students.

Research and Policy Implications

More research is needed to clarify the contextual nuances and complexities that should inform policies relating to the provision of tertiary education for the forcibly displaced, and in turn to provide a point of analysis from which to address current policy gaps. Reddick and Sadler (2019) noted that post-secondary institutions serve as catalysts for resettlement by providing academic, social, and cultural support. However, more in-depth understanding of the experiences and needs of refugee students at post-secondary institutions is essential to develop sound and reflexive policy responses. Education sector data generally combine refugees and immigrants into a single category (Shakya et al., 2010), so it is critical to clarify the particular barriers faced by refugee students and identify best practices to help foster their educational success and wellbeing.

Canada's WUSC SRP provides a distinctive roadmap for resettlement by increasing paths to educational attainment, employment opportunities, and social capital. However, the program encompasses a small subsection of refugee newcomers, both within Canada's refugee streams and in the global refugee context. Refugees who arrive in Canada through government sponsorship or the inland refugee stream are not eligible for the SRP, and no other resettlement programs to access education are available. This policy gap presents an opportunity to develop similar programs to widen access to post-secondary education for refugees arriving through all humanitarian streams. Researchers and policymakers need to interrogate barriers to tertiary education for students with precarious immigration status: lack of information or even misinformation, high international student fees, and ongoing exclusion as they attempt to access education (Villegas & Aberman, 2019).

Overall, international bodies, governments, nongovernmental organizations, and post-secondary institutions are paying more attention to widening educational access for refugee students, which has resulted in a myriad of policy interventions that vary in size, delivery method, focus, and scope (Streitwieser et al., 2018). Research suggests that tertiary education for refugees has the potential not only to provide access to professional attainment and skills, but also to contribute to post-war recovery, conflict resolution, and peacebuilding in countries of origin (Coffie, 2014; Milton & Barakat, 2016). Students who have experienced forced displacement face particular barriers that can impede their smooth transition into a new educational context. While the experiences of refugee students trying to access education share some commonalities, they also differ between groups, so responsive policy and practice must address both commonalities and differences. Previous research has clearly identified the various barriers refugees face in accessing tertiary education, but few real-world solutions at the postsecondary level have been implemented to facilitate the admissions and settlement process for this unique student group. Forced migration, resettlement, and disrupted education intersect to affect access to tertiary education, and for many, ability to bridge social capital. More research and policy analysis with a multi-stakeholder lens will be required to identify and develop pragmatic and holistic ways to address the global and local disparity in post-secondary education for students with experiences of forced migration.

Key Takeaway Points

1. Peer-to-peer support can aid in a smoother settlement experience for refugee students and develop their social capital, as illustrated by the WUSC SRP. Educational institutions can support refugee students through programs that emphasize peer connections and social support.
2. Research has revealed key barriers that impede refugee student wellness and educational success, including lack of access to information, financial resources, and credential recognition. Prospective and current refugee students need targeted support throughout application and orientation processes.
3. Multi-stakeholder collaborations represent opportunities for more long-term and responsive solutions to disrupted education among refugee students. Post-secondary education institutions can work with resettlement agencies, in tandem with governmental bodies, to carve out space for education-based resettlement within humanitarian migration streams. WUSC is a good example of this type of framework.

References

Aizlewood, A., & Pendakur, R. (2005). Ethnicity and social capital in Canada. *Canadian Ethnic Studies.* 37(2), 77-103. https://doi.org/10.1080/09620214.2013.822715

Bajwa, J., Couto, S., Kidd, S., Markoulakis, R., Abai, M., & McKenzie, K. (2017). Refugees, higher education, and informational barriers. *Refuge: Canada's Journal on Refugees.* 33(2), 56–65. https://doi.org/10.7202/1043063ar

Blount, A., & Acquaya, H. (2018). Promoting wellness in refugee populations. *Journal of Counseling & Development, 96*(4), 461-472. https://doi.org/10.1002/jcad.12227

Brubaker, R. (2002). Ethnicity without groups. *Archives Europeennes de Sociologie. European Journal of Sociology. Europaisches Archiv Fur Soziologie, 43*(2), 163–189. https://doi.org/10.1017/S0003975602001066

Coffie, A. (2014). Filling in the gap: Refugee returnees deploy higher education skills to peacebuilding. *Refugee Survey Quarterly, 33*(4), 114–141. https://doi.org/10.1093/rsq/hdu015

Crea, T., & Sparnon, N. (2017). Democratizing education at the margins: Faculty and practitioner perspectives on delivering online tertiary education for refugees. *International Journal of Educational Technology in Higher Education, 14*(1), 43. https://doi.org/10.1186/s41239-017-0081-y

Dahya, N., & Dryden-Peterson, S. (2017). Tracing pathways to higher education for refugees: The role of virtual support networks and mobile phones for women in refugee camps. *Comparative Education Review, 53*(2), 284–301. https://doi.org/10.1080/03050068.2016.1259877

Dryden-Peterson, S. (2011). *Refugee education: A global review.* Geneva, Switzerland: United Nations High Commissioner for Refugees.

Dryden-Peterson, S. (2012). The politics of higher education for refugees in a global movement for primary education. *Refuge: Canada's Journal on Refugees, 27*(2), 10–18. https://refuge.journals.yorku.ca/index.php/refuge/article/view/34718/3 1518

Dryden-Peterson, S. (2016). Refugee Education: The crossroads of globalization. *Educational Researcher, 45*(9), 473–482. https://doi.org/10.3102/0013189X16683398

Dryden-Peterson, S. (2017). Refugee education: Education for an unknowable future. *Curriculum Inquiry, 47*(1), 14–24. https://doi.org/10.1080/03626784.2016.1255935

Dryden-Peterson, S., & Giles, W. (2010). Introduction: Higher education for refugees. *Refuge: Canada's Journal on Refugees, 27(2), 3-9.* https://refuge.journals.yorku.ca/index.php/refuge/article/view/34724/31554

Ferede, M. (2010). Structural factors associated with higher education access for first-generation refugees in Canada: An agenda for research. *Refuge: Canada's Journal on Refugees, 27*(2), 79–88. https://refuge.journals.yorku.ca/index.php/refuge/article/view/34724

Gericke, D., Burmeister, A., Löwe, J., Deller, J., & Pundt, L. (2018). How do refugees use their social capital for successful labor market integration? An exploratory analysis in Germany. *Journal of Vocational Behavior, 105*(1), 46-61. https://doi.org/10.1016/j.jvb.2017.12.002

Giles, W. (2018). The Borderless Higher Education for Eefugees project: Enabling refugee and local Kenyan students in Dadaab to transition to university education. *The Journal on Education in Emergencies.* 4(1). 164-184. http://hdl.handle.net/2451/42485

Goodman, A. (2016). Three ways higher education can respond to the Syrian refugee crisis. Retrieved from https://www.brookings.edu/blog/education-plus-development/2016/05/13/three-ways-higher-education-can-respond-to-the-syrian-refugee-crisis/

Hess, J., Isakson, B., Githinji, A., Roche, N., Vadnais, K., Parker, D., & Goodkind, J. (2014). Reducing mental health disparities through transformative learning: A social change model with refugees and students. *Psychological Services, 11*(3), 347-356. https://doi.org/10.1037/a0035334

Immigration, Refugees and Citizenship Canada (IRCC). (2019). *Guide to the private sponsorship of refugees program.* Ottawa: Canada. Government of Canada.

Jack, O., Chase, E., & Warwick, I. (2019). Higher education as a space for promoting the psychosocial well-being of refugee students. *Health Education Journal, 78*(1), 51–66. https://doi.org/10.1177/0017896918792588

Lenette, C. (2016). University students from refugee backgrounds: Why should we care? *Higher Education Research & Development, 35*(6), 1311–1315. https://doi.org/10.1080/07294360.2016.1190524

Milton, S., & Barakat, S. (2016). Higher education as the catalyst of recovery in conflict-affected societies. *Globalisation, Societies and Education, 14*(3), 403–421. https://doi.org/10.1080/14767724.2015.1127749

Myers, J., Sweeney, T., & Witmer, J. (2000). The wheel of wellness counseling for wellness: A holistic model for treatment planning. *Journal of Counseling & Development, 78*(3), 251-266. https://psycnet.apa.org/doi/10.1002/j.1556-6676.2000.tb01906.x

Pendakur, R., & Mata, F. (2012). Social capital formation and diversity: Impacts of individual and place-related characteristics. *Journal of Ethnic and Migration Studies, 38*(10), 1491–1511. https://doi.org/10.1080/1369183X.2012.711030

Plasterer, R. (2010). Investigating integration: The geographies of the WUSC student refugee program at the University of British Columbia. *Refuge: Canada's Journal on Refugees, 27*(1), 59-74. https://refuge.journals.yorku.ca/index.php/refuge/article/view/34349

Prokopenko, E. (2018). Refugees and Canadian post-secondary education: Characteristics and economic outcomes in comparison. *Ethnicity, Language and Immigration Thematic Series. Statistics Canada.* Ottawa: Canada. Retrieved from https://www150.statcan.gc.ca/n1/en/pub/89-657-x/89-657-x2018001-eng.pdf?st=GUC45Olz

Putnam, R. (2007). E Pluribus Unum: Diversity and community in the twenty-first century. The 2006 Johan Skytte Prize Lecture. *Scandinavian Political Studies, 30*(2), 137–174. https://doi.org/10.1111/j.1467-9477.2007.00176.x

Ramsay, G., & Baker, S. (2019). Higher education and students from refugee backgrounds: A meta-scoping study. *Refugee Survey Quarterly, 38*(1), 55-82. https://doi.org/10.1093/rsq/hdy018

Reddick, D., & Sadler, L. (2019). Post-secondary education and the full integration of government-assisted refugees in Canada: A direction for program innovation. In E. Sengupta & P. Blessinger (Eds.), *Language, teaching and pedagogy for refugee education* (59–73). Bingley: Emerald Group Publishing. http://www.srdc.org/media/9369/helping_GARs.pdf

Ryan, L. (2011). Migrants' social networks and weak ties: Accessing resources and constructing relationships post-migration. *The Sociological Review, 59*(4), 707-724. https://doi.org/10.1111/j.1467-954X.2011.02030.x

Shakya, Y. B., Guruge, S., Hynie, M., Akbari, A., Malik, M., Htoo, S., Khogali, A., Mon, S.A., Murtaza, R., Alley, S. (2012). Aspirations for higher education among newcomer refugee youth in Toronto: Expectations, challenges, and strategies. *Refuge: Canada's Journal on Refugees, 27*(2), 65-78. https://refuge.journals.yorku.ca/index.php/refuge/article/view/34723

Shankar, S., O'Brien, H. L., How, E., Lu, Y. W., Mabi, M., & Rose, C. (2016, October). The role of information in the settlement experiences of refugee students. *Proceedings of the Association for Information Science and Technology.* Copenhagen: Denmark. https://doi.org/10.1186/1471-2458-8-293

Streitwieser, B., Loo, B., Ohorodnik, M., & Jeong, J. (2018). Access for refugees into higher education: A review of interventions in North America and Europe. *Journal of Studies in International Education.* *23*(4), 473-496. https://doi.org/10.1177%2F1028315318813201

Turner, M., & Fozdar, F. (2010). Negotiating "community" in educational settings: Adult South Sudanese students in Australia. *Journal of Intercultural Studies, 31*(4), 363–382. https://doi.org/10.1080/07256868.2010.491276

University and College Union. (2007). *UCU Scotland welcome fee waivers for asylum-seekers.* Retrieved from https://www.ucu.org.uk/article/2724/UCU-Scotland-welcome-fee-waivers-for-asylum-seekers?list=2173

UNESCO (1998, October). Declaration of higher education for the twenty first century: Vision and action and Framework for Priority Action for Change and Development in Higher Education. *World Conference on Higher Education, 9th October.* Paris, France. Retrieved from http://www.unesco.og/education/educprog/wche/declarationeng.htm

United Nations High Commissioner for Refugees (UNHCR). (2017a). *The other one percent – refugee students in higher education. DAFI Annual Report 2017.* Retrieved from https://www.unhcr.org/publications/education/5bc4affc4/other-percent-refugee-students-higher-education-dafi-annual-report-2017.html

United Nations High Commissioner for Refugees (UNHCR). (2017b). *Global Report 2017.* Retrieved from http://reporting.unhcr.org/sites/default/files/gr2017/pdf/GR2017_English_Full_lowres.pdf

United Nations High Commissioner for Refugees (UNHCR). (2019). *Tertiary education.* Retrieved from https://www.unhcr.org/tertiary-education.html

Villegas, P., & Aberman, T. (2019). A double punishment: The context of postsecondary access for racialized precarious status migrant students in Toronto, Canada. *Refuge: Canada's Journal on Refugees, 35*(1), 72–82. https://doi.org/10.7202/1060676ar

World University Service of Canada (WUSC). (2017a). *Educational pathways for refugees: Mapping a Canadian peer-to-peer support model*. Retrieved from https://wusc.ca/building-educational-pathways-for-refugees-mapping-a-canadian-peer-to-peer-support-model/

World University Service of Canada (WUSC). (2017b). *The student refugee program - 2017 annual report.* Retrieved from https://annualreport.wusc.ca/paving-pathways-resettlement-higher-education-refugees/

Zeus, B. (2011). Exploring barriers to higher education in protracted refugee situations: The case of Burmese refugees in Thailand. *Journal of Refugee Studies, 24*(2), 256–276. https://dx.doi.org/10.1093/jrs/fer011

SECTION IV

REFUGEE HEALTH

CHAPTER ELEVEN

FAYYAA-NAGAA:
HEALTH AND WELLBEING AMONG
OROMO WOMEN AND GIRLS IN ONTARIO

BAREDU ABRAHAM, TOLEE BIYA,
MARTHA KUWEE KUMSA
AND NARDOS TASSEW

Introduction

Most Oromo women and girls who come to Canada are refugees fleeing political violence in Ethiopia. They come from traumatic backgrounds, and often arrive with their health and wellbeing already compromised. They have been torn away from their social networks and cultural and spiritual resources, and find themselves struggling in isolation and despair. The combined effects of these and other forms of subtle violence affect their health and wellbeing in profound ways. This chapter explores the cultural resources that female Oromo draw on to redress the disparities they experience in their health and how they use these resources to nurture their wellbeing. We crafted our research in such a way that participation itself served as an intervention to promote healing, self-care, and self-empowerment. The study was funded by Women's Xchange at the Women's College Research Institute in Toronto and was approved by the Research Ethics Board of Wilfrid Laurier University.

We used the Indigenous Oromo concept of *maree*, (sharing circles) to inform our conceptual and methodological directions (Kumsa, 2013; 2017). In total, 44 girls and women from Oromo communities in Southwestern Ontario, including Toronto, responded to our invitation and joined us. We gathered in 19 small *maree* circles and dyads and generated rich qualitative data from June 2016 to February 2017. We used the same *maree* format for data analysis: we gathered in virtual and face-to-face circles, made collective meanings, and generated shared themes and overarching findings. Here, we present the main finding – 'loss of *fayyaa-nagaa'* – along with major themes categorized as internal and external factors. The experiences of participants were highly complex and involve interweaved themes, and we include a comprehensive description of one participant, Solane.[1] We conclude by reflecting on three prominent issues affecting Oromo and other refugee populations, as well as the implications for human services.

Overview of Findings

Loss of Fayyaa-Nagaa

The overarching theme, loss of *fayyaa-nagaa,* emerged from all *maree* circles and dyads. Participants defined health and wellbeing in multidimensional and wholistic ways, which is consistent with the traditional Indigenous Oromo conceptualization of health and wellbeing (Dugassa, 2014). The Oromo language has no accurate translation for the concepts of health or wellbeing, and the Oromo culture has no clear distinction between health and wellbeing. For Oromos, health (*'fayyaa'*) and peace (*'nagaya'*) are inseparably interwoven, and together they define wellness. As in many other Indigenous cultures (Freeman, 2011), health is understood as deeply relational and collective, so the *fayyaa-nagaa* nexus captures a relational and collective notion of health and wellbeing. When this wholistic nexus is lost, existential uncertainty can set in. Some study participants said that they feel well only when everyone and everything near and far are well. Nagesse commented:

> I am fine in my body, but I am not well. I say I am well only when my family is well, and my community is well, when my country is well, and my neighbors are well, when the land is well, and the air is well… when the plants are well, and the animals are well, when the grass is well, and the rivers are well….

Participants in all *maree* circles and dyads referred to feeling a profound loss of *fayyaa-nagaa,* but we observed an intergenerational gap in terms of redressing this loss. Older women were able to draw on their foremothers' traditional practices of women's empathic connections, solidarity, and mutual empowerment, whereas younger women and girls who felt disconnected from their culture did not have much to draw on. Girls

---

[1] Participants' names in this paper are all aliases created to protect anonymity.

expressed the need to learn their culture in order to redress the loss of *fayyaa-nagaa*. Waataate said:

> To be honest, even though I identify as Oromo and I grew up in Oromo household, I don't really know much about our culture.... girls want to learn our past, history, Oromo music, culture, language, food, dances, plants, stories and the meanings behind them... We need to learn our beautiful culture like science in school and doing it in practice, we need the same education.

Internal Factors

Four distinct themes were classified as internal factors: gender suffering, double-edged culture, normalizing *maree,* and existential uncertainty. All of these factors contributed and fed into the loss of *fayyaa-nagaa*. With regard to gender suffering, Oromo women and girls are culturally primed to swallow their own pain and care for their families and communities. This suffering in silence has tremendous effects, but they do not share their struggles for fear of shame and stigma (Poole, 2014). One excerpt from a girls' *maree* captures this theme:

> Jiitu: Everyone expects a woman to take care of everybody around her but when she needs care for herself, she is on her own.... Women cook all the food but get only leftover bites... Moms do everything for us but don't care where they land themselves.

> Lalise: Moms are not appreciated for the stuff they do, the life they lived. They feel we can never understand their experience... there is trauma for a lot of our mothers... forced to leave their home in war, families killed before their eyes. Memory stuck in their heads needs to come out, but it doesn't because mental health is not spoken in Oromo community. We stress the trauma story but don't care for the person experiencing it.

With regard to double-edged culture, participants commented that Oromo culture soothes their wounds in some ways but wounds them in other ways. One example is the institution of mediation by '*manguddoo*' (elders): when they resolve disputes fairly and make peace, this soothes women's suffering, but when they pick sides and coerce women (e.g., into remaining in abusive relationships without addressing the abuse), this can hurt women's wellbeing (Mulleta, 2014). Jaalle commented:

> Mediation is good when *manguddoo* listen to your problems, but they dismiss women's concerns. Divorce? Oh, they shut it down very quickly because divorce is like unheard of in our community... It's not fair when

you [*manguddoo*] are taking advantage of the respect everyone has for you… you're supposed to be there for guidance.

With regard to normalizing *maree*, many participants expressed their commitment to create new *maree* circles as their action part of the research. They experienced the empathic connections and solidarity in the research *maree* circles as spaces of healing and wanted to create such spaces to gather and share stories regularly. Xiicho said:

> We must organize maree circles everywhere, we must start now…. If women come together men come together; if women disperse men disperse too. Women have the key to bring our people together… In our culture folks pray for *humna bishaanii fi mala dubatii* [the ingenuity of women and the power of water]. If we play our role, we can move mountains.

With regard to existential uncertainty, participants expressed deep-seated fears and anxiety that they might be erased off the face of the earth as Oromos. Some worried that if their children and peers married non-Oromos, their identity as Oromos would disappear within the next few generations. This is consistent with previous research documenting deep concerns about identity within other minority ethnonational communities (Abulof, 2009). In Damitu's poignant words:

> It is the end of Oromos…. Everyone is isolated… we have no time to get together. Our children don't speak our language, even to us. They don't know each other. Who will they marry and have children with? I always worry. Will there be an Oromo people after the next generation? Oh God, how are we going to survive?

External Factors

Three major themes were classified as external factors contributing to the loss of *fayyaa-nagaa*: existential echoes, perpetual refugees, and transnational suffering. Existential echoes are related to participants' existential uncertainty about the insecurity and precarity of retaining their Oromo identity in Canada, as well as the uncertainty and precarity of the violent repression of Oromos in Ethiopia. Participants worried that they would disappear as a people if Oromos were killed off in Africa and their ancestral lands were taken from them. These concerns are consistent with previous research involving other communities who worry about land-grabbing as the old form of colonialism returning with the newest form of neocolonial appropriation (Nyong'o, 2013). An excerpt by Nagesse illustrates this theme:

They are killing our people and taking away our ancestral land. They are jailing and torturing those who refuse to leave. Our youths are running away in desperation. You know how many drowned in the Mediterranean and Red Sea recently. You know the 700 Oromos massacred in one day at Irrecha [thanksgiving] a few months ago. All this to grab their land! I fear my people will be wiped off the earth.

The second theme, perpetual refugees, is related to the complex processes of blatant and subtle violence that hamper participants' settlement in Canada and return them to the unsettling and dislocating experience of being refugees. It also relates to how refugees are defined and the processes of refugee-making (Gatrell, 2013; Park, 2008). As in previous research, we identified both local and global processes of refugee-making that produce perpetual refugees, and we heard how these processes disrupt health and wellbeing. Hoyyo said:

They [Western nations] put the Ethiopian regime in power; it's their puppet. They look the other way when our people are massacred, when we are tortured and exiled. Yes, they give us asylum, but we are discriminated here too. Then they continue to support Ethiopia as it kills our people and we become refugees here again but now we have nowhere to run. Back home at least we were the majority, we were on our ancestral land. Here we are nothing, a minority with no land, no voice.

The last theme, transnational suffering, is related to how the political violence participants fled in Ethiopia continues to unsettle their lives and their settlement processes. Their *fayyaa-nagaa* – health and wellbeing in Canada – is profoundly disrupted by the continued repression unfolding in their faraway homeland. At the time of our study, repression in Ethiopia was at a record high: a state of emergency had been declared and killing was continuing unabated throughout the country. Despite the silence in mainstream media, social media were bringing the tragic news 24/7. The research team was greatly affected as the bloodletting slowly seeped into our personal lives and our work; we were tense, physically ill, and depressed, and found it difficult to meet project deadlines. Our work seemed insignificant compared with the violence others were facing in Ethiopia. Our participants often could not come to *maree;* they were glued to their screens taking in the violence, curling up and crying, or gathering in places of worship to fast and pray for their people. Anane said:

I cannot sleep, I cannot eat, I cannot work… How can I, when my families are harassed in Ethiopia, when my people are being massacred? I see the bad news and cry… when I see the blood of those young Oromos, blood drops from my heart… I worry a lot... I feel sick. I can't even get out of bed. How can I come to *maree*?

For many participants, this distant violence reopened the old wounds of untreated trauma they carry deep within them. Previous research has documented how trauma is transmitted intergenerationally among refugees (Dragojlović, 2018; Hudson, Adams & Lauderdale, 2016). We found that the process of perpetual refugee-making is not just transgenerational but also transnational and transcontinental, and it blurs both temporal and spatial boundaries of colonial nation-states.

Solane's Story

This section moves away from abstract themes and explores the experiences of one participant, Solane, to illustrate how these complex elements are interwoven in the real world. We use poetic representation to present Solane's story in its fullest power and to draw readers into the power of experiencing her story in a deeply embodied way (Adame, Leitner & Knudson, 2011; Faulkner, 2009). In her *maree* session, Solane's powerful story emerged with the passionate energy of youth. It was a potent combination of excruciating pain, righteous indignation, and quiet determination: representing it poetically is our way of honouring her story and giving it back to her as powerfully as she shared it.

> Oh, Ethiopian girls are so cool
> Oh, you're so beautiful…
>
> But I'm not Ethiopian!
> I'm Oromo!
> See me for who I am,
> Don't erase my existence. It hurts!
>
> My Ethiopian peers are upset; they feel attacked
> Just because I voiced my hurt
>
> My existence is being erased here
> While war is being waged on my people there
> Ethiopia is killing!
> Genocide is happening on my people!
> So many murdered for voicing their grievance
> I see images of lifeless bodies
> strewn in the streets
>
> My heart is broken

This sweet little girl, perhaps she's six, perhaps seven
Gunned down on her way to school
She lies dead in the street, her head in a pool of blood
Life, dream, erased in an instant
I die with her instantly
They erase my people, they erase my dream, they erase my existence

Here, people see the blood; they see the killing field
But they're scared to say anything
Because Ethiopia is like the White people of Africa
And it hurts. It hurts in the pit of my stomach
At least acknowledge the pain, I cry!

Most disturbing is the denial of Ethiopians
They're good at flashing the race card here
But they don't want to know their violent history
And this genocide is not even history
It's happening right now
But it's easier for them to deny the pain
than to confront their responsibility

Ignorance is easier. I get that
What I don't get is their audacity to be upset,
to say they are attacked
When my people are massacred
I want a recognition of this pain.
Ignoring this is a choice
A choice to actively erase my existence
To tell me
I don't exist, my pain doesn't exist, my people don't exist

You ask me why I feel I belong with my people there?
When I was born in Canada?
When I haven't even set foot in my people's land?
Where I don't even know the people, the language, the culture?
Let me tell you this:
That one claims me; this one doesn't
I'm Canadian but I'm not White or Christian
That sets me apart
Canada is not helping my suffering people
It praises Ethiopia, just like my peers
Praise for what? For doing genocide?
That adds insult to injury
It erases my existence

My erasure continues in more ways

I'm erased in my own Oromo community
because I don't speak the Oromo language
They show me I don't belong there
Not good enough Oromo, I'm erased.

Among my own Muslim people
I'm Muslim, but I don't wear hijab
That makes me less of a Muslim
Although I love my faith, I practice it with love
Not good enough Muslim, I'm erased.

At home I am a girl
Not allowed to do the things boys do
I'm less valued than boys
Although I'm the smartest, the brightest
I'm erased by my family too

Excluded and erased
With no recognition of this pain coming
I swallow my rage
And channel my energy
Into refusing erasure
That's my responsibility

Reflections on Solane's Story

Solane's story is a wholistic depiction of a space where complex themes interweave. We conclude this chapter by examining three elements that underscore the complexity of Solane's narrative and discussing their implications for human services.

Nurturing Spaces

Solane's story epitomizes the loss of *fayyaa-nagaa,* and we consistently found that such loss disrupts health and wellbeing in profound ways. Solane referred to the multiplicity of erasure, which is related to the invisibility of marginalized groups; she could only express this deep pain of erasure and grieve the loss of *fayyaa-nagaa* in the safety of *maree.* Other study participants also shared that even though they felt well in their individual bodies, they felt gravely ill in terms of their collective identity; they experienced the empathic connection and solidarity of *maree* circles as spaces of healing and made commitments to sustain them. How can human services create nurturing spaces of *fayyaa-nagaa* to soothe these wounds of erasure? Human services practitioners need to support women and girls by helping them create spaces they find nurturing. Within this community, women and girls are expected to swallow their pain and care for others; it is vital to draw on their cultural resources and create sharing spaces of *maree* to encourage people to gather and share stories. The objective is to maintain community care while also creating spaces where women can care for themselves.

Subtle Violence

Solane was born in Canada and is a Canadian citizen. She is technically not a refugee, but her experience of vicarious transnational political violence positions her as a refugee. This was also the case for other participants: ongoing violence continues to disrupt their wellbeing, positioning them as perpetual refugees. This finding contests the very definition of 'refugee' as a legal political entity and a subject of international accords. According to the 1951 UN Geneva Convention, a refugee is someone who has been forced to flee his or her country because of persecution, war, or violence (Gatrell, 2013; Park 2008). The experiences of our participants revealed the need to look beyond the blatant political violence by states and non-state actors, and to focus on everyday subtle violence. It compels us to see refugees as people who long for a space free from subtle violence, oppression, and discrimination (Kumsa, 2006). Human services practitioners need to find ways to minimize spaces of subtle violence in everyday relations. Subtle violence is deeply embedded within our institutions and practices, so we need to critically examine how this violence is perpetuated and find ways to overcome it.

Sense of Belonging

Solane's story also illustrates the sense of long-distance belonging experienced by most participants. Refugees are discursively constructed within the context of modern global order by dividing the world into bounded nation-states, erasing some peoples, and assigning specific people to specific territorial belonging (Gatrell, 2013; Kumsa, 2006; Park 2008). We found that participants' sense of belonging to their ancestral homeland moves beyond the boundaries of colonial nation-states. At the same time, it is linked with a deep-seated desire for home and homeland created by the same colonial nation-states (Bhattacharya, 2018; Binaisa, 2011). The challenge for human services practitioners is to draw on these contradictory elements – both opposition to and conformity with the boundaries of colonial nation-states – to nurture the wellbeing of refugees. With regard to opposition, we need to find ways to build solidarity with Indigenous peoples by defying the colonial order that pits marginalized communities against each other. With regard to conformity, we need to advocate for ways to strengthen refugees' connections to their homeland. Finally, it is important to note that refugees may have been displaced from their own homeland, but they are also settlers on lands stolen from other Indigenous peoples.

Key Takeaway Points

1. Loss disrupts health and wellbeing in profound ways, so human services practitioners must support refugees by enabling them to create the spaces they find nurturing.
2. Vicarious transnational political violence is an issue and concern not only for refugees, but also for their children born in Canada, and needs to be considered in any assessment and when working with both individuals and families.
3. Refugees to Canada bring with them a sense of long-distance belonging that transcends bounded nation-states; we must also acknowledge the realities that national boundaries create in negatively affecting the wellbeing of refugees.

References

Abulof, U. (2009). "Small peoples": The existential uncertainty of ethnonational communities. *International Studies Quarterly, 53*(1), 227-248.

Adame, A., Leitner, L., & Knudson, R. (2011). A poetic epiphany: Explorations of aesthetic forms of representation. *Qualitative Research in Psychology, 8*(4), 370-379.

Bhattacharya, K. (2018). Coloring memories and imaginations of "home". *Cultural Studies ↔*
Critical Methodologies, 18(1) 9-15.

Binaisa, N. (2011). Negotiating 'belonging' to the ancestral 'homeland': Ugandan refugee descendants 'return'. *Mobilities, 6*(4), 519–534.

Dragojlović, A. (2018). Knowing the past affectively: Screen media and the evocation of intergenerational trauma. *Arts and Humanities in Higher Education, 17*(1), 119 -133.

Dugassa, B. (2014). Reclaiming Oromo Indigenous organizational structures and fostering supportive environments for health. *Archives of Business Research, 2*(1), 23-45.

Faulkner, S. (2009). *Poetry as method: Reporting research as verse.* Walnut Creek: LeftCoast Books.

Freeman, B. (2011). Indigenous pathways to anti-oppressive practice. In D. Baines (Ed), *Doing anti-oppressive practice.* (pp 111 – 131). Halifax: Fernwood Publishing.

Gatrell, P. (2013). *The making of the modern refugee.* Oxford: Oxford University Press.

Hudson, C., Adams, S., & Lauderdale, J. (2016). Cultural expressions of intergenerational trauma and mental health nursing implications for U.S. health care delivery following refugee resettlement: An integrative review of the literature. *Journal of Transcultural Nursing, 27*(3), 286–301.

Kumsa, M. K. (2006). "No! I'm not a Refugee!" The poetics of be-longing among young Oromos in Toronto. *Journal of Refugee Studies, 19*(2), 230-255.

Kumsa, M. K. (2013). *Songs of Exile.* Kitchener, Duudhaa Publishing.

Kumsa, M. K. (2017). *Youth violence and community healing.* Kitchener: Duudhaa Publishing.

Lev-Wiesel, R. (2007). Intergenerational transmission of trauma across three generations: A preliminary Study. *Qualitative Social Work, 6*(2), 75-94.

Lin, N., Suyemoto, K., & Kiang, P. (2009). Education as catalyst for intergenerational refugee family communication about war and trauma. *Communication Disorders Quarterly, 30*(4), 195-207.

Mulleta, A. (2014). Gender power relationship in the discourse of jaarsummaa: A traditional dispute mediation among Arsi Oromo of Ethiopia. *International Journal of Medical Science and Clinical Inventions, 1*(10), 601-623.

Nyong'o, P. A. (2013). The land question, land grabbing and agriculture in Africa. *International Journal of African Renaissance Studies, 8*(2), 23-31.

Park, Y. (2008). Making refugees: A historical discourse analysis of the construction of the 'refugee' in US social work, 1900–1957. *British Journal of Social Work, 38*(4), 771-787.

Poole, J. (2014). *Sanism and mental health* Retrieved from https://www.youtube.com/watch?v=hZvEUbtTBes

Poynton, C., & Lee, A. (2011). Affecting discourse: Towards an embodied discourse analytics. *Social Semiotics, 21*(5), 633–644.

CHAPTER TWELVE

REFUGEE MOTHERS' PERINATAL MENTAL HEALTH EXPERIENCES AND ACCESS TO HEALTH CARE

JOYCE O'MAHONY AND NANCY CLARK

Introduction

Canada has a long history of resettlement of refugees, which has contributed to strong population growth. As discussed in previous chapters, Canada's participation in global humanitarian actions has contributed to the admission of more than 50,000 refugees from Syria since 2015 (Government of Canada, 2017). If this trend continues, Canada's refugee and immigrant population will be greater than 11 million by 2031, half of whom will be female (Statistics Canada, 2015). Due to loss of their social support systems, female refugees are at increased risk of violence, sexual abuse, exploitation, and distress in the pre-migration context, all of which affect mental health and wellbeing post-migration (Winn, Hetherington & Tough, 2018).

There is paucity of studies that have focused specifically on refugee women's access to mental health care. Current evidence indicates that immigrant women are approximately 40% less likely than non-immigrant women to seek and receive the mental health care they need (Vigod et al., 2017). This suggests, by extension, that the mental health of refugee women is an urgent public health policy issue and that this population requires additional targeted supports and specialized healthcare services (Khanlou et al., 2017; Schmied, Black, Naidoo, Dahlen & Liamputtong, 2017).

Migration to a new country is a significant transition, and parenthood in the new context further complicates this process, leading to serious challenges for refugee mothers and their families. Refugee women in Canada are at five times the risk of developing postpartum depression compared with Canadian-born women (Dennis, Merry & Gagnon, 2017; Falah-Hassani, Shiri, Vigod & Dennis, 2015; Stewart, Gagnon, Saucier, Wahoush & Dougherty, 2008). Additionally, up to 50% of women who suffer from postpartum depression exhibit depressive symptoms in pregnancy (King, Feeley, Gold, Hayton & Zelkowitz, 2018; Verreault, Da Costa, Marchand, Dritsa & Khalife, 2014). Together, these findings demonstrate the urgent need to focus on perinatal mental health among refugee women.

Refugees in Canada experience significant challenges in accessing and using all forms of health care, which have "consequences for the inequitable promotion of health and well-being, disease prevention, and illness recovery and survival" (World Health Organization, 2008, p. 3). Although many refugee mothers demonstrate strength and resilience, the competing challenges that occur during resettlement can still significantly affect their mental health and wellbeing (Mental Health Commission of Canada, 2019). This chapter provides an overview of resettlement risk factors related to perinatal mental health care services from the perspectives of healthcare and community service professionals who provide these supports to refugee women.

Background

Migration Factors and Social Determinants of Mental Health for Refugee Women

Refugees face risk factors related to mental health during the pre-migration, during migration, and post-migration contexts. Government-assisted refugees receive some government services and supports during resettlement, but many still experience multiple vulnerabilities related to their minority identity status, and in some cases, single motherhood. Pre-migration circumstances can be extremely stressful for refugees who may have lost family members, homes, and livelihoods, and post-migration research has demonstrated that many refugees experience psychosocial distress related to social determinants of mental health such as affordable housing, (un)employment, and education (Fegert, Diehl, Leyendecker, Hahlweg & Prayon-Blum, 2018; Pangas et al., 2018). Difficulties in finding appropriate safe housing, lower incomes, a lack of familiarity with healthcare services, and in some instances, disability, are all factors strongly linked to unmet health care needs (Tuck et al., 2019). The early migratory phases of settlement are particularly challenging for refugees, who often experience discrimination in host countries, which can hinder their social, cultural, and economic adjustment (Rezazadeh & Hoover, 2018). Exclusionary feelings of being unwelcome have been associated with mood and stress disorders in refugee populations (Hynie, 2017; Shishehgar, Gholizadeh, DiGiacomo, Green & Davidson, 2017) and contribute to feelings of social isolation and poorer health (Dennis et al., 2017; Guruge et al., 2018; O'Mahony, Donnelly, Raffin Bouchal & Este, 2013; Schmeid et al., 2017).

Postpartum Depression: A Health Risk for Refugee Women

Perinatal mental health is a specialized field focusing on women's mental health during pregnancy and up to one year postpartum (Higgins, Downes, Carroll, Gill & Monahan, 2017). Refugee women experience mental health challenges, and these are exacerbated among women who are pregnant or postpartum. Research has consistently revealed that women who have experienced the trauma of war and displacement are at increased risk for postpartum depression (Ahmed, Bowen & Fung, 2017; King et al., 2018). The stresses of parenthood, and postpartum depression, are also highly associated with low social support, limited income, and immigration within the previous two years (Khanlou et al., 2017; Pangas et al., 2018; Schmied et al., 2017). High levels of postpartum depression symptoms have been documented among refugee women living in poverty with limited social support (Hassan et al., 2015). Refugee women are also less likely to engage with maternity care services than Canadian-born women due to lack of knowledge of the healthcare system, financial burdens, and fear that contact with clinicians will negatively affect their ability to remain in Canada (Firth & Halth-Cooper, 2018; Pangas et al., 2018).

Additionally, a substantial body of evidence has demonstrated that maternal depression and subsequent disrupted maternal-infant interactions adversely affect children (Ahmed et al., 2017; East, Gahagan & AlDelaimy, 2018; Heslehurst, Brown, Pemu, Coleman & Rankin, 2018; Stewart et al., 2015). Thus, posttraumatic stress and depressive symptoms can have long-lasting effects on both maternal and child health, contributing to further intergenerational traumatization (East et al., 2018).

Barriers to Accessing Mental Health Services

The most cited barriers to refugees accessing health care in Canada are lack of gender sensitivity, linguistic barriers, lack of information about how to navigate the healthcare system, and lack of culturally appropriate services (Clark, 2018; Guruge et al., 2018; Khanlou et al., 2017; Stewart et al., 2017). These barriers are known to disadvantage refugee women and place them at risk for negative mental health outcomes (Brown-Bowers, McShane, Wilson-Mitchell & Gurevich, 2015; Khanlou et al., 2017). Adverse pregnancy outcomes among refugee women also illustrate inequity (Firth & Halth-Cooper, 2018; Heslehurst et al., 2018).

O'Mahony and colleagues (2013) found that refugee mothers face many difficulties accessing mental health care due to cultural differences, language barriers, unfamiliarity with or unawareness of services, gender roles, and low socioeconomic status. Healthcare practices among refugee women, including whether they would seek or accept help for postpartum depression, are also influenced by cultural stigma and past encounters with the healthcare system. Stigma associated with mental illness typically leads to feelings of shame or embarrassment, social judgement, symptom masking, and difficulties and hesitancy in disclosing issues to healthcare professionals (Bina, 2019; Clement et al., 2015; Heslehurst et al., 2018; Higginbottom et al., 2013; Thomson, Chaze, George & Guruge, 2015).

Existing policies and practices are also known to shape societal views and responses to those who need mental health services. For example, healthcare professionals may take a more superficial approach based on an individual's depressive characteristics, rather than addressing the broader context of refugee mothers' experiences (Brown-Bowers et al., 2015; Clark, 2018; Floyd & Sakellariou, 2017; Spitzer et al., 2019). This can make it difficult to fully understand refugee mothers' PPD symptoms and to provide appropriate treatment. Additionally, some women who experience postpartum depression report feeling forced to internalize their feelings, stating that clinicians focus on the postpartum depression instead of the events that led to it, causing women to feel unheard and misunderstood (Schmeid et al., 2017). Poor healthcare relationships, and attitudes among healthcare providers, also affect how care is provided and received (Heselhurst et al., 2018; O'Mahony, Donnelly, Raffin Bouchal & Este, 2012). Together, these factors combine to make it difficult to fully understand postpartum depression symptoms in refugee women and provide appropriate treatment.

Findings from a Canadian Environmental Scan

A recent environmental scan was conducted among healthcare practitioners to examine gaps affecting the availability of and access to mental health care supports and services for refugee women living in the British Columbia interior (O'Mahony & Clark, 2018). It included interviews with 10 key informants (public health and mental health professionals).[2] Four main themes emerged from interviews:

1. Capacity building for refugee mothers' postpartum care
2. Barriers to care for refugee mothers
3. Healthcare provider education and accessible pathways
4. Facilitation of support and care.

Capacity Building for Refugee Mothers' Postpartum Care

The key informants embraced capacity building as a mechanism to enhance community collaboration among healthcare services through networking and developing good working relationships with ethnocultural groups, government, and immigration services within their region. They viewed collaboration between refugee service agencies and church and faith-based organizations as a health promotion strategy that would help build community capacities and increase knowledge of resources for refugee mothers. Strategies such as potluck lunches, walking groups, and cooking classes were all considered valuable ways to increasing social connections, facilitating friendships, and decreasing isolation. Participants also spoke about the need for 'shared care work' and interdisciplinary collaboration across service sectors to strengthen service delivery. One said:

> ...(we) tried to map maternity patients' experiences as they moved through different services... because some of them are rural patients and they need to see maternity providers in a different community...[O]ne of our efforts was a virtual clinic where we shared information between physicians.

---

[2] Data collection included analysis of hospital and community profiles, a grey literature search, a review of peer-reviewed literature, key informant interviews, and fluid surveys. Key informant interviews were conducted with healthcare professionals who had direct experience working with refugee women. This study received research ethics board approval from Thompson Rivers University and the British Columbia Interior Health Authority. For detailed findings, see O'Mahony and Clark (2018).

They also considered information technologies to be useful in building capacity, such as by using social media platforms like Facebook to connect and reach refugee mothers as well as the use of an online support group. One participant said: "our current influx of Syrian refugees have a Facebook page to gain much needed support with other Syrian community members." Others referred to using tele-health services to provide perinatal mental health services for patients, with one-to-one assessments that can increase capacity for outreach, support, and assessment in rural contexts.

Previous research suggests that fathers can also experience depressive symptoms and highlights the importance of including fathers in screening and early prevention efforts targeting depression during the transition to parenthood (Da Costa et al., 2017; Eddy, Poll, Whiting & Clevesy, 2019). Refugee men are also less likely to receive mental health support due to traditional masculine roles (The Affiliation of Multicultural Societies and Services Agencies of BC, 2019). Accordingly, informants suggested providing gender-sensitivity-enhanced support for refugee families, as well as screening of male partners, as a way to enhance family support during the perinatal period:

> Women back home would have their mothers, grandmothers or their aunties helping them raise the child … And so here they rely on their husbands…they [husbands] are not trained to do that [support their partners], they don't have a clue… So, it causes a lot of stress [since] they are going through a cultural adjustment in the middle of the most stressful time of their lives [while] having a new baby.

Overall, interviewees agreed that building stronger relationships and collaboration among mental health, public health, and newcomer services can benefit the mental health of refugee women. They also noted that upstream factors, such as building networks of support for education for healthcare professionals, could further enhance clinical competencies and potentially contribute to the development of better pathways to perinatal mental health care.

Barriers to Care for Refugee Mothers

Multiple levels of barriers prevent ready access to perinatal mental health services among refugee mothers. Key challenges relate to the intersection of gender, language and literacy, housing, migration stress, stigma, cultural safety, and lack of support for healthcare professionals. Our key informants identified cultural and linguistic barriers as having significant effects on their ability to provide adequate assessment services for refugee women and their families. They also noted that mistrust of the healthcare system, isolation, and stigma were factors preventing refugee women from accessing available resources. One healthcare professional noted:

> (there are) three levels of stigma... [:] one level is related to the depression and mental health... [The] second layer is around the stigma in their community... they really feel ashamed for expressing that they are depressed ...when it's supposed to be the most wonderful time of your life [having a baby] ... [The] third level is experiencing everything related to them being a newcomer... you know, the racism, all the more structural things.

Informants identified multiple barriers to care, including unfamiliarity with Canadian laws regarding parenting, interpersonal violence, limited access to language classes, and knowledge of women's rights in Canada. They also felt that stigma is an important factor preventing refugee women from accessing mainstream mental health services and supports. They noted that in some cases, refugee families valued rural areas for the anonymity they provided and did not integrate into the community, but that this kind of isolation served as another substantive barrier to seeking perinatal mental health care when needed.

They also noted that economic factors and social inequality are associated with increased psychological distress. Frequent moves due to finances, coupled with health issues of the partner and infant, long waiting periods for housing, and negative encounters with landlords all affect the mental health of refugee women and their integration into the host country (O'Mahony, 2017). The key informants involved in our environmental scan felt that housing is a main priority of most refugees, and felt that housing insecurity has significantly effects on health experiences and outcomes. One said:

> [There is] strong evidence to say what is being framed as mental issues are related to poverty... [H]ousing in [this small city] has a huge segment of the population precariously housed, they live in poverty and unfortunately it manifests itself in depression and anxiety and labelled as mental health causes.

Healthcare Provider Education and Accessible Pathways

Many participants identified the need to develop more specialized competencies related to clinical pathways and referrals. Based on geographical location and seasonal conditions, smaller communities often do not have specialized resources, community champions, or peer mentors to support healthcare professionals to build competency and improve capacities. One interviewee commented:

> Family physicians, public health, and the community organizations do not have the capacity to do mental health support...So when they identified moms with a challenge, they would refer them to mental health teams... but does the mom make it in the door or actually make contact with the clinician?

Some healthcare professionals emphasized that equity-oriented pathways to care for the perinatal needs of refugee women during the postpartum period require far more support, beginning with sustained funding. They also wanted more funding for mental health education and training of service providers. Overall, they felt that systemic barriers to accessing mental health services include limited mental health services, specialists, and resources outside of public health for perinatal mental health. Rural and remote regions lack mental health services, and pathways are urgently needed to help healthcare professionals link with mental health services. Service locations, as well as hours of operation, are also important considerations for women and families who work longer hours.

Facilitation of Support and Care

Key informants noted that culturally sensitive care should include use of 'lay language' and friendlier, more acceptable ways of explaining mental health issues to refugee women and their families. They suggested using peer mentors with similar postpartum experiences or with similar struggles with mood disorders as one way to provide more meaningful support. The mentor could be a friend or a family member selected by the mother, and would receive training to provide support and weekly check-ins. Others suggested that the stigma attached to mental health problems could be reduced by having familiar faces and perinatal services closer to home. One proposed initiating a community perinatal group support program that could include interdisciplinary healthcare professionals; this kind of group experience could enhance trust, foster relationships, and reduce stigma among new mothers. Informants also stressed the vital need for trained interpreters and materials translated into multiple languages to facilitate more culturally responsive care.

More than half of informants supported using champions to provide specialized care to clients in smaller communities or in rural and remote service areas. They felt that community champions and peer mentors are important ways to build capacity, provide education, increase competencies related to mental health and postpartum care for refugee women, and ensure long-term sustainability:

> ...Because how else do you keep those competencies up when they may only see 'certain kinds of mental health clients' once a year? ... Having the knowledge available to the local mental health teams about reproductive mental health, having people feel they are educated [so that] they can provide the service closer to home.

Informants recommended that more attention be given to educating the partners of pregnant refugee women about postpartum depression, enabling them to provide better supports after the child's birth. One said:

> (I am) always beating that drum, for many services in public health and family health exclude men from the equation. Fathers play a critical role in the health of their children...[and we need to do] very simple things to support that right from the beginning, ...[like] change our hours to include dads or when both parents are in the room include them as both being as important and ask their opinions.

Conclusion

Our findings, and those of others, demonstrate the need for immediate action to support childbearing refugee women – not only in terms of early screening for psychosocial risk, but also in response to their social support needs through intersectoral collaboration. Improvements in the provision and access of perinatal healthcare services could reduce inequalities and adverse outcomes and improve women's experiences of care. Gender-sensitive policy responses are urgently needed to harness the strengths and existing social capital within resettlement communities, as a necessary step toward improving the diverse experiences of refugee women.

It is also important to focus on the practical and contextual factors that influence migrant mental health, intercultural understanding, and interdisciplinary communications. To address these challenges, more research is needed to explore the social and cultural context and needs of newly arrived refugee families. Additionally, to mitigate potential harms related to mental health and perinatal health care, and to align with international and national migration healthcare policy and practice, healthcare providers need to understand the social and political context and pre-migration experiences of refugee women (Clark, 2018).

Many refugee women seek help from within their local community, for example through faith-based organizations or social groups. Community groups can play important roles in disclosure and help-seeking, and can empower refugee women to obtain appropriate help and exercise their right to make informed decisions about their emotional and mental health issues. Culturally appropriate interventions can foster a sense of trust, safety, stability, and control among refugee women. Increased partnerships can also increase service utilization by refugee mothers, decrease stigma, and enhance participatory engagement. To encourage personal and social healing, healthcare practitioners must listen to the stories of refugees to understand their experiences: they can provide culturally appropriate care by listening, providing safe spaces, using peer supports, offering workshops, and training mentors.

The healthcare professionals who participated in the environmental scan also indicated that refugee women need more information about mental health in general, as well as about Canadian laws and policies. They recommended that educational programs be offered within the community, as well as by public health nurses in community health clinics. Finally, they felt that more cross-sectoral partnerships are needed to develop pathways to care that service providers can more easily follow to provide care for refugee women who live in rural communities.

Key Takeaway Points

1. Development of shared care pathways can provide service providers with more explicit approaches to care for refugee mothers and their families.
2. Healthcare professionals must learn about community-based organizations that provide support for new refugee mothers on a variety of issues including language classes, breast feeding, and mutual supports.
3. Cultural safety and competency training can increase healthcare professionals' knowledge about the broader processes of social

exclusion that affect the mental health and wellbeing of identified 'at risk' populations.

References

Ahmed, A., Bowen, A., & Xin Feng, C. (2017). Maternal depression in Syrian refugee women recently moved to Canada: A preliminary study. *BMC Pregnancy and Childbirth, 17*: 240. doi.org/10.1186/s12884-017-1433-2

Beiser, M. (2009). Resettling Refugees and Safeguarding their Mental Health: Lessons Learned from the Canadian Refugee Resettlement Project. *Transcultural psychiatry, 46*(4), 539-583.

Bina, R. (2019). Predictors of postpartum depression service use: A theory-informed, integrative systematic review. *Women and Birth.* https://doi.org/10.1016/j.wombi.2019.01.006

Brown-Bowers, A., McShane, K., Wilson-Mitchell K., & Gurevich, M. (2015). Postpartum depression in refugee and asylum-seeking women in Canada: A critical health psychology perspective. *Health, 19*(3), 318–335.

Clark, N. (2018). Exploring community capacity: Karen refugee women's mental health. *International Journal of Human Rights in Healthcare, 11*(4), 244-256.

Clement, S., Schauman, O., Graham, T., Maggioni, F., Evans-Lacko, S., Bezborodovs, N., Morgan, C., … Thornicroft, G. (2015). "What is the impact of mental health-related stigma on help-seeking? A systematic review of quantitative and qualitative studies. *Psychological Medicine, 45*(1), 11–27.

Dennis, C., Merry, L., & Gagnon, A. (2017). Postpartum depression risk factors among recent refugee, asylum-seeking, non-refugee immigrant, and Canadian-born women: Results from a prospective cohort study. *Social Psychiatry Psychiatric Epidemiology, 52*(4), 411-422.

Da Costa, D., Zelkowitz, P., Dasgupta, K., Sewitch, M., Lowensteyn, I., Cruz, R., Hennegan, K., … Khalifé, S. (2017). Dads get sad too: Depressive symptoms and associated factors in expectant first-time fathers. *American Journal of Men's Health, 11*(5), 1376 –1384.

Fast, P., Gahagan, W., & Al-Delaimy, W. (2018). The impact of refugee mothers' trauma, posttraumatic stress, and depression on their children's adjustment. *Journal of Immigrant Minority Health, 20*(2), 271–282.

Eddy, B., Poll, V., Whiting, J., & Clevesy, M. (2019). Forgotten fathers: Postpartum depression in men. *Journal of Family Issues, 40*(8), 1001-1017.

Falah-Hassani, K., Shiri, R., Vigod, S., Dennis, C. (2015) Prevalence of postpartum depression among immigrant women: a systematic review and meta-analysis. *Journal of Psychiatric Research, 70*(1), 67–82.

Fegert, J. M., Diehl, C., Leyendecker, B., Hahlweg, K., & Prayon-Blum, V. (2018). Psychosocial problems in traumatized refugee families: overview of risks and some recommendations for support services. *Child and Adolescent Psychiatry and Mental Health, 12*(5), 1–8.

Firth, A., & Halth-Cooper, M. (2018). Vulnerable migrant women and postnatal depression: A case of invisibility in maternity services? *British Journal of Midwifery, 26*(2), 78-84.

Floyd, A., & Sakellariou, D. (2017). Healthcare access for refugee women with limited literacy: layers of disadvantage. *International Journal for Equity in Health, 16*:195, DOI 10.1186/s12939-017-0694-8

Government of Canada. (2017). #WelcomeRefugees:key figs. Retrieved from
https://www.canada.ca/en/immigration-refugees-
citizenship/services/refugees/welcome-syrian-refugees/key-
figures.html

Guruge, S., Sidani, S., Illesinghe, V., Younes, R., Bukhari, H., Altenberg, J., Rashid, M., … Fredricks, S. (2018). Healthcare needs and health service utilization by Syrian refugee women in Toronto. *Conflict and Health, 12*(46). doi: 10.1186/s13031-018-0181-x

Hassan, G, Kirmayer, LJ, Mekki- Berrada A., Quosh, C., el Chammay, R., Deville-Stoetzel, J.B., Youssef, A, … & Ventevogel, P. (2015). *Culture, context and the mental health and psychosocial wellbeing of Syrians: A review for mental health & psychosocial support staff working with Syrians affected by armed conflict.* Geneva: UNHCR.

Heslehurst, N., Brown, H., Pemu, A., Coleman, H., & Rankin, J. (2018). Perinatal health outcomes and care among asylum seekers and refugees: a systematic review of systematic reviews. *BMC Medicine, 16,* 89. doi:10.1186/s12916-018-1064-0

Higginbottom, G. M., Morgan, M., O'Mahony, J., Chiu, Y., Kocay, D., Alexandre, M., & Young, M. (2013). Immigrant women's experiences of postpartum depression in Canada: A protocol for systematic review using a narrative synthesis. *Systematic Reviews, 2,* 65. doi:10.1186/2046-4053-2-65

Higgins, A., Downes, C., Carroll, M., Gill, A., & Monahan, M. (2017). There is more to perinatal mental health care than depression: Public health nurses reported engagement and competence in perinatal mental health care. *Journal of Clinical Nursing, 27*(3–4), e476–e487.

Hynie, M. (2017). The social determinants of refugee mental health in the post-migration context: A critical review. *The Canadian Journal of Psychiatry, 63*(5), 297-303.

Khanlou, N., Haque, N., Skinner, A., Mantini, A., & Kurtz Landy, C. (2017). Scoping review on maternal health among immigrant and refugee women in Canada: Prenatal, intrapartum, and postnatal care. *Journal of Pregnancy, 2017,* 8783294 doi.org/10.1155/2017/8783294

King, L., Feeley, N., Gold, I., Hayton, B., & Zelkowitz, P. (2018). The healthy migrant effect and predictors of perinatal depression. *Women and Birth.* doi.org/10.1016/j.wombi.2018.07.017

Mental Health Commission of Canada (2019). Immigrant, refugee, ethnocultural and racialized populations and the social determinants of health: A review of 2016 census data. Retrieved from: https://mentalhealthcommission.ca/sites/default/files/201903/ irer_report_mar_2019_eng.pdf

O'Mahony, J. M. (2017). Hearing the voices of immigrant and refugee women for planning postpartum depression care. In A.Vollman, E. Anderson & J. McFarlane (Eds.), *Community as Partner: Theory and Multidisciplinary Practice,* 4th Ed. (pp. 377-385) Wolters Kluwer: Lippincott Williams & Wilkins.

O'Mahony, J. M. & Clark, N. (2018). Immigrant women and perinatal mental health care: Findings from an environmental scan, *Issues in Mental Health Nursing Journal, 39*(11), 924-934.

O'Mahony, J. M., Donnelly, T., Bouchal, S., & Este, D. (2013). Cultural background and socioeconomic influence of immigrant and refugee women coping with postpartum depression. *Journal of Immigrant and Minority Health, 15*(2), 300-314.

O'Mahony, J. M., Donnelly, T., Raffin Bouchal, S., & Este, D. (2012). Barriers and facilitators of social supports for immigrant and refugee women coping with postpartum depression. *Advances in Nursing Science, 35*(3), E42-E56.

Pangas, J., Ogunsiji, O., Elmir, R., Raman, S., Liamputtong, P., Burns, E., Dahlen, H., ...Schmied, V. (2019). Refugee women's experiences negotiating motherhood and maternity care in a new country: A meta-ethnographic review, *International Journal of Nursing Studies, 90*(1), 31-45.

Rezazadeh, M. S., & Hoover, M. L. (2018). Women's experience of immigration to Canada: A review of the literature. *Canadian Psychology Association, 59*(1), 76-88.

Schmied, V., Black, M., Naidoo, N., Dahlen, H., & Liamputtong, P. (2017). Migrant women's experiences, meanings and ways of dealing with postnatal depression: A meta-ethnographic study. *PLoS ONE, 12*(3), e0172385. doi.org/10.1371/journal.pone.0172385

Shishehgar, S., Gholizadeh, L., DiGiacomo, M., Green, A., & Davidson, P. (2017). Health and socio-cultural experiences of refugee women: An integrative review. *Journal of Immigrant and Minority Health, 19*(4), 959-973.

Statistics Canada. (2015). Immigrant women. Retrieved from http://www.statcan.gc.ca/pub/89-503-x/2015001/article/14217-eng.htm.

Statistics Canada. (2017). Immigration and ethnocultural diversity: Key results from the 2016 census. Retrieved from https://www150.statcan.gc.ca/n1/dailyquotidien/171025/dq171025b-eng.htm?indid=14428-4&indgeo=0

Stewart, M., Dennis, C., Kariwo, M., Kushner, K., Letourneau, N., Makumbe, K., &

Shizha, E. (2015). Challenges faced by refugee new parents from Africa in Canada. *Journal of Immigrant Minority Health, 17*(4), 1146–1156.

Stewart, M, Gagnon, A, Saucier, JF., Wahoush, O., & Dougherty G. (2008). Postpartum depression symptoms in newcomers. *Canadian Journal of Psychiatry 53*(2), 121-124.

Stewart, M., Kushner, K. Dennis, C., Kariwo, M., Letourneau, N., & Makumbe, K. (2017). Social support needs of Sudanese and Zimbabwean refugee new parents in Canada. *International Journal of Migration, Health, and Social Care, 13*(2), 234-252.

The Affiliation of Multicultural Societies and Services Agencies BC (2019). *Migration matters; newcomer men: Unique challenges and considerations.* Retrieved from www.amssa.org/resources/Infosheet" www.amssa.org/resources/Infosheet.

Thomson, M., Chaze, F., & George, U. & Guruge, S. (2015). Improving immigrant populations' access to mental health services in Canada: A review of barriers and recommendations. *Journal of Immigrant and Minority Health, 17*(6), 1895–1905.

Tuck, A., Oda, A., Hynie, M., Bennett-AbuAyyash, C., Roche, B., Agic, B., McKenzie, K. (2019). Unmet health care needs for Syrian refugees in Canada: A follow-up. *Journal of Immigrant and Minority Health.* doi.org/10.1007/s10903-019-00856-y.

Verreault, N., Da Costa, D., Marchand, A., Dritsa, M., & Khalife, S. (2014). Rates and risk factors associated with depressive symptoms during pregnancy and with postpartum onset. *Journal of Psychosomatic Obstetrics & Gynecology, 35*(3), 84-91.

Vigod, S., Bagadia, A., Hussain-Shamsy, N., Fung, K., Sultana, A., & Dennis, C. (2017). Postpartum mental health of immigrant mothers by region of origin, time since immigration, and refugee status: a population-based study. *Archives of Women's Mental Health, 20*(3), 439–447.

Watson, H., Harrop, D., Walton, E., Young, A., & Soltani, H. (2019). A systematic review of ethnic minority women's experiences of perinatal mental health conditions and services in Europe. *PLoS One 14*(1) e0210587. doi.org/10.1371/journal.pone.0210587

Winn, A., Hetherington, E., & Tough. S. (2018). Caring for pregnant refugee women in a turbulent policy landscape: perspectives of health care professionals Calgary, Alberta. *International Journal for Equity in Health, 17*:91. doi:.org/10.1186/s12939-018-0801-5

World Health Organization (2008). *Closing the gap in a generation: Health equity through action on the social determinants of health.* Retrieved from http://www.who.int/social_determinants/final_report/en/index.html

CHAPTER THIRTEEN

CONSIDERING PRIMARY HEALTH CARE AS A SOCIAL DETERMINANT OF REFUGEE HEALTH THROUGH THE LENS OF SOCIAL JUSTICE AND CARE ETHICS: IMPLICATIONS FOR HEALTHY PUBLIC POLICY

NANCY CLARK AND JOYCE O'MAHONY

Of all the forms of inequality, injustice in health is the most shocking and the most inhuman because it often results in physical death.

Martin Luther King, Jr.

Introduction

Lack of access to culturally appropriate health care is a fact of life for many people who have experienced forced displacement (Spitzer et al., 2019). Health care is a human right, and lack of access to it needs to be seen as a serious form of injustice. To ensure equity in the context of health care for refugees in Canada, primary healthcare services must take into account the social determinants of refugee health, and also ensure that the core values of social justice and care ethics, also known as the ethics of care, are integral to their explicit mandate (Clark, 2018; Hankivsky, 2014; Longhurst & Cohen, 2019). Inclusive health care for refugees requires healthy public policies based on the principles and core values of promoting health and including communities in the delivery of a sustainable public health system through meaningful and intersectoral partnerships across systems (National Collaborating Centre for Healthy Public Policy, 2013).

Refugee health is affected by multiple intersecting social determinants and structural barriers (Beiser, 2005; Hynie, 2018a; 2018b). Although Canadian government-sponsored resettlement programs have been implemented to redress social inequities in care through health policy initiatives such as the Interim Federal Health Plan,[3] many refugees have no access to universal health insurance (Pottie, Gruner & Magwood, 2018). Additionally, some health providers refuse to provide care for refugees in primary care clinics due to the complexities associated with health insurance and their understanding of the Interim Federal Health Plan (Spitzer et al., 2019; Pottie et al., 2017). The need for language interpreters is another barrier to accessing health care for many refugees (Brisset et al., 2013; Joshi et al., 2013; Mota, Mayhew, Grant, Batista & Pottie, 2015; Newbold, Cho & McKeary, 2013; Pottie et al., 2018).

Discussions of refugee health tend to focus more on healthcare utilization and health status, rather than on care-based ethics within primary health care systems (Arya & Piggott, 2018; Engster, 2014). However, previous research has demonstrated that care within primary healthcare systems can serve as a measure of justice within healthcare systems. Engster noted that "Care is the other half of health care that has been almost completely ignored in normative discussions of health policy but provides the best reason for states to continue subsidizing comprehensive health-care services" (2014, pp. 156–157). As a political and moral philosophy, care ethics provides a lens through which to examine the values and practices that shape refugee healthcare experiences. It is commensurate with the principles of social justice: it moves beyond equal accessible healthcare and brings attention to the distribution of health resources, and to the diverse factors affecting individual and community health (Kirmayer, 2011; Reimer-Kirkham & Browne, 2006).

Fraser (1996, 1999, 2001) developed a political theory outlining the key principles of social justice for enhancing primary health care for refugees. These include not only the (re)distribution of social goods and services; social justice must be reflected in the recognition of differences, and awareness of the systemic exclusion of non-dominant groups in policymaking. Most refugees have not had a voice in the construction of policies that directly affect them, and Fraser argued that equity can be enhanced not only by the redistribution of health care as a social resource, but also by the recognition of social differences within and between refugee

---

[3] The Interim Federal Health Program provides temporary coverage of healthcare benefits to some groups who are not eligible for provincial health insurance. This includes protected persons and refugee claimants (HEIA, 2017). However, this health insurance plan only provides coverage based on identity status.

groups, and ensuring parity of refugee participation in decision-making on how primary health care is structured.

Emerging practices resulting from structural changes in primary healthcare services for refugees include integration of cultural brokers, increased outreach support, accessible language interpreters, and recognition of gender-sensitive issues. These have been facilitated through shared-care approaches, as well as through intersectoral and interdisciplinary collaboration across community health centers in Canada (Longhurst & Cohen, 2019). In this chapter, we propose that an explicit value of care and social justice can be operationalized when social determinants of refugee health are integrated in primary care models to promote greater social inclusion. We also provide a case example, drawing from the experiences of Karen refugees to illustrate how gender, health literacy, and language are important determinants of health affecting the provision of primary care.

Social Determinants of Refugee Health

Raphael (2018) convincingly argued that the lack of public policy uptake of the social determinants of health threatens the health and wellbeing of all Canadians. He used a critical and social justice perspective to broaden traditional thinking about social factors such as housing, education, employment, income, and social acceptance to include how society organizes and distributes resources, and how economic and social policies promote health. Other factors including social identity, healthcare services, social exclusion, and gender also affect the achievement of equitable health outcomes. Importantly, the values of justice are embedded in liberal democracies, including Canada, where "Liberal welfare states have the greatest degree of wealth and income inequality, the weakest safety nets and the poorest population health" (Raphael, 2018, p. 29).

Hynie (2018a) extended on Raphael's analysis, exploring how both political and social structures produce inequalities within and between groups. Refugee groups experiencing forced migration face inequitable care due to discursive labels and their migrant status (Spitzer et al., 2019). In Canada, a person's legal status determines the type and quality of healthcare services they can access. Social structures also have indirect effects on health because they affect a person's perception of social inclusion and control. Hyman and Meinhard (2016) argued that structural factors and intermediary determinants of health, such as government policies, produce unequal socio-economic positions that lead to differences in both social cohesion and social capital. Systemic factors affect refugee health throughout the migration process. In the pre-migration context, refugees may experience trauma, sexual violence, political violence, and protracted camp environments. During migration, they may experience international border crossing and family separation. In the post-migration context, they may face acculturation stress, social exclusion, diminished community relationships, and access to health care (Health Equity Impact Assessment, 2019); Hynie, 2018b; Kirmayer et al., 2011).

Hankivsky noted that adopting an ethic of care can aid in the "identification and critical understanding of the structures that create relations resulting in exclusion, marginalization, suffering, and harm" (2004, p. 24). Importantly, Hankivsky also noted that an effective application of care ethics must move beyond any single determinant of health to address the processes of power that shape structural inequities. Many determinants are known to affect refugee health, but recent research has demonstrated the need for primary health care service providers to consider gender, education and health literacy, and language as vital factors affecting equitable primary health care (Clark, 2015a, 2018b; Clark & Vissandjée, 2019; Floyd & Sakellariou, 2017; O'Mahony & Clark, 2018; O'Mahony & Donnelly, 2013).

Case Example: The Karen

Karen refugee groups include diverse ethnic Burmese who were forcibly displaced and resettled across Australia, Canada, and the United States as a result of ethnic genocide and ongoing political violence in Myanmar (formerly Burma). In a 2015 study, Clark found that many Karen refugee women did not have access to formal education. These same refugee women were also primarily responsible for their family's health upon arrival in Canada, so many were forced to become highly dependent upon others, which increased their stress and anxiety, and ironically, their feelings of social isolation. The following excerpt illustrates one Karen woman's experiences of accessing and receiving health care:

> [The] last two days she called the interpreter and today she needs to go to see the doctor again. She worries. She waits and waits and waits until her daughter feels very sick . . . she tries to close her eyes and call the interpreter. But when she sees the doctor, the doctor says, "Why you not come earlier? Your child is very sick . . . it will be too late." But she says, "I'm worried because I'm scared to call the interpreter."

This experience reveals the importance of not only having easily accessible culturally trained interpreters, but also of having culturally safe approaches that address the diverse needs of refugees. In most contexts, health system planning and preparation has not accommodated the needs of refugees, including those resettled into smaller communities across Canada (Pottie et al., 2017). The lack of interpreters, as well as some relationships with interpreters, can force women to depend on those whom they do not fully trust. Within the Karen community, dependency on interpreters tended to result in increased stress and feelings of shame, particularly among women with less education and lower social status. Many Karen women felt that they were a burden on the system, and thus postponed seeking care or did not access health care at all. Delays in care can have serious health consequences for those who are most vulnerable, including children and older family members. In some instances, refugee women were turned away from specialist appointments due to lack of interpreter services, and many said they had experienced fear and lack of trust when adequate translation was not provided.

Few studies have explored health provider perspectives in relation to structures of primary health care for refugees, but Clark's 2015 study of Karen resettlement revealed that social determinants of health are key issues affecting quality of care. One nurse practitioner working in a specialized refugee health clinic explained:

> [A] lot of the issues in regard to mental health, social determinants of health and so on, transcend all the refugee groups . . . the literacy affects things because . . . that affects your whole ability to access resources in your community and deal with social assistance and paperwork and stuff . . . even just keeping your appointments or knowing about appointments and how to take your meds and how to navigate a system between different populations that don't have literacy and have some literacy or education before they came.

Gender, language, and health literacy are key challenges affecting the provision of primary health care and the development of trust, cultural safety, and social support (Floyd & Sakellariou, 2017; Kohler et al., 2018; O'Mahony, Donnelly, Raffin Bouchal & Este, 2013). As noted above, effective health care requires not only acts of egalitarian justice such as distribution of resources, but also more understanding of social differences between and within refugee groups. At a minimum, health care should involve "helping individuals to meet their basic physical and emotional needs so that they can survive, develop their basic capabilities, function in society and avoid or mitigate unnecessary pain and suffering" (Engster, 2014, p. 157).

Social Justice and Care Ethics

Social justice can be linked to political and moral philosophy to craft and validate health equity approaches that move beyond distributive justice frameworks such as healthcare resource allocation. Structural processes that integrate the voices of marginalized populations are required to adequately respond to "gender, racial, ethnic, cultural and class differences, and oppression" (Hankivsky, 2004, p. 24). Additionally, primary healthcare systems must include shared responsibility of care across all levels of government, health providers, and the public sector with regard to provision of primary health care for refugees (Pottie et al., 2018).

Social justice has largely been equated with egalitarian claims of just distribution of resources and goods, including health care. However, social justice viewed from the perspective of a politics of recognition (Fraser, 1999, 2001) moves beyond a distributive justice framework to include recognition of group difference (i.e., healthcare providers not being 'difference-blind'), the ability to participate in policies (i.e., parity of participation by refugees in policies that affect them), and redistribution of resources (i.e., alternative primary care models). Fraser also argued that "assimilation to dominant cultural norms is no longer the price of equal respect ... [but rather] claims for recognition of distinct perspectives of ethnic 'racial' and sexual minorities as well as gender differences [are accepted as valid]" (1996, p. 4). This view of social justice is particularly relevant, given the fact that almost half of refugee submissions to the United Nations High Commissioner for Refugees involve women and girls (UNHCR, 2019).

Care ethics can serve as a moral and political corrective measure when applied to health care for refugees. For example, the Immigrant Refugee Protection Act requires that government policies (e.g., those set out by Immigrant, Refugee and Citizenship Canada) include gender-based analysis as well as analysis of their effects, in annual reports to parliament. These analyses must go beyond biological (sex) and socio-cultural (gender) differences to consider how race and ethnicity, age, disability, and sexual orientation affect people's experience of policies and programs (IRCC, 2018). Tronto (2010) referred to this kind of application as institutional care ethics. In an institutional context, care ethics has three central foci: (a) the purpose of care, (b) a recognition of power relations, and (c) a pluralism that entails tailoring care to meet an individual's needs. Engster asked: "Is there any reason for society to support universal access to comprehensive healthcare when spending on the social and environmental determinants of health will do more to improve people's health?" (2014, p. 156). The response to this question rests squarely on a broader orientation toward social justice and the potential for improved integration of the social determinants of health for refugees accessing primary health care. Drawing from political and moral philosophy, social justice, and care ethics, it can be argued that both the politics of recognition and acts of redistribution are required to mitigate inequities in care. For example, gender roles, responsivities, and expectations for refugees are not static in the post-migration context and thus are often overlooked in health and social services planning and policy (Clark & Vissandjée, 2019; O'Mahony & Clark, 2018). A responsive healthcare approach based on a care ethics requires collecting more information about post-migration developments in the experience of refugees, both as groups and as individuals, to clarify how diverse social identity categories intersect to shape health-care experiences and broader health inequities in care.

Public Policy Implications

Hankivsky argued that "what is required for real change in social policy is a distinct shift in the existing normative orientation of justice; a shift that will make a central place for the values of care" (2004, p. 40), and also that values of care are not impartial – they are rooted in human interconnectedness and interdependencies. Policy must mitigate the barriers to effective care and address the basic health needs of refugees (Pottie et al., 2017). A brief overview of primary care models reveals that traditional distributive understandings of social justice are being challenged, and also that there is an increasing need to operationalize social justice through the lens of care ethics. Many healthcare services are moving toward more equity-oriented approaches to address both the recognition of difference and redistribution of healthcare resources for refugees. Changes to funding structures and provision of health care for refugees are occurring from traditional primary models to community health centres across Canada (Batista et al., 2018). These structural changes reflect an increasing awareness of collective social responsibilities beyond liberal notions of justice.

Care ethics is closely related to human relationships and the ways care can promote wellness and rectify social problems (Hankivsky, 2004). Many refugees in Canada have accessed community-based primary healthcare services, suggesting that many refugees value the relationship with community-based primary care practitioners (Pottie et al., 2018), who may be structurally well-placed to deliver care-ethical services. Community health centres also provide health-promotion and community-based programs where services are offered at no charge for people without a health card. Health providers in these settings tend to be inter-disciplinary and on a salary-based fixed payment method that is not related to patient volume (Werner & Woodgate, 2017). This kind of structure allows them to take more time to provide care, build trusting relationships, and address the social determinants of refugee health. During Clark's 2015 study, one Karen woman explained:

> I think for the doctor and the nurse they need to understand Karen people . . . so they can understand so that the family will be happy to go . . . because the doctor they don't have the time. . . . So, all they want to do is fast, fast, fast, they speak fast you have to answer them fast, feel more patient, a little bit patient and then the family will feel more comfortable to see their doctor.

In addition to increasing the time allocated to healthcare provision, outreach support can facilitate better access to care as well as address barriers related to system navigation. For example, the Umbrella Multicultural Health Co-op community health centre in British Columbia offers translation support and outreach support through mobile clinics; it also offers one of the only cultural broker programs in British Colombia, linking minority newcomer language groups with primary healthcare services. Similar outreach services are provided in Toronto and Edmonton through the Multicultural Health Brokers Co-operative, which provides co-operative perinatal outreach health care services to immigrant and refugee women (Avery, 2017). Integration of cross-cultural health brokers is an important care practice: it promotes health literacy between service providers and service users and can improve knowledge related to the social determinants of health, including cross-cultural literacy (Najafizada, Bourgeault, Labonte, Packer & Torres, 2015). The following excerpt from a Karen outreach worker from Clark's 2015 study illustrates the significance of outreach support:

> So, the reality is that I can understand how the government wants to streamline or create greater effectiveness in use of money that's puts towards the families. . . . I think that's why some of these policies have been put in place but unfortunately what happens is [. . .] that there's been relationships established with the families that [. . .] create stronger network and support system to enable families and build that resiliency.

Overall, creating caring practices that include outreach support facilitates trust and enhances support for refugee families who arrive with minimal social capital. Primary healthcare models can foster social capital by assisting refugee groups to strengthen social networks and social cohesion (Batista et al., 2018). It is also necessary to engage refugee communities in policies that directly affect them to ensure that health care is responsive to differential determinants such as gender, education, and health literacy (Floyd & Sakellariou, 2017; Pottie et al., 2017). According to Tronto, imagining a world organized to care requires "politics: recognition and debate/dialogue of relations of power" (2010, p. 162). One good example is the RISE Collingwood Neighbourhood House in British Columbia; this community health centre is build on the explicit values of resilience, integration, social justice, and equity, and is governed by community members, including refugee groups. Health care must be structured by an explicit focus on care ethics and social justice paradigms in order to build in mechanisms to include refugee experiences and advocacy for change toward improving health and addressing healthcare inequities.

Conclusion

Ethics of care are firmly rooted in the moral obligation to promote health and minimize inequities. Healthcare practices should also be framed by a lens of social justice. We must move beyond a merely minimalist approach to fair distribution of resources and instead further examine the individual and systemic factors that intersect to shape health outcomes. Primary healthcare providers and policymakers have an ethical obligation to address gender, health literacy, and education as well as other determinants of refugee health through the restructuring of funding, developing a shared-care framework and increased inter-sectoral collaboration, and providing outreach support in order to build healthy public policy.

Overwhelming evidence has demonstrated that the social determinants of health affect refugee health, so there is a need to move toward social justice and a more explicit focus on values of care. Recognition of social difference is a moral imperative that allows for parity of participation with others in social action (Fraser, 1996). If we consider primary health care itself to be a social determinant of health, then the provision of health services must reflect values of care. Unique refugee contexts such as those of the Karen help illustrate how social determinants intersect in complex ways through human interaction to shape the way health care is distributed.

When health care is justified in terms of care – rather than only health – a different set of priorities emerges for measuring the justice of healthcare systems (Engster, 2014).

Key Takeaway Points

1. Adopting an ethic of care is critical to clarify how the exclusion and marginalization of refugees adds to their suffering and harm.
2. The provision of appropriate, needed, and targeted health care promotes social justice.
3. An ethic of care framework can directly improve social and health policies related to refugees.

References

Aery, A. (2017). *Innovations to champion access to primary care for immigrants and refugees.* Retrieved from http://www.wellesleyinstitute.com/publications/innova-ons-to-champion-accessto-primary-care-for-immigrants-and-refugees/

Arya, N., & Piggott, T. (2018). Introducing under-served populations and their determinants of health. In N. Arya & T. Piggott (Eds.), *Under-served: Health determinants of Indigenous, inner-city, and migrant populations in Canada* (pp.1-10). Toronto, ON: Canadian Scholars Press.

Batista, R., Pottie, K., Bouchard, L., Ng, E., Tanuseputro, P., & Tugwell, P. (2018). Primary health care models addressing health equity for immigrants: A systematic scoping review. *Journal of Immigrant and Minority Health, 20*(1), 214-230.

Beiser, M. (2005). The health of immigrants and refugees in Canada. *Canadian Journal of Public Health, 96*(Suppl.2), S30-S44. Retrieved from https://www.ncbi.nlm.nih.gov/pubmed/16078554

Brisset, C., Leanza, Y., Rosenberg, E., Vissandjée, B., Kirmayer, L. J., Muckle, G., . . . Laforce, H. (2013). Language barriers in mental health care: A survey of primary care practitioners. *Journal of Immigrant Minority Health.* doi:10.1077/s10903-013-9971 9

Clark, N. (2015). *Examining community capacity to support Karen refugee women's mental health and well-being in the context of resettlement in Canada.* University of British Columbia. Retrieved from https://open.library.ubc.ca/collections/ubctheses/24/items/1.0166208

Clark, N. (2018). Exploring community capacity: Karen refugee women's mental health. *International Journal of Human Rights and Health Care*, *11*(4), 244-256. doi:10.1108/IJHRH-02-2018-0025

Clark, N., & Vissandjée, B. (2019). Exploring intersectionality as a policy tool for gender-based policy analysis: Implications for language and health literacy as key determinants of integration. In O. Hankivsky & J. Jordan-Zachery (Eds.), *The Palgrave handbook of intersectionality in public policy. The politics of intersectionality* (pp. 603-623). doi:org/10.1007/978-319-98473-5_28

Collingwood Neighbourhood House. (2019). Retrieved from https://www.cnh.bc.ca/about/who-we-are/

Engster, D. (2014). The social determinants of health, care ethics and just health care. *Contemporary Political Theory, 13*(2), 149-169.

Floyd, A., & Sakellariou, D. (2017). Healthcare access for refugee women with limited literacy: Layers of disadvantage. *International Journal for Equity in Health, 16*(1), 195. doi:org/10.1186/s12939-017-0694-8

Fraser, N. (1996). *Social justice in the age of identity politics: Redistribution, recognition, and participation.* Presented at the Tanner Lectures on Human Values, Stanford University. Retrieved from http://tannerlectures.utah.edu/_documents/a-to-z/f/Fraser98.pdf

Fraser, N. (1999). Social justice in the age of identity politics: Redistribution, recognition, and participation. In G. Henderson & M. Waterstone (Eds.), *Geographic thought: A praxis perspective.* London and New York: Routledge.

Fraser, N. (2001). Recognition without ethics? *Theory, Culture & Society, 18*(2-3), 21-42.

Immigration, Refugees and Citizenship Canada. (IRCC). (2018). Government of Canada Annual Report to Parliament on Immigration 2018. Retrieved from https://www.canada.ca/content/dam/ircc/migration/ircc/english/pdf/pub/annual-report-2018.pdf

Hankivsky, O. (2004). *Social policy and the ethic of care.* Vancouver, BC: UBC Press.

Hankivsky, O. (2014). Rethinking care ethics: On the promise and potential of an intersectional analysis. *The American Political Science Review, 108*(2), 252-264.

Health Equity Impact Assessment. (HEIA). (2019). Immigrant supplement for the Ontario MOHLTC heath equity impact assessment program. Retrieved from http://www.health.gov.on.ca/en/pro/programs/heia/

Hynie, M. (2018a). Social determinants of refugee health. In Akshaya Neil Arya& Thomas Piggott. (Eds.), *Under-served: Health determinants of*

Indigenous, inner-city, and migrant populations in Canada (204-225).
Toronto, ON: Canadian Scholars Press.

Hynie, M. (2018b). The social determinants of refugee mental health in the
post-migration context: A critical review. *Canadian Journal of
Psychiatry, 63*(5), 297-303. doi:10.1177/0706743717746666

Hyman, I., & Meinhard, A. (2016). Public policy, immigrant experiences,
and health outcomes in Canada. In D. Raphael (Ed.), *Immigration,
public policy, and health: Newcomer experiences in developed nations*
(pp. 96-131). Toronto, ON: Canadian Scholars' Press.

Joshi, C., Russel, G., Cheng, I-Hao., Kay, M., Pottie, K., . . . Harris, F. M.
(2013). A narrative synthesis of the impact of primary health care
delivery models for refugees in resettlement countries on access, quality
and coordination. *International Journal for Equity in Health 12*(88).
doi:org/10.1186/1475-9276-12-88

Kirmayer, L. J. (2011). Multicultural medicine and the politics of
recognition. *Journal of Medicine and Philosophy, 36*(4), 410-423.

Kirmayer, L. J., Narasiah, L., Munoz, M., Rashid, M., Ryder, G. A., Guzder,
J., . . . Pottie, K. (2011b). Common mental health problems in
immigrants and refugees: General approaches to primary care. *Canadian
Medical Association Journal, 183*, E959-967. doi:10.1503/cmaj.090292

Kohler, G., Holland, T., Sharpe, A., Irwin, M., Sampalli, T., MacDonell, K.,
. . . & Kanakam, A. (2018). The Newcomer Health Clinic in Nova
Scotia: A beacon clinic to support the health needs of the refugee
population. *International Journal of Health Policy Management, 7*(12),
1085-1089.

Longhurst A., & Cohen, M. (2019). *The importance of community health
centres in BC's primary care reforms: What the research tells us.* BC
office: Canadian Centre for Policy Alternatives. Retrieved from
https://www.policyalternatives.ca/sites/default/files/uploads/publicatio
ns/BC%20Office/2019/03/ccpa-bc_march2019_chcs-in-bc.pdf

Moore, A. (2013). "Tracking down Martin Luther King, Jr.'s words on
health care."

Huffington Post, January 18. Retrieved from
http://www.huffingtonpost.com/amanda-moore/martin-luther-king-
health-care_b_2506393.html

Mota, L., Mayhew, M., Batista, R., & Pottie, K. (2015). Rejecting and
accepting international migrant patients into primary care practices: A
mixed-method study. *International Journal of Migration, Health and
Social Care, 11*(2), 108-129. doi:org/10.1108/IJMHSC-04-2014-0013

Najafizada, S. A., Bourgeault, I. L., Labonte, R., Packer, C., & Torres, S.
(2015). Community health workers in Canada and other high-income

countries: A scoping review and research gaps. *Canadian Journal of Public Health, 106*(3), e157-164. doi:10.17269/CJPH.106.4747

National Collaborating Centre for Healthy Public Policy. (2013). Public policy models and their usefulness in public health: The stages model. A briefing note for up-to-date knowledge relating to healthy public policy. Montreal, QC: Author.

Newbold, K. B., Cho, J., & McKeary, M. (2013). Access to health care: The experiences of refugee and refugee claimant women in Hamilton, Ontario. *Journal of Immigrant & Refugee Studies, 11*(4), 431-449.

O'Mahony, J., & Clark, N. (2018). Immigrant women and mental health care: Findings from an environmental scan. *Issues in Mental Health Nursing, 39*(11), 924-934.

O'Mahony, J., & Donnelly, T. T. (2013). How does gender influence immigrant and refugee women's postpartum depression help-seeking experiences? *Journal of Psychiatric and Mental Health Nursing, 20*(8), 714-725.

O'Mahony, J., Donnelly, T. T., Raffin Bouchal, S., & Este, D. (2013). Cultural background and socio-economic influence among immigrant and refugee women coping with postpartum depression. *Journal of Immigrant and Minority Health, 15*(2), 300-314.

Pottie, K., Gruner, D., & Magwood, O. (2018) Canada's response to refugees at the primary health care level. *Public Health Research Practice. 28*(1), e2811803. Retrieved from http://www.phrp.com.au/issues/march-2018-volume-28-issue-1/canadas-response-to-refugees-at-the-primary-health-care-level/

Pottie, K., Hui, C., Rahman, P., Ingleby, D., Akl, E. A., Russell, G., . . . Brindis, C. D. (2017). Building responsive health systems to help communities affected by migration: An international Delphi Consensus. *International Journal of Environmental Research and Public Health, 14*(2), 144. doi:10.3390/ijerph14020144

Raphael, D. (2018). The social determinants of health of under-served populations in Canada.

In N. Arya & T. Piggott (Eds.), *Under-served: Health determinants of Indigenous, inner-city, and migrant populations in Canada* (pp. 23-38). Toronto, ON: Canadian Scholars Press.

Reimer-Kirkham, S., & Browne, A. (2006). Toward a critical theoretical interpretation of social justice discourse in nursing. *Advances in Nursing Science, 29*(4), 324-339.

Spitzer, D. L., Torres S., Zwi A. B., Khalema, E. N., Palaganas, E. (2019). Towards inclusive migrant healthcare. (2019). *British Medical Journal*; 366: l4256, 1-4. doi:10.1136/bmj.l4256

Tronto, C. J. (2010). Creating caring institutions: Politics, plurality, and purpose. *Ethics and Social Welfare, 4*(2), 158-171.

Umbrella Multicultural Health Co-op. (2017). *Cooperative community health centre.* Retrieved from http://umbrellacoop.ca/cchc/

United Nations High Commissioner for Refugees. (2019). *Resettlement at a glance.* Retrieved from https://www.unhcr.org/5c594ddf4

Wener, P., & Woodgate, P. (2017). Looking for help: Primary care providers' need for collaboration to deliver primary mental healthcare services. *Canadian Journal of Community Mental Health, 36*(3), 29-39.

SECTION V

WHERE DO WE GO NEXT?

CHAPTER FOURTEEN

CHANGE MAKING

BHARATI SETHI

Our opening reflections about 'belonging' and 'home' reflect the fear about refugees (read: 'foreigners' or the 'Other') in Canada and beyond: in India (Citizen Amendment Act), Italy (refusing permission of rescue ships to dock), the United Kingdom (Brexit), the United States (Build the Wall), and elsewhere. As Canada competes with other developed nations for skilled labour in the global capitalist economy, concerns have emerged that refugees are taking away jobs from Canadians or that they are a drain on the Canadian healthcare and social service systems. The scholarly and applied evidence in this edited volume demonstrates that the reality is quite the opposite: individuals and families who are displaced and forced to resettle in a new land tend to exist in the margins of their host nations. We can all learn from the resilience of refugees and their desire to contribute to Canadian social, cultural, and economic capital – despite the multiple barriers preventing them from doing so. At the beginning of the book, we asked you what type of changemaker you need to be to respond to the myriad of issues faced by refugees coming to Canada. The book has provided you with some ideas to begin to address and resolve the challenges faced by this population.

We end this collection with an eye toward the future. Where do we go next as change-makers? Our summaries of key takeaway points at the end of each chapter are a good starting point for considering the answer. We hope that these key lessons will be a useful guide to you in your continued efforts to challenge false self /Other dichotomies that perpetuate fearmongering about refugees. Individually and collectively as a nation, Canadians must reanalyze our global responsibility in the refugee crisis. As changemakers, we have an ethical responsibility to influence public and social policies through advocacy, and to foster safe and dignified conditions to displaced populations. We can be part of the solution to the worldwide problem of forced displacement by providing sanctuary to people who are displaced and by continually working to enhance diversity and foster inclusion in our homes, workplaces, community, and nation. The following discussion summarizes future directions in practice, policy, and research:

Practice

The authors contributing to this volume, many of whom have lived experiences of oppression, are committed to advancing social justice in their practice, research, and teaching. Their evidence-based work has helped unpack the discourses on social, economic, cultural, and political inclusion/exclusion of refugees at the community, organizational, and national levels. Unpacking these discourses is vital to make connections between policy and practice. The chapters in this volume have identified some of the barriers preventing the full participation of individuals and families postmigration: language difficulties, lack of affordable and culturally relevant childcare, transportation challenges, inaccessibility to health care, loss of social capital, and experiences of trauma, racism, and discrimination. Social and health inequalities are further exacerbated by the mechanisms of power, privilege, and exclusion, both overt and covert, as illustrated by Siham Elkassem, Rick Csiernik, Andrew Matulak, Gina Kayssi, Yasmine Hussain, Kathryn Lambert, Pamela Bailey, and Asad Choudhary in Chapter Six.

The contributing authors have also demonstrated the need for practitioners and service providers to recognize the unique experiences of specific refugee populations and how these experiences shape their acculturation experiences. In Chapter Seven, for example, Edward Lee stressed the importance of working from the perspective that the LGBTQI service users and communities themselves are experts; by listening to their stories, practitioners can understand the systemic factors serve as barriers or facilitators to this population. In Chapter Eight, Ei Phyu Smith, Sheila Htoo, Michaela Hynie, and Susan McGrath explored the specific factors and processes involved in the resettlement of the underserved Karen refugee community into Canadian society.

In Chapter Three, Nimo Bokore explored the lived experiences of refugees, such as accessing and maintaining employment and housing, and how these often differ based on the type of refugee protection program (Government-Assisted Refugees, Privately Sponsored Refugees or Blended Visa Office-Referred) through which they were granted permanent residency in Canada. She concluded that integrating culturally appropriate care and trauma-informed approaches into refugee post-resettlement services can help build trust and create safety. Similarly, in Chapter Five Abdelfattah Elkchirid and Bree Akesson provided compelling evidence that family-based assessments and interventions must integrate the complexities of pre-flight, flight, and resettlement phases of refugee's lives to strengthen parent and child relationships.

Refugee students can rebuild their lives through the promise of education – which is also the promise of hope in difficult times. Snežana Obradović-Ratković, Dragana Kovačević, Neelofar Ahmed, and Claire Ellis (Chapter Nine) and Claire Ellis, Courtney Oreja, and Emma Jankowski (Chapter Ten) explored how education can be a site of social justice. Many refugee children face challenges to accessing education at the intersections of forced migration, settlement, and disrupted education. Every refugee child must have access to equitable, safe, and affordable education. The authors of Chapters Nine and Ten make persuasive arguments that such education must be grounded on a vision of a society that is inclusive, transformative, and responsive to the root causes of economic, social, political, and health inequities. Refugee children and youth experience loss of social capital (pre-exile friendships) and lack of post-migration capital (post-exile peer support) during resettlement, but inclusive education built on the principles of social justice can create a positive, safe, supportive, and healing learning environment for them, both within and outside the classroom.

Along with social factors, refugee health is shaped by economic, environmental, and political contexts related to migration. Joyce O'Mahony and Nancy Clark (Chapters Twelve and Thirteen) demonstrate that refugees are subjected to inequities related to accessible language resources, gender-sensitive supports, and promotion of cultural and health literacy practices, compared with other populations. Canada has committed to fostering health for all, and this will require integrating high-level structural supports into primary health care services. O'Mahony and Clark both concluded that primary care models should include an explicit focus on care ethics and broader notions of social justice to address the increasing inequities in health care experienced by diverse refugee groups and to foster social inclusion. These ethical and social justice-oriented principles are in alignment with emerging trends in primary healthcare services. O'Mahony and Clark also demonstrate that Canada's commitment to provide high-quality health care will also necessitate attention to mental health to reflect the needs of refugee service users. In Chapter 5, Abdelfettah Elkchirid and Bree Akesson also stress the importance of supporting the emotional health of refugee parents in the context of pre-flight, flight, displacement, and resettlement as parents struggle with their loss of cultural identity.

Research

In Chapter Eleven, Baredu Abraham, Tolee Biya, Martha Kuwee Kumsa, and Nardos Tassew demonstrated that culturally safe and holistic research approaches, which centre on refugee empowerment and healing, can create intentional spaces to explore meanings of health and wellness across time and place. Non-traditional approaches to research can be helpful ways to engage populations that have experienced structural trauma and violence, such as Photovoice and poetry (Bharati Sethi and Snežana Obradović-Ratković, Chapter Four) and sharing circles (Baredu Abraham, Tolee Biya, Martha Kuwee Kumsa, and Nardos Tassew, Chapter Eleven). The authors of Chapters Four and Eleven also stress the need for community-engaged arts-based methods to gather information on gender-specific resettlement supports for refugee women. Creative approaches can also be used to explore the utility of practice and policy initiatives intended to foster social equity among refugees in refugee camps (Abdelfettah Elkchirid and Bree Akesson, Chapter Five). In Chapter Seven, Edward Lee reminds us that community-engaged and social justice research necessitates ongoing reflection on one's own social location (as a researcher, social worker, healthcare practitioner, community worker) when engaging in anti-oppressive practice with vulnerable populations such as queer and trans migrants with precarious status.

Policy

The contributors to this volume agree that issues of justice at the intersection of race, gender, sexual orientation, and other multiple social categories can only be addressed if institutional/organizational policies, programs, and practices include the voices, worldviews, and histories of refugees. Policy and practise are inextricably linked, and the chapters in this volume demonstrate the importance of recognizing that policies play a significant role in fostering equity, inclusion, and equality – or in compounding the difficulties experienced by refugees at the personal, institutional, and systemic levels. We must move beyond a focus on cultural factors and carefully access how immigration policies contribute to economic, social, and health inequities (Bharati Sethi and Snežana Obradović-Ratković, Chapter Four; Edward Lee, Chapter 7).

Policies that are responsive to the settlement and integration of vulnerable populations can lead to positive health outcomes. For example, Canada's commitment to gender-based analysis of immigration policies has been beneficial in evaluating the effects of immigration on women, but more needs to be done to translate policy into practice in supporting certain segments of the population, such as Karen refugee women refugee mothers (Nancy Clark and Joyce O'Mahony, Chapter Thirteen), The Canadian government must dedicate funds for training, to help agencies integrate gender perspective and culturally appropriate lenses into settlement interventions. Some of the contributing authors have captured the nuances and complexities of settlement and displacement experiences. In Chapter Eleven, Baredu Abraham, Tolee Biya, Martha Kuwee Kumsa, and Nardos Tassew discussed gender suffering of Oromo women and girls. Nancy Clark and Joyce O'Mahony (Chapter Thirteen) demonstrated the need for immediate action to support childbearing refugee women. Snežana Obradović-Ratković, Dragana Kovačević, Neelofar Ahmed, and Claire Ellis (Chapter Nine), highlighted gender roles in the context of refugee education. Therefore, when designing holistic interventions and policies, it is also important to be attentive to how gender intersects with other locations of social diversity, such as race, class, and immigration status.

Together, the chapters in this volume advance evidence on racism, implicit or explicit biases, and discrimination experienced by refugees (Bharati Sethi and Snežana Obradović-Ratković, Chapter Four; Siham Elkassem, Rick Csiernik, Andrew Mantulak, Gina Kayssi, Yasmine Hussain, Kathryn Lambert, Pamela Bailey, and Asad Choudhary, Chapter Six; Baredu Abraham, Tolee Biya, Martha Kuwee Kumsa, and Nardos Tassewm, Chapter Eleven). Discrimination and exclusion are contributing factors to negative health effects (Baredu Abraham, Tolee Biya, Martha Kuwee Kumsa, and Nardos Tassewm, Chapter Eleven), so policy initiatives must integrate racism as determinants of refugee health.

In the current digital age with increased access to information – both fact-based and fabricated – many of the contributing authors have noted that fostering refugee individual and family resettlement requires grass-root, community-based, multi-stakeholder, and holistic approaches to policymaking that build on the resilience of service users and honour their collectivist nature. For example, the work of Ei Phyu Smith, Sheila Htoo, Michaela Hynie, and Susan McGrath with Karen refugees (Chapter Eight) demonstrates that while community self-organizing may vary based on the needs and characteristics of each community, it is a potentially powerful integration strategy, and its success depends upon collaboration and working relationships between community leaders and a network of service providers in their respective cities and neighbourhoods.

Another vital component of social justice is advocacy. To prevent discrimination against refugees, helping professionals including social workers, healthcare practitioners, and other service providers must engage in advocacy during day-to-day practice advocacy efforts, and also speak up about any discriminatory practices and policies within our organizations and communities. Broader and more collective advocacy efforts can also be achieved through community organizing and capacity-building.

Policymakers must establish and sustain cross-cultural/global networks and dialogues about refugee resettlement and wellbeing (Karun Karki and Dhruba Neupane, Chapter Two). In Chapter 10, Claire Ellis, Courtney Oreja, and Emma Jankowski discuss global initiatives for providing post-secondary education opportunities for refugee students; this is an important example of global collaboration between states, international and local NGOs, and post-secondary institutions. More policies in Canada should be responsive to the humanitarian crisis in the developing world. For example, most current resettlement policies are focused on the postmigration context. In Chapter 5, Abdelfettah Elkchirid and Bree Akesson make a compelling argument that policy discussions must be incorporate the pre-flight, flight, and displacement experiences of refugee families.

Finally, Canada must play an active role in fostering critical dialogue about the increasing characterization of refugees as 'not genuine, but rather 'bogus,' or a 'burden.' Karun Karki and Dhruba Neupane (Chapter Two) and Edward Lee (Chapter Seven) demonstrated that this kind of labelling, especially stigmatizing stereotypes about refugees perpetuated by the media, creates fear and creates a false dichotomy among displaced populations as deserving/undeserving based on their religious, ethnic, social, or immigration status. The dissonance between the media portrayal and the reality of refugee lives is, at the very least, ineffective in integrating refugees into their host communities. Treating all human beings with dignity – regardless of their immigration status – is an important step toward fostering belonging. As Canada becomes home to larger refugee populations, policy efforts must be directed toward engaging refugees in the economic, social, and political spheres so that they can carve their own path to resettlement and have opportunities to contribute their own skills in the creation of transformational change at local, transnational, and global levels.

Given your new knowledge regarding this field of practice, we invite you to consider the questions below. In doing so, we encourage you to reflect on the courage refugees have repeatedly shown in the face of extreme vulnerability and the many contributions they have made to Canada.

1. How can you foster meaningful dialogue about immigration around your kitchen table and in your community? How can you dispel myths about refugees and the GAR, BVOR, and PSR resettlement programs?
2. Working as an advocate with refugees in a camp overseas, draft an outline of a letter to the UNHCR authority indicating why the individual/family you are working with should be considered for resettlement in Canada. Include the appeals of reason (why this case deserves immediate attention), emotion (emotionally moving language and narrative), and trustworthiness (why the UNHCR should trust you as an advocate and trust this individual or family).
3. In appealing to the federal government to consider allowing more refugees into Canada, how would you describe what successful resettlement would look like and how we should track this to counter anti-immigrant sentiments throughout Canada?
4. Group resettlement was effective in the case of the Karen because of their close community ties. Other group resettlement initiatives such as those arising out of civil wars (e.g., previously in Vietnam and presently in Syria) have been more problematic due to internal strife among refugees from those war-torn nations. What would you do to create greater cohesion among these migrating individuals who bring tension from their homeland to Canada?
5. Consider the relationship of power, social attitudes about refugees, and the difficulties in accessing health care among refugees being resettled in Canada. What forms of education and action could encourage more social equity among this population? What actions could you personally take?
6. What recommendations do you have to help refugees and Canadian-born citizens work together in building individual and collective resilience to benefit past and future refugees in Canada?
7. Outline some creative, innovative, and culturally relevant methods that could be used to help children and youth understand and support the integration and settlement experiences of refugees, within and outside the classroom. How could these methods be applied in clinical interventions and community awareness projects?
8. How could Muslim and non-Muslim practitioners promote and practice advocacy and ally-ship with Muslim communities, incorporating a social justice framework in practice, education, and research?

9. How could human service practitioners critically examine the everyday violence perpetrated against immigrants and refugees at the intersection of gender, race, and sexuality, and how could they minimize spaces for such violence?
10. Consider the accumulative effects of being a foreigner or the 'Other' on physical and mental health. Given that racism and discrimination are contributing factors to declines in physical and mental health status of minoritized and racialized groups, what strategies from this volume might you adopt in your community to address these? How would you begin to implement them?
11. In closing, reflect on the question: Is a refugee *always* a refugee?

References

Bartolomei L, 2015, 'Surviving the city: Refugees from Burma in New Delhi', in Urban Refugees: Challenges in Protection, Services and Policy, pp. 139 – 163

Forced Migration Research Network, University of New South Wales (2017). THE WORLD'S

BIGGEST MINORITY? Refugee Women and Girls in the Global Compact on Refugees. Retrieved from http://www.unhcr.org/59e5bcb77.pdf

Olivius, E. (2014). (Un)Governable Subjects: The Limits of Refugee Participation in the Promotion of Gender Equality in Humanitarian Aid. *Journal of Refugee Studies*, *27*(1), 42–61. https://doi.org/10.1093/jrs/fet001

CONTRIBUTING AUTHORS

Baredu Abraham is a member of the central research team and the lead research assistant on a project exploring the health and wellbeing of Oromo women and girls in Ontario, and she has presented the findings at an international conference. She has experienced the health disparities affecting refugees: she was born in Oromia, Ethiopia and moved to Kenya as a child when her family fled Ethiopia. She arrived in Canada in 2000. Professionally, she has been exposed to health disparities while training as a nurse and working as a personal support worker. Her role as research assistant neatly wove together her passion for relearning her Oromo culture and addressing the disparities in her community.

Neelofar Ahmed is a doctoral candidate at the University of Toronto. She holds an M.Ed. from Brock University (Canada), and has completed three degrees, M.A., M.B.A., and M.S. from different universities in Pakistan. Her career spans more than 20 years of national and international transdisciplinary work experience. She last served as the regional head for the Virtual University of Pakistan in 2018, and is now a team member on projects funded by SSHRC and Brock University. She has presented at various international conferences, participated in three videos and a webinar, and serves as a reviewer for international journals. She was interviewed for the Voice of America in Washington D.C. to discuss the education of refugee students in North America and Pakistan.

Bree Akesson, Ph.D., is an Associate Professor at Wilfrid Laurier University's Faculty of Social Work and Social Justice and Community Engagement program. She is the Associate Director of the Centre for Research on Security Practices and a Research Associate with the International Migration Research Centre. Her research focuses broadly on international social work, ranging from micro-level understandings of the experiences of children and families affected by war to macro-level studies on strengthening social service and mental health systems. She is the principal investigator on a mixed-methods study investigating mobility and wellbeing among Syrian families, for which she has already received several awards including the Early Career Researcher Award from Wilfrid Laurier University and the Early Researcher Award from the Government of Ontario.

Pamela Bailey B.S.W., M.S.W.., R.S.W., is a Child and Family Therapist at Vanier Children's Services in London, Ontario. She has many years experience working in children's mental health, individual and family counselling, and child protection. She practices from an anti-oppressive, feminist and family-focused lens, using narrative therapy and cognitive behavioural therapy as her primary treatment modalities.

Tolee Biya is an active member of the larger research team in the research exploring the health and wellbeing of Oromo women and girls in Ontario. She is passionate about addressing the disparities in the health and wellbeing of women and girls, and has presented her findings at an international conference. She is an Oromo woman residing in Toronto, and graduated in International Development Studies from the University of Toronto. Currently, she works with Shelter Movers, an organization that helps retrieve the belongings of women and children after they flee violent/unstable homes.

Nimo Bokore, B.S.W.., M.S.W., Ph.D., is an Assistant Professor in the School of Social Work at Carleton University. She earned her B.S.W. at Ryerson University, M.S.W. at the University of Toronto, and her Ph.D. and Graduate Diploma in Neuroscience from York University in Toronto. For more than a decade, her research and publications have focused on practice-based immigrant and refugee resettlement including past and present traumas, transference, and intervention. As a resettled refugee herself, she also brings a rich perspective to her work.

Asad Choudhary M.Ed., Ph.D. candidate, is currently the Principal at the London Islamic School and is also a co-founder of Tarbiyah Learning, an Ottawa-based private school. He has been an educator in both Canada and the Middle East. He is involved with many Muslim youth programs and is frequently invited by various organizations to conduct workshops and lectures across Canada, including the Muslim Mind workshop for school educators and administrators.

Nancy Clark, R.N., Ph.D., is an Assistant Professor in the Faculty of Human and Social Development at the University of Victoria. She is also affiliated with the University of British Columbia Research Excellence Cluster in Migration, which works to support ethical research with newcomer communities and organizations. Her research and practice focus on community mental health with structurally vulnerable groups, including groups affected by displacement. She is motivated to understand the social determinants of mental health and integration with healthcare services.

Rick Csiernik (he/him/his) BSc, BSW, MSW, PhD, RSW, CCAC, Professor, School of Social Work, King's University College is a White settler currently living on Dish With One Spoon Treaty Territory. The privileges he enjoys today are due to the sacrifices of the Original Peoples of that He has written and edited 18 books, authored more than 200 peer-reviewed articles and book chapters, and has presented at more than 200 national and international conferences, workshops, and seminars. He has been part of research teams that have received more than CAD$4.5 million in funding and has been the recipient of both the King's University College and McMaster University Continuing Education Teaching Excellence Awards, as well as the Hugh Mellon Award for Research Excellence and the Ontario Volunteer Service Awards.

Siham Elkassem, B.S.W, M.S.W., R.S.W., is a Child and Family Therapist at Vanier Children's Services in London, Ontario, Canada. Her clinical practice is based in both decolonizing and justice-seeking frameworks and focuses primarily on the use of narrative therapy combined with anti-oppressive practice approaches. As an active Muslim community member in London, Ontario, she is involved in research and community-based work, specifically by blending activism, research, theory, and practice. She is currently completing her doctoral studies at Memorial University of Newfoundland.

Abdelfettah Elkchirid is an Assistant Professor at Wilfrid Laurier University's Faculty of Social Work. The main focus of his research is social work, particularly cross-cultural and international social work, and social work involving survivors of trauma and torture. He is currently involved in two research projects: one is developing a guide to implement men's support groups for refugees and exploring the intersection of gender, culture; the other is exploring the past migration experiences of Moroccan female migrant farm workers returning from Spain. He is a board member for Muslim Social Services and works with the Islamic Centre of Cambridge and Reception House Waterloo Region. In 2018, he was presented with an Award of Distinction by Waterloo Region for World Refugee Day.

Claire Ellis is a doctoral student in Policy Studies (Migration Stream) at Ryerson University. She holds a B.A. in Sociology from the University of British Columbia and an M.A. in Immigration and Settlement Studies from Ryerson University. Her M.A. research examined Canadian refugee smuggling policy and governmental discourse surrounding irregular migration. She serves on the Executive Committees of the Emerging Scholars and Practitioners on Migration Issues Network and the Canadian

Association for Refugee and Forced Migration Studies. Her research interests include refugee policy, critical institutionalism, education and displacement, citizenship and political belonging, human rights, and state responses to irregular migration.

Sepali Guruge, Ph.D, is Professor in the Daphne Cockwell School of Nursing at Ryerson University. She is known in Canada and internationally for her work in the area of immigrant and refugee health. Sepali's research with immigrant communities began more than 25 years ago, and pays particular attention to the health inequities resulting from socio-economic marginalization; lack of/limited access to healthcare, education, employment, and language training; housing insecurity; racism and discrimination; and the interactive effects of these issues. Her research findings have been disseminated in various formats in over 15 languages, making her work accessible beyond English-speaking audiences. Sepali has received numerous awards in recognition of her work. Her work can be found at: www.ImmigrantHealthResearch.ca

Sheila Htoo came to Canada from remote refugee camps in Thailand as a sponsored refugee student. Since 2006, she has been working with refugee and immigrant populations in Toronto as a medical interpreter, outreach worker, and community leader. She worked as a peer researcher and knowledge exchange leader on several community-based research projects led by Access Alliance. She is currently Chair of the Karen Community of Toronto and a leading member of the Karen Community of Canada's Research and Advocacy Team. She holds a M.Sc. in Planning from the University of Toronto and is a Ph.D. candidate in the Faculty of Environmental Studies at York University. Her dissertation research explores the Salween Peace Park, an Indigenous Karen conservation initiative.

Yasmine Hussain is the Manager of Community Services at the Muslim Resource Centre for Social Support and Integration in London, Ontario. She co-creates community-based strategies and carries out community work with youth and women, applying participatory and anti-oppressive models of community development and social action, as such open spaces where voices, stories, and leadership shape narratives and solutions that affect communities.

Michaela Hynie is a Professor in the Department of Psychology and the Centre for Refugee Studies at York University. Her research focuses on how social and institutional factors affect health and wellbeing in different cultural, political, and physical environments, and the development and evaluation of interventions that can strengthen social capital. She is particularly interested in social integration and inclusion in situations of social conflict or forced migration. Her research in Canada, Rwanda, Kenya, India, and Nepal has been funded by Grand Challenges Canada, the Canadian Institutes of Health Research, and the Social Sciences and Humanities Research Council of Canada. She is currently working on a five-year longitudinal study of how social integration affects long-term health outcomes among Syrian refugees in Canada.

Emma Jankowski has a M.A. in Immigration and Settlement Studies from Ryerson University. She is an International Student Advisor at International Student Support at Ryerson University. She acts as the Staff Advisor to the Ryerson WUSC Local Committee and coaches students who arrive at Ryerson through the SRP throughout their resettlement and educational journey.

Karun Karki is an Assistant Professor in the School of Social Work and Human Services at the University of the Fraser Valley, BC, Canada. His academic and professional interests are grounded in critical theories, intersectionality, and social justice praxis. His scholarly inquires include socio-economic, cultural, and civic inclusion/exclusion of immigrants/ refugees based on their race, ethnicity, gender identity, sexual orientation, skin colour, geographical location, and disability. In his social work research and practice, he applies collaborative and community-based methods that foreground the values of diversity, equity, inclusivity, and social justice.

Gina Kayssi has a B.A. in political science and French and a M.A. specializing in Canadian environmental policy. Over the last several years, she served as project assistant on the Reclaim Honour project and community engagement facilitator supporting Syrian newcomers at the Muslim Resource Centre for Social Support and Integration. Currently, she works as a Research Assistant at King's University College.

Dragana Kovačević is an Admissions Advisor at Sheridan College in Ontario. She arrived in Canada in 1997 as a refugee child from the former Yugoslavia. She has a M.Ed. specializing in Administration and Leadership. She is passionate about globalization and forced migration: her M.Ed. major research project explored the challenges and barriers faced by refugee students from the former Yugoslavia faced as they transitioned to the Canadian education system, as well as the strategies these students and their educators used to ease the transition. Her M.Ed. major research paper was nominated as an Outstanding Major Research Paper Award at Brock University. She continues to focus on forced migration and the experiences of refugee students within Canadian K-12 schools.

Martha Kuwee Kumsa is the Principal Investigator and a member of a community-based participatory action research team exploring health and wellbeing among Oromo refugee women and girls in Ontario. She was born and raised in Oromia, Ethiopia. She was a refugee in Kenya, arrived in Canada in 1991, and earned her Ph.D. from University of Toronto. Currently, she is a Professor in the Faculty of Social Work at Wilfrid Laurier University. Her research combines her passion for broader social justice issues and the need to address the specific health disparities affecting the health and wellbeing of Oromo refugee women and girls in Ontario.

Kathryn Lambert, M.S.W., R.S.W., is the Director of Clinics Services at Vanier Children's Services. She has extensive experience working within the child welfare and infant, children, and youth mental health sectors. Her areas of practice include working with families who have experienced violence, and supporting parents who have mental health difficulties. In her current role, she provides clinical supervision, develops and improves programs, leads quality improvement activities, and influences systemic and organizational change issues.

Edward Ou Jin Lee is an Assistant Professor at the School of Social Work at the Université de Montréal. Edward applies critical, community-based, participatory, and digital media methodologies. He also engages in critical reflexive decolonizing and anti-oppressive social work, and in particular transformative learning within social work field education. He works in social policy advocacy and community organizing with Queer, Trans, Black, Indigenous, and other People of Colour communities, and particularly with Queer and Trans migrants with precarious status.

Andrew Mantulak, M.S.W., Ph.D., R.S.W., is an Associate Professor in the School of Social Work at King's University College at Western University. He teaches primarily direct practice-based courses at the undergraduate and graduate levels. His current research involves exploring how social media is changing face-to-face social interaction and the effects on social work field education.

Susan McGrath, C.M., is a Professor Emerita at the School of Social Work, York University, and served as Director of the Centre for Refugee Studies from 2004–2012. She has a Ph.D. in Social Work from the University of Toronto. She is a past president of the International Association for the Study of Forced Migration and a founding member of the Canadian Association for Refugee and Forced Migration Studies. She was awarded the 2015 SSHRC Partnership Impact Award for forging innovative, interdisciplinary, equitable, and cross-sector partnerships in the field of forced migration. In 2014, she was invested into the Order of Canada in recognition of her outstanding achievement in research and policy on refugee rights and for fostering collaboration among scholars in her field.

Dhruba Jyoti Neupane is a Lecturer in the Department of Rhetoric at the University of Iowa. He specialized in Rhetoric and Writing Studies at the University of Waterloo. His research investigates the language, migration and race interface, specifically how immigrants negotiate and navigate academic, social, and civic demands and re-imagine themselves in new contexts that are often not of their own choosing. His publications are situated in the discourse around diversity and argue for engaging in diversity differently from what how it is practised in the neoliberal s/State – with the goal of enabling meaningful negotiation across difference and new exchanges of relationships.

Snežana Obradović-Ratković is a Research Officer and an Instructor in the Faculty of Education at Brock University. She has a B.Sc. in Biology and Chemistry and a B. Ed. Honours Intermediate/Senior degree from the University of Osijek in Croatia (then Yugoslavia). Since her immigration to Canada in 1998, she has obtained a B.Sc., in Biotechnology, a M.Ed. in Teaching and Learning, and a Ph.D. in Educational Studies from Brock University, St. Catharines, Ontario, Canada. Her scholarship focuses on migration and Indigeneity, transnational and transdisciplinary teacher education, social justice leadership, decolonizing research methodologies, research education, and knowledge mobilization.

Joyce O'Mahony, Ph.D., has expertise in public health nursing practice, immigrant and refugee women's mental health research, and education. Her program of research includes health promotion values and central tenets of equity, empowerment, collaboration and participation to improve the health of immigrant and refugee women in Canada. Specifically, she focuses on immigrant women's postpartum depression experiences, access to mental healthcare services, and intervention strategies for postpartum care. Her work is motivated by the need to improve understanding of immigrant women's postpartum health, their social support needs, and their treatment preferences in order to provide culturally sensitive and equitable care.

Courtney Oreja is a doctoral candidate in Ryerson University's Policy Studies Program (Immigration, Settlement and Diaspora Stream). She holds an M.A. in Immigration and Settlement Studies from Ryerson University, and a Post-Baccalaureate diploma in International Studies and B.A. in Communications from Simon Fraser University. Her doctoral research focuses on the implementation of the International Education Strategy and immigration-related programs at Canadian universities, exploring international education as a tool for immigration.

Eid Phyu Smith completed her Ph.D. at the Department of Geography at York University and has an active research program in the field of Feminist Political Geography. Her dissertation examined how displaced individuals of Karen ethnicity from Burma engage with the notion of 'home' at multiple sites of dispossession. Her post-doctoral research, which is funded by the National Geographic Society, will examine the role of civil society and transnational meanings of home in times of political transition. She is currently a Research Associate at the York Centre for Asian Research at York University in Toronto, Canada and lives in Andover, Massachusetts.

Bharati Sethi, Ph.D., is an immigrant from India and an Associate Professor in the School of Social Work, King's University College, Western University. She applies participatory action research, arts-based methodologies, and intersectionality to investigate the social determinants of health among immigrants and refugees and how these relate to social justice. She teaches in the areas of community practice, policy, and transnationalism; drawing from evidence-based research, field stories, and her own lived experiences she emphasizes the importance of bridging micro- and macro-levels of social work practice to serve the most vulnerable segments of the population. She supervises students from diverse disciplines and currently serves as a co-investigator on four multi-site community-based research projects totalling nearly $2,000,000 (funded by SSHRC and CIHR). She has been awarded the Vanier Canada Graduate Scholarship, Hilary Weston Graduate Scholarship, Ontario Women's Health Scholar Award, Newcomer Champion Award, and Governor General's Award. In 2013, her community advocacy efforts and research earned her the Citizen Award by her Member of Provincial Parliament and in 2012 she was nominated as one of the 'top 25' immigrants to Canada.

Nardos Tassew is a senior researcher exploring the health and wellbeing of Oromo women and girls in Ontario. She earned her Ph.D. in Chemistry from the University of Toronto and completed post-doctoral training at the Scripps Research Institute, La Jolla, California and the University Health

Network, Toronto, Ontario. She was a researcher at the Krembil Neuroscience Centre in Toronto and has published several papers on the mechanisms underlying neurodegenerative diseases. She has been working as a scientist in the Safety Assessment Department of Genentech, South San Francisco since 2016 and provides pre-clinical toxicological support for various programs in immunology, ophthalmology, and neuroscience.